GROVER CLEVELAND
THE MAN AND THE STATESMAN

VOLUME TWO

❧

GROVER CLEVELAND

IN HIS HOME AT PRINCETON

⌊GROVER CLEVELAND⌋

THE MAN AND THE STATESMAN

An Authorized Biography

BY

ROBERT ⌊McELROY⌋ PH.D., LL.D., F.R.H.S.

EDWARDS PROFESSOR OF AMERICAN HISTORY
PRINCETON UNIVERSITY

VOLUME
II

HARPER & BROTHERS PUBLISHERS
NEW YORK AND LONDON
MCMXXIII

CONTENTS

VOLUME II

GROVER CLEVELAND
THE MAN AND THE STATESMAN

GROVER CLEVELAND

CHAPTER I

THE FIRST BATTLE WITH BRYAN—THE REPEAL OF THE SHERMAN LAW

"Patriotism is no substitute for a sound currency."
—GROVER CLEVELAND.

THE election of November, 1892, placed Grover Cleveland in a position unique in American history. He was the only President ever re-elected after a defeat. Furthermore, he was the first President-elect since 1840 who was manifestly a greater political figure than any man whom he could conceivably select for his Cabinet

Harrison and Tyler had been outclassed by many leaders in their own party. James K. Polk had his William L. Marcy, his Robert J. Walker, his George Bancroft; Zachary Taylor, his John M. Clayton, Reverdy Johnson, and Thomas Ewing; Franklin Pierce, to his own generation, looked small beside Marcy, Guthrie, and Caleb Cushing; and James Buchanan was clearly eclipsed by Lewis Cass. Lincoln started his presidential career with both Seward and Chase to overshadow him. Andrew Johnson was outclassed in the public mind by most of the Cabinet which he inherited from Lincoln. Grant, though eminent as a soldier, was politically of small stature beside Elihu Washburn or Hamilton Fish. Hayes was dwarfed by Evarts, Sherman, and Carl

I

1882-86

Schurz. Blaine, as Secretary of State, completely over-topped both Garfield and Arthur, while Cleveland himself in 1884 was far less eminent than either Tilden or Thomas F. Bayard. But with Grover Cleveland's restoration, the older and better tradition was resumed, for, with the single exception of Monroe's first term, every administration down to that of William Henry Harrison had begun with a President more eminent than any of his advisers.

In addition to this personal prestige, Mr. Cleveland returned to power with the added advantage of being the first President since Pierce whose party was in a position to control both Senate and Congress. During his first term Congress had been Democratic; but the Republicans had controlled the Senate, and from that stronghold had wrought havoc upon many of his cherished plans. Now, however, for a brief but satisfying period, he found himself riding the crest of the wave, his triumphant party eagerly hailing him chief, and even the Republicans admitting that he had "qualities."

In the House of Representatives he was entitled to expect the support of two hundred and nineteen out of a membership of three hundred and fifty-five, with one seat vacant. Out of a Senate of eighty-eight the Democrats numbered forty-four, while the three seats yet to be filled gave them hope of a majority, especially as the five Populist Senators might reasonably be expected to train with them. To all appearances, therefore, Mr. Cleveland could count upon the support of both Houses, and but for the break in his own party when the testing time came, he might have commanded the storm for many a day.

When ready to choose his Cabinet, Mr. Cleveland felt it wise to select new men who would bring new points of view and new suggestions to bear upon the problems confronting the country. And so, while freely seeking the personal advice of his old Cabinet associates, he persistently looked elsewhere for official advisers.

On January 25, 1893, he wrote to L. Clarke Davis:

"Bayard came to me night before last and left this morning. We had a very frank and unrestrained talk, as we have always had, and so far as he can do so, he has, like the good patriotic friend he is, left matters almost entirely in my control.

"I am dreadfully perplexed and bothered. I cannot get the men I want to help me, but strange to say, my greatest trials come through those professing to be near and attached friends, who expect things.

"I hope the skies will lighten by and by, but I have never seen a day since I consented to drift with events that I have not cursed myself for yielding; and in these particular days I think I curse a little more heartily than ever. This is strange talk and perhaps seems ungracious and unappreciative. It is nothing of the kind. It presents only the personal side of the matter; and sometimes when I feel that perhaps I may after all be the instrument of doing good to the American people whom I know I love, I am quite happy."

That night he offered Bayard's old post, the portfolio of State, to Judge Walter Q. Gresham, of Indiana, a man who, except for the year 1864, when he had been unable to go to the polls, had voted the Republican ticket at every presidential election since the party was organized. Gresham had served as Secretary of the Treasury for one month during Arthur's administration, and at the opening of the campaign of 1892, had been in the minds of many

anti-Harrison leaders, a possible Republican nominee
for the Presidency. Indeed, according to the memoir published by his widow, he had been actually asked to lead
the Republicans in a fight for the nomination, but had
answered: "I am out of politics, and have no political
aspirations." The People's party, too, had offered him
their nomination, and this also he had declined, declaring
to his son that he thought the thing for him to do was to
take the stump for Grover Cleveland, largely because of
the latter's tariff views. Gresham's support under such
circumstances had been of great value to the Democratic
ticket, but the offer of the leading place in the Cabinet
came as a surprise, and he at first declined. Mr. Cleveland met his objections with the assurance that "prior
political affiliations matter not a bit." Whitney, Carlisle,
Henry Watterson, and other prominent Democrats added
their arguments, and Mr. Gresham finally accepted the
appointment. In acknowledging the acceptance, Mr.
Cleveland wrote:

Confidential.

Lakewood, N. J.

Feby. 9, 1893.

Hon. Walter Q. Gresham.
My dear Sir:
    Your letter of the 7th instant came to hand two or
three hours ago, and causes me the greatest satisfaction.
I know perfectly well that only considerations of patriotism and duty have constrained you to accede to my wishes,
and I assure you this vastly increases my appreciation
of what you have done. . . .
    I would certainly be exceedingly glad to have a chat
with you between now and the 4th of March, and hope
that your work will so close up as to enable you to come
to me.

I have settled, I think, on five members of the Cabinet. I mean to have Carlisle for the Treasury—Lamont for War—Bissell (of Buffalo, one of my oldest friends and former partner) for Postmaster General, and Hoke Smith, of Georgia (a very able representative of the new and progressive South), for Interior. This leaves Navy, Attorney General and Agriculture still to be selected. I want George Gray, Senator from Delaware, to accept the Attorney General's place, but he has thus far, strangely enough, declined. If there was a first-rate man in Alabama, Mississippi, or that neighborhood, I would like to consider him. If not, I am prepared to take a man from almost any quarter.

I offered Agriculture to Bliss of Iowa; but he and his friends are reckoning on his making a successful canvass for United States Senator next fall, and he declined my invitation. The Navy ought not to be a very hard place to fill, but I have not just the man in view yet. It is barely possible that I may induce Senator Gray to take the Attorney Generalship after all, but I hardly expect it.

I would be very glad to receive any suggestions you may make concerning incumbents for these vacant places. Now that I have secured the head of my Cabinet, I feel that it should be completed as soon as possible.

If your leisure and convenience permit, I hope you will write to me. Please address me by letter or dispatch at this place.

Very sincerely yours,
GROVER CLEVELAND.

Disappointed in his hope of securing Senator Gray as Attorney General, Mr. Cleveland appointed Richard Olney, whom he had met but once, but whose qualifications he had carefully investigated. Mr. Olney's success as counsel for the Eastern Railroad in 1875, during a period of peculiar difficulty, had established his reputation as a lawyer, and he had ably sustained the reputation thus secured.

As Secretary of the Navy, Hilary A. Herbert, of Alabama, was finally selected, while Julius Sterling Morton, of Nebraska, accepted the post of Secretary of Agriculture. Thus the Cabinet was complete, and of the men chosen only Lamont had been associated with his first administration.

In describing his Cabinet to Richard Watson Gilder, the President-elect said of John G. Carlisle: "We are just right for each other. He knows all I ought to know, and I can bear all we have to bear." And already his daily mail showed many premonitory symptoms of what he would have to bear.

Office seekers of every conceivable type once more employed every means to impress upon him the duty of a President with power to bestow. Some of these appeals were pathetic, some patriotic; but the vast majority were grotesque, almost illiterate pleas for pay for alleged party service.

One bore the distressingly familiar ring, which had called forth so many pension vetoes during his first term: "I congratulate you with greetings of love. Forget not the noble soldier. Procrastinate not. Strike at once. Give pensions to all that fought."

Another of equally well-known purport ran: "Please send me immediately $1,000, to which you are indebted to me, to say nothin about the pain and sufferin endured, caused by a pure accident when celebratin your election."

A third mingled his good wishes with a request for $45, giving as his reason: "I had ben votin the Democrat ticket ever sense the War, and I have never received anything for my trouble. goin to the election whitch some of the Republicans has been payed for votin there own ticket."

"A young lady aged 17 years old," opened her epistle with the words: "Thou ruler of the United, as such you are and have a rite to be, bein Democratic." And a New Englander, less effusive but doubtless equally sincere, modestly apologized for the form of his congratulations in the words: "I am not very mutch on the writin and spelin but then you will excuse I bein Born in Maine."

Thus again Mr. Cleveland knew what the psychologists call "the reality feeling." The burden which he had shifted to another Atlas in 1889 was his again, and while grateful for the confidence of the people, he was far from elated. "Every feeling of jubilation," he wrote, "and even my sense of gratitude is so tempered as to be almost entirely obscured by the realization, nearly painful, of the responsibility I have assumed in the sight of the American people."

Although executive authority was not yet his, his sense of responsibility drove him ruthlessly. At his office in the Mills Building, New York, he received the brunt of the office seekers' attacks. At his retreat in Lakewood, he welcomed his friends and those political leaders whose advice and assistance he requested. But whether in New York or in Lakewood, he avoided no obligation, and worked at the people's problems as though he were already once more the people's sworn servant.

"I have just been to see Mr. Cleveland at Lakewood," wrote Thomas F. Bayard to Judge Lambert Tree, "and his self-abnegation and simple devotion to the great work which confronts him touch and impress me greatly. No small purpose has any right to be brought into view where he is concerned, and self-seeking should stand rebuked in his presence."

The month before inauguration Mr. Cleveland devoted largely to work upon his address, abandoning his office hour at the Mills Building. Toward the end of that period Dr. Wilton Merle Smith, pastor of a New York church which Mr. Cleveland frequently attended, paid a visit to Lakewood.

"Come into my den," said Mr. Cleveland, "I want to read you my inaugural speech." When he had finished the final paragraph: "Above all I know there is a Supreme Being who rules the affairs of men, and whose goodness and mercy have always followed the American people, and I know He will not turn from us now if we humbly and reverently seek His powerful aid," his visitor remarked, "I like it immensely and its conclusion best of all." "I will never forget," said Dr. Smith later, "the way this strong man then paced up and down the floor, and returned and returned, with these words, 'I suppose at times you will not approve many things I do, but I want you to know that I am trying to do what is right. I have a hungry party behind me, and they say I am not grateful. Sometimes the pressure is almost overwhelming, and a President cannot always get at the exact truth, but I want you to know, and all my friends to know, that I am trying to do what is right—I am trying to do what is right.'"

Shortly before the date fixed for Mr. Cleveland's departure for Washington, a number of his intimate friends presented him with a watch. In his letter of thanks to Mr. Gilder, he wrote: "I expected to see you this evening and did not suspect any such conspiracy as was developed when the beautiful gift sent to me by yourself and your 'pals' reached my hands. I don't know what to say to 'you fellows'—and no wonder, for I never had so fine a present before.

"I can only say that I am perfectly delighted, and that this reminder of real friendliness comes to me at a time when my surroundings do not indicate that all friendship is sincere and disinterested. I thank you from the bottom of my heart."

Cleveland took his second oath as President with the ground white with snow. Before him spread an audience in which appeared at points the glint of Indian costumes, denoting not real red men but Tammany tigers. Led by Richard Croker and other of Mr. Cleveland's ancient opponents, Tammany, for the moment, celebrated Cleveland's return.

As he faced the sea of upturned faces awaiting his inaugural address, he boldly resumed the topic which four years earlier had caused his defeat. "The verdict of our voters which condemns the injustice of maintaining protection for protection's sake," he declared, "enjoins upon the people's servants the duty of exposing and destroying the brood of kindred evils which are the unwholesome progeny of paternalism." The fact that in his message of 1887 he had doomed himself and his party to defeat by a frank avowal of the same view, induced no caution. To his mind, personal or party defeats were merely incidents in the operation of great forces. It was his intention to bring about a sweeping reform of the tariff, and his method was to let the country know it at the earliest possible moment.

To those Democrats who despite his previous utterances still hoped that Grover Cleveland would promise to "do something for silver," he presented an uncompromising front. And he as frankly disappointed those who had ventured to suggest that he would "soft-pedal" when touching questions of wastefulness, civil service, and pension reform.

His speech was a reiteration of his past speeches. Four years' relief from executive cares had altered none of his fundamental conceptions. Simply, frankly, and uncompromisingly, he declared not new views but old: "Nothing is more vital to our supremacy as a nation . . . than a sound and stable currency"; "the injustice of maintaining protection for protection's sake"; "a challenge of wild and reckless pension expenditures"; "the waste of public money is a crime"; "to secure the fitness and competency of appointees to office and remove from political action the demoralizing madness of spoils"; "legitimate strife in business should not be superseded by an enforced concession to the demands of combinations that have the power to destroy."

The address made a profound impression in Europe. The President of the Paris Council caused extracts from it to be printed for use in the public schools of France, and the Papal Nuncio declared that it was: "One of the grandest spectacles of modern times to see the head of a great nation inculcate such lessons of morality and practical religion."

No sooner was the ceremony of inauguration over than Mr. Cleveland encountered, with regard to almost every article of his creed, bitter and determined opposition, not only from the Republicans, but from his own party as well. In the lower House, which had been elected under the same popular inspiration which had restored him, the adverse current remained within bounds, thanks to the high-minded leadership of Mr. Wilson, of West Virginia, and many of his efforts to carry out the promises made to the people found a fair

degree of party support. But the Democratic contingent
of the Senate was controlled by men who hated Cleveland
and spared no pains to block his measures. To such
opposition the Republicans gave assistance, for to them
Grover Cleveland was only the first successful leader of
Democracy since the small years of the century, and
their business was to add party opposition to personal
opposition, that the days of his power might prove as
few as possible.

Thus the new President soon saw that his expected
majority in the Senate was not to be realized. He was,
in short, in the unenviable position of a leader determined to lead, at the head of a band of followers who
refused to follow, and this at a time when the situation
was most perplexing and difficult.

His party was pledged to tariff reform, but there
seemed little chance of securing it in the face of such a
combination. Civil service, too, was part of its promise
to the people, but the Democratic leaders, with reform
ardor cooled by victory, found satisfying absolution in
the fact that the Republicans had packed the federal
offices with their henchmen as rapidly as vacancies had
occurred, thus restoring the inequality which had prevailed for a quarter of a century before Mr. Cleveland's
coming.

To upset this iniquitous situation, so at variance with
the will of the people as expressed in the recent elections, they boldly declared a necessary preliminary to
real reform. They pointed out the fact that of the
200,000 employees in the civil service of the United States
only 43,000 were classified according to the rules of civil
service reform, and that of this 43,000 a large percentage
were but examples of how a defeated party can, in the
last few hours of its power, use civil service reform laws

to furnish permanent berths for its members. Particularly did they denounce Amended Postal Rule No. 1, signed by President Harrison two months before his retirement, which brought some 7,500 federal employees of the free delivery post-offices within the protection of the civil service laws.

"This is perhaps the most important extension that has ever taken place under the civil service law," runs the Commissioners' annual report, signed by Theodore Roosevelt and Charles Lyman. ". . . It is needless to point out the very great benefit conferred upon the public at large and upon the cause of decent politics by this extension of the classified service."

Doubtless Mr. Roosevelt and Mr. Lyman were sincere in this opinion, but the minority report signed by the third Commissioner, George D. Johnston, gave a different interpretation, and one more favorable to the case of Democratic politicians desirous of removals. Writing to President Cleveland, on November 21, 1893, Johnston declared the action the very opposite of reform: "The extension of the classified service does not of necessity mean civil service reform. . . . When such an extension is ordered by an administration and goes into effect shortly before the government is turned over to another administration of different political faith and party affiliation, known to be friendly to the cause of civil service reform, it is difficult to reconcile it to fair-minded men of all parties as a non-partisan measure."

While inclined to accept the minority interpretation, Mr. Cleveland showed his confidence in Theodore Roosevelt by the announcement that he would be retained as Civil Service Commissioner, and this decision was hailed with enthusiasm by the reformers of both parties. Carl

Schurz declared it "A great event, and in itself a large program for the next four years."

Mr. Roosevelt fully agreed with the President's view that "public office is a public trust," but, being far more ardent in his desire to hold public office, was far more active in seeking it. "He who has not wealth owes his first duty to his family," he once declared, "but he who has means owes his to the State."

Mr. Cleveland, on the other hand, believed that a citizen should not court public place. The *Inter-Ocean,* of May 3, 1903, recalls a conversation between him and Mr. Roosevelt shortly after the latter's reappointment as Civil Service Commissioner. To the question, "Do you intend to remain active in politics?" Mr. Roosevelt returned an instant affirmative. "I am sorry to hear it," Mr. Cleveland replied. "It is enough to be a good citizen."

But though anxious to retain Roosevelt's services, Mr. Cleveland had no intention of allowing any one element, even the civil service reformers, to run the government. He believed that the Democrats, as the victorious party commissioned by the people, were entitled to control, and he did not scruple to appoint competent Democrats, chiefly because they were Democrats. Nor did he hesitate to appoint competent Republicans, whatever the opposition, when the situation demanded it. Incompetent candidates, whether Democrats or Republicans, he stoutly refused to appoint, however great the political pressure back of their applications. He was, moreover, always ready to correct injustice when convinced that injustice had been done, as is shown by the following correspondence between Mark Twain and the President's daughter Ruth, aged one.

"My dear Ruth,

"I belong to the mugwumps, and one of the most sacred rules of our order prevents us from asking favors of officials or recommending men to office, but there is no harm in writing a friendly letter to you and telling you that an infernal outrage is about to be committed by your father in turning out of office the best consul I know [Captain Mason, Consul General at Frankfort] (and I know a great many) just because he is a Republican and a Democrat wants his place."

Mr. Clemens then related what he knew of Captain Mason and his official record, and continued:

"I can't send any message to the President, but the next time you have a talk with him concerning such matters, I wish you would tell him about Captain Mason and what I think of a government that so treats its efficient officials."

Three or four weeks later Mr. Clemens received a tiny envelope postmarked Washington, in which was a note, written in President Cleveland's own hand. It read:

"Miss Ruth Cleveland begs to acknowledge the receipt of Mr. Twain's letter, and to say that she took the liberty of reading it to the President, who desires her to thank Mr. Twain for his information and to say to him that Captain Mason will not be disturbed in the Frankfort Consulate. The President also desires Miss Cleveland to say that if Mr. Twain knows of any other cases of this kind he would be greatly obliged if he will write him concerning them at his earliest convenience."

But despite his readiness to accept advice from disinterested sources, Mr. Cleveland took every step possible to strip from Congressmen and Senators the harness by which they were accustomed to draw the chariot of the spoils system. To this end, and to the indignation of Senators with expectant officials in tow, he issued the following executive order:

Executive Mansion,
May 8, 1893.

It has become apparent after two months' experience that the rules heretofore promulgated regulating interviews with the President have wholly failed in operation. The time which under those rules was set apart for the reception of senators and representatives has been spent almost entirely in listening to applications for office, which have been bewildering in volume, perplexing and exhausting in their iteration, and impossible of remembrance.

A due regard for public duty, which must be neglected if present conditions continue, and an observance of the limitations placed upon human endurance oblige me to decline from and after this date all personal interviews with those seeking appointments to office, except as I, on my own motion, may especially invite them. . . .

I earnestly request senators and representatives to aid me in securing for them uninterrupted interviews by declining to introduce their constituents and friends when visiting the executive mansion during the hours designated for their reception. Applicants for office will only prejudice their prospects by repeated importunities and by remaining at Washington to await results.

This did not, of course, solve the problem, but it did something to relieve the strain, leaving him a little freer to follow his conscience in matters which the Constitution had made his responsibility.

During the remainder of his term he worked slowly toward the ideal of the reformers, and by the end the 42,950 classified officers mentioned in the Commissioners' tenth annual report had grown into 84,000, while only 100 civil servants at the National Capitol were outside the graded service.

But the outstanding conflict of Mr. Cleveland's first year of restored power was not civil service but currency reform, the state of the nation's circulating medium when President Harrison surrendered the reins of government making prompt action imperative. The situation which culminated in the panic of 1893 had begun, long before Mr. Cleveland's restoration, with a widespread business prostration, the responsibility for which he laid at the door of those who had yielded to the oft-repeated plea: "Do something for silver." During his first term he had made clear his attitude toward what he called "the free silver heresy," and through his Secretary of the Treasury, Daniel Manning, had devoted himself whole-heartedly to conserving the gold balance in the Treasury. He had suspended for a time the bond purchases, discontinued the issue of $1 and $2 greenbacks, in order to increase the demand for silver certificates, and had sold to New York City bankers $5,915,000 worth of subsidiary silver coin, receiving gold in payment. These measures he had taken by executive action alone, existing conditions not being serious enough to justify an extra session of Congress.

In his first message, he had denounced the existing silver purchase law, the Bland-Allison Act in these words:

"Since February, 1878, the government has under the compulsory provisions of law purchased silver bullion and coined the same at the rate of more than $2,000,000 every month. By this process up to the present date, 215,759,431 silver dollars have been coined. . . . Only about 50,000,000 of the silver dollars so coined have actually found their way into circulation, leaving more than 165,000,000 in the possession of the government, the custody of which has entailed a considerable expense for the construction of vaults for its deposit. Against this latter amount there are outstanding silver certificates amounting to about $93,000,000.

"Every month two millions of gold . . . are paid out for two millions of silver dollars, to be added to the idle mass already accumulated.

"If continued long enough, this operation will result in the substitution of silver for all the gold the government owns applicable to its general purposes.

"It will not do to rely upon the customs receipts of the government to make good this drain of gold, because the silver thus coined having been made legal tender for all debts and dues, public and private, at times during the last six months, 58% of the receipts for duties has been in silver or silver certificates, while the average within that period has been 20%.

"This proportion . . . will probably increase as time goes on, for the reason that the nearer the period approaches when it will be obliged to offer silver in payment of its obligations, the greater inducement there will be to hoard gold against depreciation in the value of silver or for the purpose of speculating.

"This hoarding of gold has already begun.

"When the time comes that gold has been withdrawn from circulation, then will be apparent the difference between the real value of the silver dollar and a dollar in gold, and the two coins will part company. Gold, still the standard of value and necessary in our dealings with other countries, will be at a premium over silver; banks which have substituted gold for the deposits of their customers may pay them with silver . . . thus making a handsome profit; rich speculators will sell their hoarded gold to their neighbors who need it to liquidate their foreign debts, at a ruinous premium over silver, and the laboring men and women of the land, most defenceless of all, will find that the dollar received for the wages of their toil has sadly shrunk in its purchasing power.

"If this silver coinage be continued, we may reasonably expect that gold and its equivalent will abandon the field of circulation to silver alone. This, of course, must produce a severe contraction of our circulating medium, instead of adding to it.

"It will not be disputed that any attempt . . . to cause the circulation of silver dollars worth 80 cents side by side with gold dollars worth 100 cents . . . to be successful must be seconded by the confidence of the people that both coins will retain the same purchasing power and be interchangeable at will."

He was willing to concede that, with the concurrent action of the other great nations, the problem of maintaining a set ratio between gold and silver would present a different aspect; but all efforts in that direction had failed, "and still we continue our coinage of silver at a ratio different from that of any other nation. . . . Without an ally or friend we battle upon the silver field in an illogical and losing contest."

He reminded Congress that the five countries composing the Latin Union had not only refused, as had the leading countries of Europe, to join in a movement to maintain a fixed ratio between gold and silver, but had "just completed an agreement among themselves that no more silver shall be coined by their respective governments and that such as has been already coined . . . shall be redeemed in gold by the country of its coinage."

Such conditions, he concluded, make it the duty of the President to "recommend the suspension of the compulsory coinage of silver dollars, directed by the law passed in February, 1878." This recommendation had, however, not been heeded, and the mints had continued to turn out silver dollars, a large percentage of whose declared value was merely psychological. By December, 1886, there were in circulation 247,131,549 of these dollars, worth barely seventy-eight cents each.

By 1890 Mr. Cleveland's dire prophecies had begun to be realized. Prosperity was giving place to hard times. Cautious men were unloading securities, and values had begun to shrivel in the hands of holders. During the first six months of 1890 the mortgages of over a score of railroad companies were foreclosed, and the Barings's collapse in England later in the year caused widespread consternation.

Then there had appeared again, with their customary attendant disasters, two ancient heresies: the first, that when business languishes the enactment of a high tariff law will restore prosperity and bring financial stability. But the McKinley tariff, with its unprecedented protective features, failed to accomplish this result.

The other delusion is to the effect that a sure remedy for failing confidence and hard times may be found in a sudden increase in the volume of money, irrespective of the foundations upon which that volume rests. This remedy was also applied in 1890 by the enactment of the so-called Sherman Act, which made it imperative for the Treasury Department to purchase 4½ million ounces of silver each month. But the business decline was not stopped by the operation of the Sherman Act. On the contrary, those monthly purchases of silver only added to existing uncertainties the portentous question whether, if the issues of the government against silver purchases were continued, it would be possible to maintain the parity between gold and silver which the law required.

When retiring from office, at the end of his first term, Mr. Cleveland had turned over to Harrison a cash balance of $281,000,000 of which $196,689,614 was in gold. From Harrison he received back in 1893 only $112,-450,577 of which only $103,500,000 was in gold; and this gold reserve would certainly have been below the $100,-000,000 mark, the point fixed by the act of July 12, 1882, as the danger point, had not Secretary Foster during January and February, 1893, obtained several millions in gold from greenbacks sold to New York bankers, with the definite purpose of keeping the gold reserve secure, at least until the end of his period of direct responsibility. By such a makeshift, Foster had managed to keep the gold reserve within the $100,000,000 limit, but, as Mr. Cleveland clearly understood, now must come the deluge, unless he could find some way to check the financial forces which had so disturbed the last days of the Harrison administration.

Even before the repeal of the Sherman Law, far-sighted financiers had foreseen the necessity of issuing bonds in purchase of gold, if the gold standard was to endure, for they felt certain that it was hopeless to look to Congress for legislation sufficient to stem the tide which was setting so hard toward the disaster of a silver basis.

On February 28, 1893, August Belmont had written to the President-elect: "I have cabled to London very fully and hope for a reply which will enable me to bring before you the basis of an actual plan. The more I think the subject over, the more fully satisfied I am that not only will it be best to sell $50 million of bds., but it is essential that they should be sold abroad if they are to serve the purpose at all. . . . I am going to work to sound the Bank Presidents. I have two supporters already. Of course I have betrayed nothing.

"The difficulty is there is not 'anything in it' so to speak for the Banks in my plan."

Inauguration day found the President still searching a solution other than the issuance of bonds in time of peace.

"In our effort to meet the emergency without an issue of bonds," he wrote in after years, "Secretary Carlisle immediately applied to banks in different localities for an exchange with the government of a portion of their holdings of gold coin for other forms of currency. The effect was so far successful that on the twenty-fifth of March the gold reserve amounted to over $107,000,000, notwithstanding the fact that considerable withdrawals had been made in the interval.

"The slight betterment thus secured proved, however, to be only temporary; for under the stress of continued and augmented withdrawals, the gold reserve, on the twenty-second day of April, 1893, for the first time since its establishment, was reduced below the $100,000,000 limit—amounting on that day to about $97,000,000."

While this fact, which a generation of financiers had learned to couple with thoughts of inevitable financial collapse, was not followed by any sudden and distinctly new disaster, it had the effect of increasing the hoarding of gold and its exportation. Furthermore, gold almost ceased to come into the Federal Treasury through customs and other revenue charges.

During the anxious weeks in which the President had been seeking a remedy which would check these inroads upon the gold reserve, and avert disaster, he had let it be known that suggestions from men skilled in currency questions would be welcome, and advice now came in a deluge from men urging action, from men urging caution, from silver men, gold men, bimetallists, special pleaders for every conceivable type of currency reform. Henry Clews, an eminent figure in the world of finance, called the President's attention to the fact that "eighty-three cents per ounce or thereabouts in New York and thirty-eight pence in London is now recognized as the world's value for silver, being equal to in the neighborhood of twenty-five silver to one gold," and suggested that if the government would recoin its silver, allowing such a ratio, "silver certificates or silver coin dollars will be of equal value to gold certificates or gold coin dollars."

Mr. Clews also contributed a summary of facts regarding the existing currency: "There are now outstanding $346,000,000 of U. S. legal tender notes (called greenbacks), $328,226,504 legal tender treasury notes issued under the Bland Act, and $135,490,148 of notes issued under the Sherman 1890 Act, making in all $809,-716,652. All these notes are direct obligations of the government, all possess the legal tender quality alike; the three different acts authorizing their issue specify that they are payable at the U. S. Treasury in coin.

"Since the resumption of gold payments these notes have all been treated alike and have been redeemed in gold coin, not silver. Now it is feared that Secretary Car-

lisle intends to change their present status into two classes
—the $346,000,000 greenbacks to remain as gold notes,
and the $328,226,504 Bland notes, together with the
$135,490,148 issued under the Sherman Act, to be recog-
nized as silver obligations."

As the Sherman Act allowed the Secretary of the
Treasury to redeem the notes issued in payment of this
silver bullion "in gold or silver coin at his discretion,"
it would have been easy to establish the policy of paying them in silver, even to holders desiring gold, but
for the fact that the law declared it the established policy
of the United States to maintain the two metals at a
parity.

This clause, to quote Mr. Cleveland, "had the effect
of transferring the discretion of determining whether
these Treasury notes should be redeemed in gold or silver
from the Secretary of the Treasury to the holder of the
notes. Manifestly, in the face of this assertion of the
government's intention, a demand for gold redemption
on the part of the holders of such notes could not be
refused, and the acceptance of silver dollars insisted
upon, without either subjecting to doubt the good faith
and honest intention of the government's professions, or
creating a suspicion of our country's solvency. The
parity . . . would be distinctly denied, if the Secretary
of the Treasury persisted in redeeming these notes,
against the will of the holders, in dollars of silver instead
of gold."

At this point, the rumor was circulated that Secretary
Carlisle was nevertheless planning so to redeem them.
At once financial circles poured in upon the President a
flood of protest.

"The report . . . has created very grave alarm here,"
wrote L. Clarke Davis from Philadelphia. "I have just

received a letter from a leading banker, your friend Mr. Drexel, who . . . says: 'If the arrangement is made that the silver notes will only be paid in silver the result will be that all public dues will be gradually paid in those notes, in which case where will the gold accrue from to pay the gold interest on the public debt, as the receipts of the Sub-Treasury will all be in silver? The feeling here is (in which I cordially join) that it will be far better to encroach upon the hundred million reserve if the department is not willing to sell bonds abroad.' "

A few hours before this letter was received, Secretary Carlisle issued a statement, designed but not calculated to relieve the public mind of doubt in this important regard. It was so ambiguous as to increase rather than to quiet public apprehension, and made it necessary for the President himself to declare publicly that gold payments would continue so long as he remained President. A letter from Andrew Carnegie, written two days after Carlisle's announcement, strongly urged this course:

"Let me assure you that in my opinion the decision to pay notes in gold saved this country from panic and entire confusion in its industrial interests. From my own experience I can tell you that foreigners had taken alarm and had begun to withdraw their capital in gold. Unless all doubt is put to rest, there is still great danger of the country being drained of its gold."

He urged the President to make a public declaration. "If I might suggest," he said, "the announcement should be somewhat like the following: 'As long as I am President of the United States, the workingman is going to be paid in as good dollars as the foreign banker is.' " Such a statement would be "good politics," he said, and added: "I have spoken to many Republicans, and without exception they agree that in standing for sound money, and the parity of gold and silver, you will receive almost the unanimous support of the Republican party."

On April 2d the President's public declaration was issued, in the spirit though not in the words which Mr. Carnegie had suggested:

"The inclination on the part of the public to accept newspaper reports concerning the intentions of those charged with the management of our national finances, seems to justify my emphatic contradiction of the statement that the redemption of any kind of Treasury notes, except in gold, has at any time been determined upon or contemplated by the Secretary of the Treasury or any other member of the present Administration.

"The President and his Cabinet are absolutely harmonious in the determination to exercise every power conferred upon them to maintain the public credit, to keep the public faith and to preserve the parity between gold and silver and between all financial obligations of the Government. . . ."

Such a declaration of executive intention, however, the President knew to be vain unless Congress could be induced to alter the laws responsible for the nation's financial plight, and the repeal of the Sherman Law thus became the first item on his program. This meant, of course, a special session of Congress, for which the sound money men of both parties and the general public were clamoring.

On May 12th, Carl Schurz wrote: "Before leaving Washington I had a conversation with Secretary Carlisle about the financial situation, in the course of which he expressed himself as more and more inclined to think that the earliest possible calling together of Congress—

earlier than September—would be advisable. I am very much of the same opinion. The financial situation of the country is becoming more critical every day. The failures and restrictions of credit which have already occurred are only a premonitory symptom. Whatever measures the Executive alone can take, will only be palliatives, temporary makeshifts. I fear you take too great a responsibility upon yourself for what may happen if the meeting of Congress is put off 'unnecessarily long."

August Belmont warned him of confidential news from England to the effect that the Indian mints were about to be closed to silver. "The race between India and the United States to get upon dry ground first," he said, "is all in favor of India, unless we act with the greatest promptitude."

Harvey Fisk and Sons issued a circular letter declaring "the actual intrinsic value of our present silver dollar is but fifty-three cents and growing less each day. Still this great American nation is obliged to calmly face inevitable ruin—the sweeping away of far more wealth than was involved in the great war between the North and the South, simply because its representatives are not called together, in accordance with the authority vested in its Chief Executive, and forced to remove from the Statute Books the law which is eating away the vitals of American honesty."

Hundreds of resolutions to the same effect were passed by chambers of commerce, business men's clubs, bankers' associations, churches, congresses of voters, mass meetings, etc., and sent by telegram, by special messenger, by solemn delegation. They warned, they coaxed, they threatened; but they did not cause the President to act hastily.

On June 4th, however, Mr. Cleveland intimated to a representative of the United Press that Congress would be speedily summoned and asked to stop the silver purchases. Again his letter pouch jumped to twice its normal size. Again prophecies of calamity came from free silver men, again gold men praised him for his sane financial views and clamored for the program of reform.

At this point, the President suddenly faced the appalling discovery that a virulent growth in the roof of his mouth menaced him with death unless an operation were immediately performed. Dr. W. W. Keen gives this account of the case: "On Sunday, June 18, 1893, Dr. R. M. O'Reilly—later Surgeon-General of the United States Army—the official medical attendant on officers of the government in Washington, examined a rough place on the roof of Mr. Cleveland's mouth. He found an ulcer as large as a quarter of a dollar, extending from the molar teeth to within one third of an inch of the middle line, and encroaching slightly on the soft palate, and some diseased bone."

A small fragment was subjected to the scrutiny of a pathologist and pronounced strongly indicative of malignancy. The President's personal physician and intimate friend, Dr. Joseph D. Bryant, was therefore summoned to Washington and, after a careful examination of the malignant area, urged an immediate operation. The President accepted the verdict, but insisted that absolute secrecy be observed, as he feared the effect which an announcement of his peril might have upon the already alarming financial situation.

With this in view, it was decided that the operation should be performed on Commodore Benedict's yacht, the *Oneida,* in which Mr. Cleveland had already traveled over fifty thousand miles, and which he could therefore board without arousing suspicion. As Dr. Bryant was of the opinion that he ought to be in condition to return to Washington within about five weeks after the operation, Mr. Cleveland prepared a proclamation summoning Congress to meet in special session on August 7th, to consider the repeal of the Sherman Law; and on the day of its publication, June 30, 1893, with every precaution for secrecy, he joined his surgeons on the *Oneida* in New York Harbor.

"I reached New York City in the evening," writes Dr. Keen, "went to Pier A, and was taken over to the yacht, which was lying at anchor at a considerable distance from the Battery. Dr. E. G. Janeway, of New York; Dr. O'Reilly; Dr. John F. Erdmann, Dr. Bryant's assistant; and Dr. Hasbrouck had also secretly gone to the yacht. The President, Dr. Bryant and Secretary Lamont, at a later hour, arrived from Washington, and openly drove to Pier A, whence they were taken to the yacht. . . . On arriving on the yacht, the President lighted a cigar, and we sat on deck smoking and chatting until near midnight. Once he burst out with, 'Oh, Doctor Keen, those office seekers! Those office seekers! They haunt me in my dreams!'"

For the time at least he was secure from their intrusion. Early the next morning, the *Oneida* weighed anchor and proceeded at half speed up the East River, the President, under nitrous oxide, stretched upon the operating table, the doctors performing the extremely delicate operation of removing "the entire left upper jaw . . . from the first bicuspid tooth to just beyond the last molar, and nearly up to the middle line. . . . A small portion of the soft palate was removed" also.

The operation was performed without external incision, and was completed at 1.55 P.M. "At 2.55 P.M. a hypodermic of one sixth of a grain of morphine was given—the only narcotic administered at any time."

Five days later the *Oneida* dropped anchor at Gray Gables, and the patient walked from the launch to his residence with little apparent effort.

A second slight operation twelve days later, and the surgical work was over. Dr. Kasson C. Gibson, of New York, then fitted Mr. Cleveland with an artificial jaw of vulcanized rubber and "when it was in place the President's speech was excellent, even its quality not being altered." "He was," concludes Dr. Keen's interesting monograph, "the most docile and courageous patient I ever had the pleasure of attending."

Upon this point there appears a difference of opinion. In an intimate letter to Colonel Lamont, Dr. Bryant laments the President's tendency to disobey orders regarding the medicines prescribed: "I . . . found him grunting as you know full well, suffering from an excess of medicine rather than the lack of it. He always believes that if a little will do some good, a bottle full must be of great advantage indeed. On that theory he had secured the full effects of the prescription I sent him, as well as some after effects."

To this we may add his wife's view of his docility as later expressed in a letter to Mrs. Joseph Jefferson: "He is hard at work on his letters. It is so dreadfully hard to do anything with him. This morning when no one noticed he got a peach and ate it. Wouldn't you think a *child* would have more sense after the narrow escape he had?"

In memory of his insubordination, Commodore Benedict sent him the following lines, which he greatly enjoyed:

"Friday sorry, yet defiant,
Next day, send for Doctor Bryant."

Mr. Cleveland, however, defended his defiance with the words: "I am not so dreadfully heedless of the care I owe myself (for others' sake) as is suspected of me; and touching the Doctor's accusation of indiscretion, is it not in the very nature of faithful, devoted, and anxious medical ministrations to find patients indiscreet?"

At times also he expressed misgivings regarding the science of healing. To Richard Watson Gilder he gave the following enigmatical advice: "I hope that either by following your Doctor's directions or defiantly disobeying them (the chances probably being even in both contingencies), you will soon regain your very best estate in the matter of health. Don't forget at any time—whatever you do—that 'good men are scarce.'"

But though the President's docility is thus called into question, none can doubt the justice of Dr. Keen's second attribute—that of courage. Terribly weakened by loss of blood, and believing himself still under the shadow of death, Mr. Cleveland strove to prepare a message for the pending special session of Congress. For some time after the operation he received no visitors, until, in view of the menacing condition of national finances, he admitted Secretary Olney, who in a brief memorandum gives the story of his part in the preparation of Mr. Cleveland's silver message:

"After an interval of a fortnight, more or less, during which I made frequent attempts to see Mr. Cleveland, I succeeded in having an interview. He had changed a good deal in appearance, and lost a good deal of flesh, and his mouth was so stuffed with antiseptic wads that he could hardly articulate. The first utterance that I understood was something like this: 'My God, Olney, they nearly killed me.' He did not talk much, was very much depressed, and at the same time acted, and I believe felt, as if he did not expect to recover."

After a painful attempt to discuss with Mr. Olney the great issue to be laid before the coming session, Mr. Cleveland produced the manuscript of the message upon which he was spending his remaining strength.

"There were perhaps twenty or thirty lines," writes Mr. Olney, "forming the first two paragraphs of the message as eventually sent to Congress. He was very depressed about the progress he was making and complained that his mind would not work, and, upon my suggestion that I might perhaps be of assistance, was evidently much relieved. In the course of two or three days I went to Gray Gables with a draft of a message, which was approved by Mr. Cleveland practically as drawn. . . . So far as I know, Mr. Carlisle was the only member of the Cabinet who saw the message before it was sent in."

A comparison of Mr. Olney's draft with the message as finally sent to Congress shows that only fifty-three lines out of one hundred and seventy-eight were adapted from the Olney draft. The body of the argument is clearly the President's own work and proves beyond question that, despite his forlorn appearance, he was still determined to write his own state papers.

Mr. Cleveland reached Washington on August 5th, prepared to give his personal direction to the launching of the movement to repeal the Sherman Law. Among his papers is a poll of Congress, name by name, designed to inform him of their attitude. It shows 114 silver men, 173 anti-silver men, and 69 marked doubtful, and bears testimony to the fact that he understood the very difficult task which awaited him.

His special message was read to Congress on August 8, 1893, and demanded "the prompt repeal of the provisions of the act passed July 14, 1890, authorizing the purchase of silver bullion." It is a document difficult to condense or epitomize, for it is itself an epitome, the compact argument of a singularly concrete mind. It is the case against free silver compressed into two thousand words.

"Our unfortunate financial plight is not the result of untoward events, nor of conditions related to our natural resources, nor is it traceable to any of the afflictions which frequently check national growth and prosperity. With plenteous crops, with abundant promise of remunerative production and manufacture, with unusual invitation to safe investment, and with satisfactory assurance to business enterprise, suddenly financial distrust and fear have sprung up on every side. Numerous moneyed institutions have suspended because abundant assets were not immediately available to meet the demands of frightened depositors. . . . These things are principally chargeable to Congressional legislation touching the purchase and coinage of silver by the general Government.

"Undoubtedly the monthly purchases by the Government of 4,500,000 ounces of silver, enforced under that statute, were regarded by those interested in silver production as a certain guarantee of its increase in price. The result, however, has been entirely different, for immediately following a spasmodic and slight rise, the price of silver began to fall after the passage of the act, and has since reached the lowest point ever known. This disappointing result has led to renewed and persistent effort in the direction of free silver coinage.

"The policy necessarily adopted of paying these silver

notes in gold has not spared the gold reserve of $100,-000,000 long ago set aside by the Government for the redemption of other notes. . . . Between the first day of July, 1890, and the 15th day of July, 1893, the gold coin and bullion in our Treasury decreased more than 132 million dollars, while during the same period the silver coin and bullion . . . increased more than a hundred and forty-seven million. Unless Government bonds are to be constantly issued and sold to replenish our exhausted gold, only to be again exhausted, it is apparent that the operation of the silver purchase law now in force leads in the direction of the entire substitution of silver for gold in the Government Treasury, and that this must be followed by the payment of all Government obligations in depreciated silver. . . . Our Government cannot make its fiat equivalent to intrinsic value, nor keep inferior money on a parity with superior money. . . .

"The people of the United States are entitled to a sound and stable currency, and to money recognized as such on every exchange and in every market of the world. Their government has no right to injure them by financial experiments opposed to the policy and practice of other civilized states."

Confidently, almost imperiously, in the interest of the whole nation, the message demanded the repeal of the Act of July 14, 1890, "condemned by the ordeal of three years' disastrous experience."

The appearance of this Cleveland-Olney message marks the stage in the silver conflict which placed Mr. Cleveland and Mr. Bryan squarely before the country as leaders of opposing factions in the Democratic party. Bryan was at that time a member of the lower house, elected as a Democrat, and abundantly willing to defend the position that free silver was a proper article in the Democratic creed. Until after the launching of the Cleveland boom of 1892, he had been a consistent Cleveland man; but a change had recently taken place in his attitude toward his party chief. In a letter to Jesse D. Carr, dated May 22, 1903, Mr. Bryan wrote:

"I was an enthusiastic supporter of Mr. Cleveland in 1884 and in 1888. But between '88 and '92 I began to study the money question, and when I came to understand its principles, I became an opponent of Cleveland's renomination, but it required his second administration to fully enlighten me upon the designs and methods of Wall Street. I have no doubt from my observation of his course that the financiers put up the money that secured his nomination in 1892, and I know they furnished large sums of money to secure his election. His Committee spent $900,000 in the state of New York and among the contributors to his campaign fund was the Sugar Trust which gave $175,000.

"When he made up his Cabinet he deliberately ignored the silver men who represented the majority of the voters, and put gold men into the Cabinet. When he called Congress together in extraordinary session, he used all the patronage in his possession to corrupt members and he used important positions in the foreign service to reward men who had betrayed their constituents. He was completely dominated by the banking influence in New York City."

That "the interests" contributed largely to Mr. Cleveland's campaign of 1892 is unquestionably true, but the innuendo that Mr. Cleveland sold himself to Wall Street in order to win his way back to the White House is not justified by a single line of evidence, and is most unquestionably untrue.

Though his own acts were often unfairly criticized, Mr. Cleveland himself habitually refrained from ascribing unworthy motives to his political opponents. "Because . . . views are various and conflicting, some of them must be wrong," he once wrote, "and yet when they are honestly held and advocated, they should provoke no bitterness nor condemnation." He did not doubt Mr. Bryan's loyalty to the country, but he did not think that this excused Mr. Bryan's financial heresies. As he himself expressed it: "Patriotism is no substitute for a sound currency." He acknowledged that free silver men could be loyal Americans, but he emphatically denied that they could be real Democrats, for he read into the Democratic party the principle of devotion to a currency system which would force no American to accept as a dollar that which was not intrinsically worth a dollar.

On August 11th, Congressman Wilson, of West Virginia, presented a bill to repeal the Sherman Law. With unfortunate lack of skill, if the aim was to rally Democrats, it was drawn in close imitation of a bill which Senator Sherman had presented to the Senate on July 14, 1892, a fact which made it easier for free silver Democrats to deny that it embodied Democratic doctrines.

Taking advantage of this fact, the free silver leader, Richard P. Bland, of Missouri, offered a substitute looking toward the free and unlimited coinage of silver at a fixed ratio; and over these rival measures, both Democratic in origin, there began at once a fierce debate, during which it speedily became evident that all calculations based upon titular party labels in the House were likely to prove misleading. Democrats who had been counted upon at the beginning of the administration to support the President, openly scorned his leadership, and the Populists sympathized with their insurgency. Most of the Republicans, on the other hand, showed marked sympathy with him. Thus party lines, already wavering and uncertain when the debate opened, grew more uncertain as it continued. If the question of the repeal of the silver purchase clause transcended old party lines, why might not the larger question of free silver be made the basis of new party lines?

That such a thought had entered Mr. Bryan's mind at an earlier date appears likely, and when he rose to speak, on August 16th, the thought of the fate of silver obliterated all thought of the fate of the Democratic party. Twice he had been elected to Congress as a Democrat, and had there won the right to regard himself as the man best fitted to lead the hosts of free silver. Richard P. Bland was manifestly too old to head a new movement; Grover Cleveland, the titular Democratic leader, did not count, for he, according to Mr. Bryan's judgment, had betrayed the party, deserted the people, and joined with the Israelites of Wall Street in the sacrilegious worship of the Golden Calf.

For almost three hours Mr. Bryan occupied the floor, the one hour limit allotted to each speaker being, by common consent, extended in his case. The magic of his personality, the unrivaled beauty of his voice, and the compelling eloquence, which were later to charm millions, were fully in evidence. The inspiration which Mr. Cleveland's message lacked breathed in every sentence of Mr. Bryan's impassioned speech. But the evidence of patient study and searching thought, which appears in every line of the President's argument, is missing from the Congressman's appeal. The one instructed the mind, the other played upon the emotions; the one appealed to reason, the other to sentiment; the one dealt in specific facts, the other in vague generalizations.

"Does any one believe," asked Mr. Bryan, "that Mr. Cleveland could have been elected President upon a platform declaring in favor of the unconditional repeal of the Sherman Law? Can we go back to our people and tell them that, after denouncing for twenty years the crime of 1873, we have at last accepted it as a blessing?" The answer to the first of these questions must remain purely speculative, although Mr. Cleveland's entire record had been a prophecy of the action which he was now taking, and if the voters of America had re-elected him in ignorance of his views on the Sherman Law, theirs was the fault, not his. As to the second question, the vote of the House, on August 28, 1893, repealing the debated clause by a majority of 239 to 109, answered it fully, making it necessary for every Congressman to return to his constituency with the news that Congress had agreed with Grover Cleveland that the "crime of 1873" had been but an example of sound finance.

On account of his weakened condition Mr. Cleveland had remained only five days in Washington, returning to Gray Gables on August 11th, weary, but confident of victory. When Congressman Wilson's telegram arrived announcing the vote of the House, he wired in return: "Please accept for yourself and associates in to-day's achievement my hearty congratulations and sincere thanks."

To those who had closely followed the situation, however, it was evident that the victory was the President's victory. "The country," wrote Jacob H. Schiff, on August 29th, "is to be congratulated that you, Mr. President, while others doubted and despaired, did not falter, and succeeded in carrying the adoption of the only measure which will restore the confidence at home and abroad which the country so sorely needs."

To the extreme silverites, however, the President's victory was susceptible only of sinister interpretation, and it goaded them to excesses of denunciation. *The Rocky Mountain News* of August 29, 1893, declared the repeal "John Bull's Work," its headlines announcing that "British Gold and Federal Patronage" had been used "to bribe the American Congress." Beneath the headline appeared a cartoon representing "Grover and J. Bull," unsteadily dancing together, with hands clasped and thick voices roaring the gin-house melody, "We won't go home till morning."

As the repeal had still to pass the Senate they again spread, with an energy worthy of a better cause, the story that Grover Cleveland was the hired agent of unscrupulous manipulators bent upon enslaving the masses of the United States.

Up to this time the secret of the President's operation had been kept from the press. But at this point appeared an announcement, fairly accurate in detail, as to what had transpired upon the *Oneida,* and though every effort was made by the President's friends to convince the public that it had no foundation in fact, the report soon spread over the country and to foreign lands.

On September 2d, Ambassador Bayard wrote to his daughter:

"I have been all along since I came abroad uneasy, feeling that all was not right with Mr. Cleveland. I have written to him, but neither expected nor desired that he should increase his labors by writing to me—but yesterday an English newspaper contained a statement from a surgeon dentist Dr. Hasbrouck detailing the very serious surgical operation which had been performed upon his mouth. I confess I bent my head and wept when I thought of the pain he had suffered & the danger to the country.

"Few know so well as I do the devotion of this plain true man to his great duties—what energies—what toil, what anxieties have been his in the high performance of his duties—and at last his natural force has abated— and his weak link in the chain of vitality has been found.

"Oh how ineffably base, mean, cruel & poor have been the assaults upon him—such wretched suspicions & surmises, when all the while he was struggling with disease & fighting the good fight for the welfare & honor of his country. Dear soul! how my heart goes out to him & how much I feel my absence from his side,

"I have just written to him what I feel about him, but I am deeply concerned & distressed. This pending issue of the currency is fraught with the most profound & farreaching results. You may remember how for years I have dinned it into the ears of those around me & how little it seemed to be comprehended. Now the poisonous effects have been felt of a false assertion of values— & it is to be hoped that the costly experience of this summer will bring men to their sober senses.—Should this struggle cost Mr. Cleveland his life, & also eventuate in the vindication of his wisdom & devotion he will be glorified in men's memories, & generations yet unborn will rise up & call him blessed."

Upon receipt of the letter mentioned by Mr. Bayard, the President sent his Ambassador the following characteristic compound of politics and family affairs:

Private

Executive Mansion, Washington.

Sept 11, 1893.

My dear Mr Bayard:

I received to-day your letter of Sept 1st and thank you for it as well as for two or three preceding it and thus far unacknowledged. I especially want to thank you for the splendid picture of yourself you sent. I think it is the best and most faithful likeness I have ever seen.

I can well believe how interested you are in the subject just now occupying the time of the Senate. The action of the House was wonderfully gratifying and the majority we secured was beyond our expectations and to me was a demonstration that behind these direct representatives of the people there was a sentiment that actually *drove* them to duty.

The Senate is making a shameful display, but no one doubts that we have a good sound majority when the vote comes. With this conceded by all, the result hangs on, keeping back the day of better things. I shall not be much surprised however if the break occurs and a vote is reached sooner than the most of us expect. Isn't it queer that Voorhees and Gorman should be the leaders in a cause in which I am so vitally interested? "Strange bedfellows!" They are I believe both working well but every day is an anxious one for me, fearing that something may occur to distract time and attention, from the pending topic. . . .

Day before yesterday (the 9th) my wife presented me with what is always called I believe "a fine baby." It's a little girl and they do say it's a healthy one. The mother is as well as she can be and Ruth thus far seems to think the newcomer's advent is a great joke. You were only one of many who were trapped by a fool of a newspaper man into the premature expression of kind congratulation. I laid yours away and applied it to the event of last Saturday.

The report you saw regarding my health resulted from a most astounding breach of professional duty on the part of a medical man. I tell you this in strict confidence for the policy here has been to deny and discredit his story. I believe the American public and newspapers are not speculating further on the subject.

The truth is, office seeking and office seekers came very near putting a period to my public career. Whatever else developed found its opportunity in the weakened walls of a constitution that had long withstood fierce attacks. I turned the corner to the stage of enforced caretaking almost in a day. And this must be hereafter the condition on which will depend my health and life. Another phase of the situation cannot be spoken of with certainty but I believe the chances in my favor are at least even.

I have learned how weak the strongest man is under God's decrees and I see in a new light the necessity of doing my allotted work in the full apprehension of the coming night.

You must understand that I am regarded here as a perfectly well man and the story of an important surgical operation is thoroughly discredited.

I think I never looked better and I am much stronger than I have lately been. You have now more of the story than any one else outside of the medical circle.

Mrs. Cleveland sends love to you and Mrs. Bayard and with mine added in plenteous degree I am

Yours very sincerely

GROVER CLEVELAND.

HON. T. F. BAYARD.

Meanwhile, free silver Senators were exhausting every known parliamentary device to prevent action. The entire machinery of obstruction, which in the hands of a skillful and determined minority has proved fatal to so many worthy measures, was called into play. With equal skill, and backed by the consciousness of a stronger following, sound money Senators worked for a speedy trial of strength, and John Sherman worked with the President's friends.

In a spirit of compromise, Sherman had given his name to the Sherman Bill, in order to prevent the enactment of a more extreme free silver law, and he was as eager as was the President himself to see it repealed. In this, as in many previous currency conflicts, he merited the praise which Mr. Cleveland bestowed upon him: "No man in public life, certainly no Republican, has rendered a greater service to sound finance than John Sherman."

These weeks of steady conflict and ceaseless anxiety told heavily upon the impaired vitality of the President. His letters breathe the spirit almost of despair, but in them one looks in vain for the slightest sign of surrender. "I know there is a God," he wrote to Richard Watson Gilder, on October 12th, "but I do not know his purposes, nor when their results will appear. I know the clouds will roll away, but I do not know who, before that time, will be drowned in their floods." And to L. Clarke Davis, two days later, he said: "I am growing very tired physically and if I did not believe in God I should be sick at heart.

"I wonder if the good people of the Country will see before it is too late the danger that threatens, not only their financial well-being, but the very foundations upon which their institutions rest.

"I suppose it is wrong, but sometimes I feel very despondent and very much deserted. I believe in the people so fully, and things are often so forlorn here, that I want to feel and hear my fellow Countrymen all the time. Are they still about me? I think so often of Martin Luther's 'Here I stand—God help me.' "

Two weeks later, Ambassador Bayard wrote to Frederic Emory: "Assuming that the miserable makeshift of Sherman shall be wiped out, it seems to me there could be no better time than now to recall the words of James Russell Lowell, addressed to President Cleveland in his oration at the 250th anniversary of Harvard, in Cambridge:—The pilot of Seneca, 'Oh! Neptune, you may sink me, you may save me, but I will hold my rudder true.'

"Were I a painter, I should depict the scene of confusion, insubordination, and selfishness on deck, and the calm, steadfast pilot at the helm with his eye on the pole star, keeping the ship in her unswerving course."

Fortunately victory came before the President's depleted vitality had collapsed under the strain of keeping his rudder true. On October 30th, repeal in the form of a Senate substitute for the House bill passed the Senate by 43 to 32, 23 Republicans voting yea. Two days later, by 194 to 94, the House accepted the Senate bill, and Mr. Cleveland had won a truce over the increasing hosts of free silver.

In the *Atlantic Monthly* of March, 1897, Woodrow Wilson, then Professor of Jurisprudence in Princeton University, thus interpreted the meaning of this Cleveland victory:

"It was the President's victory that the law was at last repealed, and everyone knew it. He had forced the consideration of the question; he had told Senators plainly, almost passionately, when they approached him, that he would accept no compromise,—that he would veto anything less than absolute repeal, and let them face the country as best they might afterwards.

"Until he came on the stage, both parties had dallied and coquetted with the advocates of silver. Now he had brought both to a parting of the ways. The silver men were forced to separate themselves and look their situation in the face, choose which party they should plan to bring under their will and policy, if they could, and no longer camp in the tents of both.

"Such a stroke settled what the course of Congressional politics should be throughout the four years of Mr. Cleveland's term, and made it certain that at the end of that term he should either have won his party to himself or lost it altogether. It was evident that any party that rejected the gold standard for the currency must look upon him as its opponent."

From the point of view of the peace and effectiveness of the new administration, it was a costly victory. The necessities of the conflict had forced the President to cut across his own party and its Republican opponent, forming thereby a temporary coalition, dangerous alike to party discipline and party solidarity. He had, furthermore, admitted by his actions that the Republicans were nearer to soundness upon the great question of the hour than were the representatives of his own party. And by these actions he had won the bitter and lasting resentment of a vast body of Democrats who now denied, not only that Grover Cleveland was a Democrat, but even that he was an honest man, and who henceforth dedicated themselves to the task of reading him out of the party.

CHAPTER II

BLOCKING "MANIFEST DESTINY" IN HAWAII

"I mistake the American people if they favor the odious doctrine that there is no such thing as international morality; that there is one law for a strong nation and another for a weak one."

—GROVER CLEVELAND.

FEW of Mr. Cleveland's public actions have been more bitterly denounced, more needlessly misunderstood, or more deliberately misrepresented, than was his attitude toward the Hawaiian situation. Yet in refusing to connive at the annexation of Hawaii by methods sanctified by long usage, he but sounded, in the nineteenth century, the note which is the hope of the twentieth, the right of men everywhere "to choose their own ways of life and of obedience." As in the case of Germany and Samoa, he had uncompromisingly opposed a powerful nation in the interests of a helpless one, so in the case of the United States and Hawaii he took a ground no less just and impartial, although this time the aggressor was his own nation.

It would have been easy, had he been fitted with a less exacting conscience, for President Cleveland to allow the process of Hawaiian annexation to go smoothly on to its culmination. Instead, however, he invited conflict, which he hated, solely in the interest of international justice, solely that another weak and defenseless people might remain free. It was not annexation that he opposed, but conquest disguised as annexation.

45

v.2 c.2

From the beginning of our contact with the Hawaiian Islands, many Americans had felt that control by the United States, perhaps annexation, was inevitable. But until the days of President Harrison, the actions of American statesmen were in the main considerate of the sovereign rights of the Hawaiian people. In 1851 a menacing move on the part of France caused King Kamehameha III. to deliver to Mr. Severance, American Commissioner in Honolulu, an executed deed of gift, granting the islands in full sovereignty to the United States, and requesting him to take possession as soon as it should become evident that the king could not resist the French encroachments.

Instead of taking advantage of this situation to establish an American control over the islands, as he might easily have done, our Secretary of State, Daniel Webster, to the credit of the nation, directed that the deed be returned to the Hawaiian government, and notified France that it was the intention of the United States to keep her "naval armament . . . in the Pacific Ocean in such a state of strength and preparation as shall be requisite for the preservation of the honor and dignity of the United States and the safety of the government of the Hawaiian Islands."

In 1854 President Pierce's Secretary of State, William L. Marcy, marred this record by negotiating a treaty providing for the annexation of the islands, but the death of the Hawaiian king upset the scheme, and Hawaii was still free.

Meanwhile, commercial connections between the two countries grew rapidly. American merchants and planters immigrated in considerable numbers, and, in 1875, the United States and Hawaii entered into a treaty of commercial reciprocity. In this treaty appeared no menace to Hawaiian independence, save the provision which bound her not to alienate any of her territory to nations other than the United States. In 1884 a supplementary convention was negotiated by which Pearl Harbor was set aside for the exclusive use of the United States and her commerce.

Owing to delay in ratification, this supplementary convention was still pending when Mr. Cleveland first became President; and, after carefully studying its provisions, he strongly advised the Senate to approve it.

"I express my unhesitating conviction," he declared in his second annual message, "that the intimacy of our relations with Hawaii should be emphasized. As a result of the reciprocity treaty of 1875, those islands, on the highway of Oriental and Australasian traffic, are virtually an outpost of American commerce and a stepping-stone to the growing trade of the Pacific. The Polynesian island groups have been so absorbed by other and more powerful governments that the Hawaiian Islands are left almost alone in the enjoyment of their autonomy, which it is important for us, should be preserved. Our treaty is now terminable on one year's notice, but propositions to abrogate it would be, in my judgment, most ill-advised. The paramount influence we have there acquired, once relinquished, could only with difficulty be regained, and a valuable ground of vantage for ourselves might be converted into a stronghold for our commercial competitors. I earnestly recommend that the existing treaty stipulations be extended to a further term of seven years."

The treaty was proclaimed on November 9, 1887, and in the meantime the Bayonet revolution in Hawaii had forced the Hawaiian king to consent to a liberal constitution, enfranchising his numerous Western guests and making of himself a limited monarch. The character of this constitution was clearly the work of American minds, and is evidence that the Republic of the West was rapidly coming into control in Hawaii in the persons of men bred to American law and American ideals of government.

And so, when President Cleveland retired from office in 1889, although the sovereignty of the Hawaiian Islands was unimpaired, and her form of government entitled her to be called a constitutional monarchy, the process of peaceful penetration was well advanced, and it was evident to all men trained in the arts of imperialistic expansion that the days of Hawaiian independence were numbered.

Had the annexationists exercised patience, and respected the sovereign rights of the Hawaiian people, they might have reached their goal without the opposition which Grover Cleveland later accorded them. He saw no crime in annexation, should it come to be the free choice of the inhabitants of the islands, and while he perhaps never definitely approved, there is no indication that he ever disapproved the views of his Secretary of State, Thomas F. Bayard, who later declared: "The obvious course was to wait quietly and patiently, and let the islands fill up with American planters and American industries, until they should be wholly identified in business interests and political sympathies with the United States. It was simply a matter of waiting until the apple should ripen and fall."

Unfortunately, the administration which superseded Mr. Cleveland had not Mr. Cleveland's patience, and it was not long before our Minister to Hawaii, John S. Stevens, began consciously working by political means in the direction of the annexation of the country to which he was accredited, while the American Secretary of State failed to rebuke, if he did not actually encourage, this ambition. "The near future," Minister Stevens wrote to Secretary Blaine, on March 20, 1890, "is to show conclusively that only the strong pressure and continual vigilance of the United States can enable American men and American ideas to hold ascendency here and make these islands as prosperous and valuable to American commerce and to American marine supremacy in the north Pacific as the isles of the Mediterranean have been and are to its adjacent nations." Eagerly Stevens awaited the psychological moment for a brilliant stroke which would land the islands in the lap of his own country—waited, worked, and planned.

In 1891, King Kalakua died while on a visit to the United States, and his sister, the Princess Liliuokalani, ascended the throne by virtue of the twenty-second article of the Hawaiian Constitution of 1887. The new queen, imbued, as had been her late brother, with autocratic theories and possessed of a despotic temperament, was out of harmony with the liberal tendencies clearly manifest in her kingdom and specifically embodied in the constitution under which she reigned, and which she had sworn to defend.

This constitution was too modern for Queen Liliuokalani, who hated the white intruders, hated the missionaries, hated all the paraphernalia of what the West had labeled progress, and dreamed of reaction to the dark old ways of primitive autocracy. What she and her reactionary advisers longed for, was to be freed from the shackles of the constitution theory. This done, it would be easy to drive out the white man, confiscate his property, if necessary take his life.

Within a month after her accession, the ill-advised queen attempted to force the resignation of her ministers, and to select a cabinet composed of her tools. The opium ring, the lottery ring, and other parasites that flourish best upon autocracy, were pressing upon her plans, which they knew would have scant shrift should the American element gain control, and she was readily countenancing their advances, conscious that she needed their support in her contemplated return to the ways of earlier times. On January 14, 1893, professing to act under pressure of popular demand, she declared her intention to overthrow the constitution which had enfranchised the hated foreigner, and to substitute another more in accordance with her temperament and aspirations. But Hawaii had progressed beyond the point at which a restoration of autocracy was possible. The monarchy was a shell, ready to crumble at a touch of opposition, and the Queen's action was at once interpreted by Stevens and the small but powerful minority of annexationists as abdication, an interpretation based on ideas purely Western.

As soon as Liliuokalani understood the interpretation put upon her autocratic threat by her dangerous guest-citizens and their fellow disciples of Western law, she issued á recantation. But it was already too late. A committee of safety had been organized, and plans had been made for arming those who resented her disloyalty to the Constitution. It was revolution, and the days of Hawaiian royalty were over.

It is an interesting fact that Minister Stevens was not in Honolulu when the revolution broke. On January 4, 1893, he had sailed on the *Boston* for a cruise to Hilo, a hundred miles away. It is still more interesting to discover that he returned just as the revolution needed the support of American marines, and that, ten months before, he had written to Secretary Blaine: "I have little doubt the revolutionary attempt would have been made ere this but for the presence here of the United States ship-of-war. I still incline to the opinion that the revolutionary attempt will not be made so long as there is a United States force in the harbor of Honolulu."

As soon as the *Boston,* with the American Minister on board, re-entered the harbor, Mr. Stevens was asked by the leaders of the revolution to land the marines, and he at once complied. Admiral Skerrett later commented that: "the American troops were well located if designed to promote the movement for the Provisional Government, and very improperly located if only intended to protect American citizens in person and property."

The revolution moved rapidly. Before the close of the seventeenth of January, the monarchy was declared at an end, Stevens had recognized the Provisional Government, and the latter had assumed full control "until such time as terms of union with the United States of America should have been agreed on. Two weeks later, at the request of President Dole of the Provisional Government, Stevens raised the American flag over the government buildings, and thus established a protectorate pending annexation.

These facts furnish an excellent basis for what the theologians term "argument from design." They tally also with the defense which Murat Halstead later made of Stevens: "He was an American himself, with a partiality for white folks, and, we presume, had the common American sentiment that the islands belonged to us, and our title would be perfected some day," and Stevens' own dispatches, both the published and the unpublished, make it quite clear that he gloried in the belief that manifest destiny had thus marked Hawaii as American property.

Meanwhile the Provisional Government had dispatched five commissioners, four Americans and one Englishman, to request President Harrison to annex the islands of the Hawaiians to the United States. They were received, on February 4th, by Secretary of State Foster, and eleven days later Harrison sent to the United States Senate a treaty providing that: "the government of the Hawaiian Islands hereby cedes . . . absolutely and without reservation to the United States forever all rights of sovereignty of whatever kind in and over the Hawaiian Islands and their dependencies." The document bore six signatures—John W. Foster, Lorin A. Thurston, William R. Castle, William C. Wilder, Charles L. Carter, and Joseph Marsden. There was not one Polynesian name on the list.

In his accompanying message President Harrison informed the Senate that "the overthrow of the monarchy was not in any way promoted by this Government," and this President Harrison unquestionably believed, having been so informed by the promoters of "Manifest Destiny," that ancient altar piece which the annexationists were employing to give sanctity to their plans and value to their plantations.

As President Harrison's term was drawing toward its close, friend and foe of the pending annexation treaty began to speculate what would be the policy of the returning President, Grover Cleveland. But the latter, while watching carefully the progress of the annexation movement, scrupulously avoided any expression of opinion upon the subject until the responsibility should again become his.

In the absence of facts, the newspapers, of course, published fiction. The day before the inauguration, the Omaha *Bee* confidently assured its readers, upon the basis of that most untrustworthy witness, "good authority," that Mr. Cleveland could be counted upon "to promote as far as possible the 'Manifest Destiny' doctrine which contemplates the ultimate extension of the United States over the entire North American continent and the absorption of whatever 'outposts' it may be found expedient or desirable to possess."

This illusion was soon dispelled by the new President. Within a week after his inauguration, he sent to the Senate a curt message of five lines: "For the purpose of re-examination I withdraw the treaty of annexation between the United States and the Provisional Government of the Hawaiian Islands now pending in the Senate, which was signed on February 14, 1893, and transmitted to the Senate on the 15th of the same month; and I therefore request that said treaty be returned to me. Grover Cleveland."

He was not content that Hawaii should be annexed upon the mere assurance of annexationists that "the overthrow of the monarchy was not in any way promoted by this Government." Beneath the insistent demand for immediate annexation, in order that there might be, as Harrison had expressed it, "decent administration of civil affairs," might lurk the ancient Anglo-Saxon thirst for empire. Perhaps in Hawaii his own nation had been guilty of the very sin which he was seeking to prevent the German Imperial Chancellor from committing in the Samoan Islands—the ruthless subversion of a weak and helpless nation.

As he studied the documents in the State Department he became increasingly suspicious. To annex the islands in response to the free will of their population would be entirely justifiable, but to annex them in response to the desire of American officials would be something quite different. What he had learned of the history of Hawaii's recent past inclined him to give ear to an appeal lately received from the dethroned queen herself, a passionate appeal for justice, based upon the contention that the revolution had been planned and carried out by Americans, chief among whom was the American Minister:

To His Excellency
Grover Cleveland
President Elect of the
United States.
My great and good friend:

In the vicissitudes which happened in the Hawaiian Islands and which affect my people, myself and my house so seriously, I feel comforted the more that beside the friendly relations of the United States, I have the boon of Your personal friendship and good will.

The changes which occurred here need not be stated in this letter. You will have, at the time at which it reaches You the official information, but I have instructed the Hon. Paul Neuman whom I have appointed my representative at Washington, to submit to You a precis of the facts and circumstances relating to the revolution in Honolulu, and to supplement it by such statements which you may please to elicit.

I beg that You will consider this matter in which there is so much involved for my people, and that you give us your friendly assistance in granting redress for a wrong which we claim has been done to us under color of the assistance of the naval forces of the United States in a friendly port.

Believe me that I do not veil under this a request to You the fulfillment of which could in the slightest degree be contrary to Your position, and I leave our grievance in Your hands confident that in so far as you deem it proper we shall have Your sympathy and Your aid.

I am Your good friend

LILIUOKALANI.

Looking only upon the surface, it seemed reasonable to accept the vociferous assurances of the annexationists that Stevens had landed the marines only for the entirely legal and proper task of protecting American lives and American property. But in his study of the documents, Mr. Cleveland soon became convinced that Stevens had deliberately furthered the revolution in order the sooner to make Hawaii American territory. "To a minister of this temper, full of zeal for annexation," he later informed Congress, "there seemed to arise in January, 1893, the precise opportunity for which he was *watchfully waiting* . . . and we are quite prepared for the exultant enthusiasm with which, in a letter to the State Department dated February 1, 1893, he declares: 'The Hawaiian pear is now fully ripe, and this is the golden hour for the United States to pluck it.'"

Having withdrawn the treaty from the Senate, President Cleveland next sent the Honorable James H. Blount, recently Chairman of the House Committee on Foreign Affairs, as his special personal agent to Hawaii to discover the facts. In his testimony before the Senate Committee at a later date, Blount made under oath the statement that President Cleveland never gave him the least intimation as to what his own views regarding the situation in Hawaii were. "I was impressed," he said, "with the belief that he wanted information."

Pending Blount's report, the President of course received information from Minister Stevens, whose new dispatches presented the history of the revolution in the most favorable light, and made it quite clear that the landing of troops, in Stevens's opinion, had insured its final success.

"The supporters of the Provisional Government," he wrote, on April 4, 1893, "having had little or no military experience, an organized military force could not be created at once. Time was absolutely necessary. The presence of the few United States soldiers with their country's flag was of incalculable importance to the only existing and the only possible government for Hawaii. When the men of the *Boston* went to their ship April 1st, the Provisional Government had at its command a military force of four hundred men,—the most effective ever known in the islands, and an organized police with a tried and efficient man at the head. The remarkable change accomplished in seventy-five days had been without the loss of life or the destruction of property. Had the United States Minister and the Naval Commander not acted as they did, they would have deserved prompt removal from their places and the just censure of the friends of humanity and of civilization."

Thus Stevens's own dispatches justified the President's uneasy suspicions. But when Blount's report of July 17th reached him, it changed suspicion into a sense of certainty. After studying it and numerous items of documentary evidence furnished by his personal agent, Mr. Cleveland reached a definite conclusion. Stevens and certain American associates were the real authors of the Hawaiian revolution, made with the express purpose of annexation. "Mr. Stevens," Blount boldly declared, "consulted freely with the leaders of the revolutionary movement from the evening of the 14th. These disclosed to him all their plans. They feared arrest and punishment. He promised them protection. They needed the troops on shore to overawe the Queen's supporters and government. This he agreed to and did furnish. . . . The leaders of the revolutionary movement would not have undertaken it but for Mr. Stevens's promise to protect them against any danger from the government. . . . But for this no request to land troops would have been made. Had the troops not been landed no measures for the organization of a new government would have been taken.

"The American Minister and the revolutionary leaders had determined on a new addition to the United States and had agreed on the part each was to act to the very end."

Blount's report made it further evident that the revolution rested little upon the wishes of the native Hawaiians. "If the votes of persons claiming allegiance to foreign countries were excluded," he confidently informed Mr. Cleveland, "it (annexation) would be defeated by more than five to one." And this view was independently confirmed by Charles Nordhoff, a veteran Washington correspondent, whom the New York *Herald* sent to Honolulu to check up Blount's statements and report to the American people, and whom the Provisional Government vainly tried to silence.

"No one unprejudiced," declared the New York *Herald's* leading editorial of November 22, 1893, "can read Mr. Blount's report without the conviction that it goes into the archives of the State Department at Washington as the darkest chapter in the diplomatic annals of this country."

The New York *Times* declared, editorially, that it "reveals a conspiracy . . . which if not repudiated by this nation, would sully the honor and blacken the fair name of the United States."

"The people of this country," said the Savannah *Morning News,* "if they accept Mr. Blount's report, cannot do otherwise than sustain the position taken by the President and his Cabinet. The only way to create a sentiment against that position is to show that Mr. Blount's report is not correct."

This suggestion the annexationists promptly adopted. Blount was accused of working for a verdict against the white "crusaders of Democracy," and in favor of "the lady who looks like the inside of a package of Arbuckle's coffee"; he had seen only the queen's friends; he was the man who had hauled down the American flag. But Blount's work had been conscientiously and intelligently done, his facts were in the main identical with those presented by Nordhoff and other disinterested spectators, and the attempts of the annexationists to prove the contrary met with little success.

The Cleveland press challenged Stevens or ex-President Harrison, or any one else to point to a statement in the report which was not true. "Mr. Stevens," declared the Chicago *Herald,* "was asked to show wherein Mr. Blount has misstated facts. Mr. Stevens had a peremptory engagement out of town for several days. . . . Ex-President Harrison was also invited to show that Blount erred in any statement of fact. The ex-President diplomatically avoided the issue."

A few days later, however, Stevens sent forth from his retreat in Maine an elaborate reply to Blount's report; and the Hawaiian Minister, Lorin A. Thurston, in columns of argument, denounced what he termed Blount's "gross inaccuracies." But Stevens was now in the position of a deposed official, and Thurston was regarded as merely a special pleader paid for the work.

The New York *Tribune,* in its issue of November 22,

1893, ventured upon a psychological argument designed to discredit Mr. Cleveland's policy. "The secret springs or motives are out of sight, hidden in personal relations," it impressively declared, ". . . In this, as in a great many other things, the unwritten, personal factor is potential. It is easily stated. The present Secretary of State (Mr. Gresham) has been for many years the personal enemy of ex-President Harrison, as he was also of the late Secretary Blaine. . . . Minister Stevens was an intimate personal friend of Mr. Blaine. He was an appointee of President Harrison. The policy he pursued in Hawaii was approved by the Harrison administration."

And so Grover Cleveland had faced his own nation and thwarted a movement which strongly appeals always to the strain of Anglo-Saxon blood, in order that Secretary Gresham's personal hatreds might be avenged. To such strange lengths will party spirit go, even in great affairs. And this is one of the dangers of democracies.

With little attention to disputes regarding his methods or motives, President Cleveland now faced the difficult question of action. One thing was clear to his mind: Whatever the cost, he must see justice done to the sovereignty of Hawaii.

In his search for a method by which the United States could undo the wrong which had been done by men serving in her name, the President suggested that Secretary Gresham ask specific advice from the members of the Cabinet. The opinion furnished by Attorney General Richard Olney anticipates in essential features the plan finally adopted. After a convincing summary of the American origin of what he terms "the Stevens Government," Mr. Olney suggested:

"1. All the resources of diplomacy should be exhausted to restore the *status quo* in Hawaii by peaceful methods and without force.

"2. If, as a last resort, force is found to be necessary . . . the matter must be submitted to Congress for its action.

"3. In addition to providing for the security of the queen's person pending efforts to reinstate the queen's government . . . the United States should require of the queen . . . authority to negotiate and bring about the restoration of her government on such reasonable terms and conditions as the United States may approve and find to be practicable.

"Among such terms and conditions must be, I think, full pardon and amnesty for all connected with the Stevens government who might otherwise be liable to be visited with the pains and penalties attending the crime of treason."

In the light of this and other opinions, Secretary Gresham wrote to the President an elaborate summary of the case. His recommendations were less specific than Olney's, but their general tenor was the same. And he added a moral interpretation which he knew would strike a responsive chord in the President's heart: "Should not the great wrong done to a feeble but independent state by an abuse of the authority of the United States be undone by restoring the legitimate government? Anything short of that will not, I respectfully submit, satisfy the demands of justice. . . ."

A consultation followed and that evening Secretary Gresham wrote to inform the new Minister, Albert S. Willis, of the President's decision, and to give confidential instructions for his guidance:

"You will . . . inform the Queen that, when reinstated, the President expects that she will pursue a magnanimous course by granting full amnesty to all who participated in the movement against her. . . . Having secured the Queen's agreement . . . you will then advise the Executive of the Provisional Government and his ministers of the President's determination of the question . . . and they are expected to promptly relinquish to her her constitutional authority." In case of failure to accomplish a peaceful settlement by agreement, Willis was ordered to report the facts and await further directions.

From this and many subsequent letters, it is evident that Mr. Cleveland had no idea of attempting by force to restore the queen of Hawaii. On the contrary, on December 3d, Secretary Gresham again wrote to Willis: "Should the Queen ask whether if she accedes to conditions, active steps will be taken by the United States to effect her restoration or to maintain her authority thereafter, you will say that the President cannot use force without the authority of Congress." And Blount, in his sworn testimony before the Morgan Committee, later declared: "I never heard it [the idea of a restoration by force] suggested until my return to the United States."

A busy press had, however, already managed to interpret the necessary operations of the navy as proof that armed intervention in favor of Liliuokalani was the President's program. The Newport, R. I., *Herald* had informed its readers, on November 16th, that "it is said on good naval authority that as soon as the United States ships, *Ranger* and *Mohican* . . . can be made ready for sea the Secretary of the Navy will order their commanders to proceed direct to Honolulu. . . . The combined crews of the *Ranger* and *Mohican* would enable the landing of a larger marine force than from the *Philadelphia* (already there)."

Upon the basis of this evidence of heroic intent, the enthusiastic colored citizens of Newport met and dispatched to the President a letter of congratulation that in his blow for justice he had not regarded color, nor been prejudiced by the fact that "the sun has blared heavily upon the dark skin Queen's ancestry."

As it chanced, on that very sixteenth of November, Minister Willis was preparing a dispatch containing the discouraging details of his first interview with the dethroned queen: "In the forenoon of Monday . . . [November 13th] the Queen, accompanied by the Royal Chamberlain . . . called at the Legation. . . . After a formal greeting, the Queen was informed that the President . . . had important communications to make to her, and she was asked whether she was willing to receive them alone and in confidence. . . . She answered in the affirmative.

"I then made known to her the President's sincere regret that through the unauthorized intervention of the United States, she had been obliged to surrender her sovereignty, and his hope that with her consent and co-operation, the wrong done to her and her people might be redressed. To this she bowed her acknowledgment.

"I then said to her: 'The President expects and believes that when reinstated you will show forgiveness and magnanimity.' . . . To this she made no reply.

"After waiting a moment, I continued: 'The President not only tenders you his sympathy but wishes to help you. Before fully making known to you his purposes, I desire to know whether you are willing to answer certain questions which it is my duty to ask.' She answered: 'I am willing.' "

The Minister then asked whether, if restored to her

throne, she would grant full amnesty to those concerned in her overthrow.

"She hesitated for a moment and then slowly and calmly answered: 'There are certain laws of my government by which I shall abide. My decision would be, as the law directs, that such persons should be beheaded and their property confiscated.'"

The Minister, dumbfounded at so frank a statement, asked: "Do you fully understand the meaning of every word which I have said to you, and of every word which you have said to me?" The queen replied: "I have understood and mean all I have said. . . . These people were the cause of the revolution and Constitution of 1887. There will never be any peace while they are here. . . .'"

Immediately after this interview, Willis telegraphed to Washington: "Views of first party so extreme as to require further instructions."

These facts were, of course, not made public and, with the newspaper stories of a projected forcible restoration of the queen in mind, the President's annual message was eagerly awaited. When, on December 4, 1893, it came, it was disappointingly lacking in dramatic quality. Simply, unimpassionedly, Mr. Cleveland informed Congress that he was conscientiously seeking "to undo the wrong that had been done by those representing us and to restore, as far as practicable, the status existing at the time of our forcible intervention." More than that he was not yet ready to say.

A fortnight later, the President received from Willis a list of perplexing questions: ". . . Assuming the restoration of the Queen, with the temporary acquiescence of the Provisional Government, what next? If left to itself it would fall to pieces like a card house. Would it be just to restore her and have another revolution at once—

which seems probable? If restored, would she not be
entitled to our protection until she was securely seated?
How long would this require, and what immediate announcement (after restoration) if any, should be made?

"Shall our Government suggest to the restored
queen (in the interest of peace and good government)
that the Constitution of 1887 should not be overturned
except as therein provided? Shall anything be said about
the opium license law and lottery law which have been
repealed by the Provisional Government and the passage
of which had as much to do with the late uprising as the
threat of the Queen to promulgate a new Constitution?

"In restoring the status ante shall men like Mr. Dole
be put back on the Supreme Bench? Shall vacancies (as
now intimated) be declared because of participation in
the Queen's overthrow? . . .

"If the Queen should, while under our quasi protection, again promulgate a new Constitution, shall we make
no remonstrance? This question is uppermost in Hawaiian hearts."

Such questions asked by the perplexed Minister
reached far beyond the realm which the Constitution had
assigned to the executive branch of the Government. The
President, therefore, decided to mass his evidence regarding the origin and meaning of the Hawaiian revolution into a special message to Congress, and thus force it
and the nation to face squarely and without the distraction
of other topics what he conceived to be a great moral
issue. On December 18th, this special Hawaiian message was sent to Congress. It is a document of arraign-
ment, of denunciation, ballasted by carefully substanti-
ated facts. Never, not even in his suppressed message
concerning Germany's secret intrigues against Samoan
independence, nor in his later and more famous arraign-

ment of what he believed to be the British disregard of Venezuela's sovereign rights, did he denounce a foreign government more uncompromisingly than he here denounced his own government.

It mattered not to him that expansion into the Pacific was a popular policy; that the American public could not easily be aroused to sympathy with a dethroned, dark-skinned Oriental queen; that the wrong which he denounced was an accomplished fact, and that it requires more than courage and a good cause to set back the hands of time. He poured his withering scorn upon a great and powerful nation which will stoop to countenance intrigue on the part of its own officials, that a few more acres of soil, a few more harbors and clear lagoons may be added to its vast estate. "The control of both sides of a bargain," such were his words, ". . . is called by a familiar and unpleasant name when found in private transactions."

In acknowledging his failure to secure justice to Hawaii, although executive power had been employed to the full, he laid before Congress his vision of a foreign policy worthy of a great, powerful Christian nation. In begging that justice be done, he urged upon them a standard than which no loftier has ever been presented to that body, whether by President, Secretary, or duly elected Senator or Representative:

"It has been the boast of our Government," he said, "that it seeks to do justice in all things, without regard to the strength or weakness of those with whom it deals. I mistake the American people if they favor the odious doctrine that there is no such thing as international morality; that there is one law for a strong nation and another for a weak one, and that even by indirection a strong power may with impunity despoil a weak one of its territory. . . . The law of nations is founded upon reason and jus-

tice, and the rules of conduct governing individual relations between citizens or subjects of a civilized state are
equally applicable as between enlightened nations.

"The considerations that international law is without
a court for its enforcement and that obedience to its com-
mands practically depends upon good faith instead of
upon the mandate of a superior tribunal only give additional sanction to the law itself and brand any deliberate
infraction of it not merely as wrong, but as a disgrace.
A man of true honor protects the unwritten word which
binds his conscience more scrupulously, if possible, than
he does a bond a breach of which subjects him to legal
liabilities, and the United States, in aiming to maintain
itself as one of the most enlightened nations, would do its
citizens gross injustice if it applied to its international
relations any other than a high standard of honor and
morality. On that ground the United States cannot be
properly put in the position of countenancing a wrong
after its commission any more than of consenting to it in
advance. On that ground it cannot allow itself to refuse
to redress an injury inflicted through an abuse of power
by officers clothed with its authority and wearing its uniform; and on the same ground, if a feeble but friendly
state is in danger of being robbed of its independence and
its sovereignty by a misuse of the name and power of the
United States, the United States cannot fail to vindicate
its honor and its sense of justice by an earnest effort to
make all possible reparation."

Henceforth, while diligently furnishing to Congress
all information which reached him, the President was no
longer the chief actor. As it chanced, on the very day
when his Hawaiian message was presented, Queen
Liliuokalani capitulated, sending to Mr. Willis a letter
which declared: "I must not feel vengeful to any of my

people. If I am restored by the United States, I must forget myself, and remember only my dear people and my country. . . ." With it she sent a solemn pledge promising, in the event of her restoration, full pardon and amnesty to all who had taken part in the revolution.

The same day brought to Minister Willis, from President Dole, the curt inquiry: "Will you inform me if . . . you are acting in any way hostile to this government?" Willis's reply was a demand that the Provisional Government restore to the queen the authority of Constitutional Monarch of Hawaii, upon which the Provisional Government declared that, even if the revolution had been made possible by the assistance of American troops and American officials, which was stoutly denied, "the President was not thereby given the least right to control the actions of the *de facto* government of Hawaii," a proposition which Mr. Cleveland would have been the last to controvert.

Willis here ventured upon dangerous ground. In order to test the courage of the Provisional Government he resorted to the menace of violence, and in so doing violated the whole spirit of his instructions. Taking advantage of the arrival of the revenue cutter, *Corwin*, with dispatches from the State Department the nature of which was of course unknown to the Provisional Government, Willis had the troops drawn up on the decks of the *Adams* and the *Philadelphia*, as though preparing to land an attack. "He had the guns of our ships pointed at the palace in Honolulu," reported the San Francisco *Evening Bulletin* of January 10, 1894, "but he did not succeed in scaring anybody. . . . The Provisional Government did not come down. . . . President Dole . . . knew just how far Willis dared go. It would have been as much as his official neck was worth to have done more than beat the tom-tom."

This incident served to give the enemies of the administration a shadowy pretext for circulating the report that the President was invading the precincts of Congress, by presuming to menace a friendly sovereign nation with a war which Congress had never sanctioned. The cry of impeachment was raised, was gravely re-echoed on the floors of Congress, only to sink into deserved oblivion; for those who knew the facts knew that the President had never contemplated force in Hawaii, but only an honorable settlement by mutual agreement.

Meanwhile, Congress, to whose wide discretion he had committed the task, as too large for mere executive control, was unsteadily but certainly yielding to "Manifest Destiny." The House of Representatives, while condemning the filibustering which had brought on the Hawaiian revolution, and declining to sanction annexation under such conditions, was naturally unwilling to take steps to restore the deposed queen by force; while the Senate felt that the United States should let Hawaiian affairs alone, insisting that other nations do the same. This was equivalent to allowing the revolution to stand, and annexation to await a more convenient season.

During the six months which followed, the Hawaiian revolution developed into the Hawaiian Republic, which was formally proclaimed on July 4, 1894. The stability of this new government becoming clear, President Cleveland, before the end of the month, withdrew the American vessels from the harbor of Honolulu and, on August 7th, sent to President Dole a formal letter of recognition. He thus accepted in its fullness the logic of the facts. Dole and his fellow white men in Hawaii had succeeded in establishing an orderly government, demonstrably able to fulfil the obligations of statehood. They were, there-fore, entitled to the legal recognition which alone could make them responsible agents among the nations of the world.

In recognizing the new republic President Cleveland logically committed himself to the proposition that it was able to speak with the voice of Hawaiian sovereignty. His subsequent refusal to countenance annexation at its request was, therefore, illogical and of doubtful wisdom. Had he not thus refused, the revolt of 1895 might have been avoided. As it was, the Royalists made a final effort to re-enlist him in their now hopeless cause, soon to end in a bloody defeat. They sent to Washington a commission to plead for his assistance. But when the date set for the audience arrived, Mr. Cleveland was ill in bed. He therefore sent them the following address, with which they were forced to depart:

Executive Mansion, Washington.

Gentlemen:

You must permit me to remind you that this inter-view is not an official one, and that instead of receiving you in any representative capacity, I meet you as indi-viduals who have traveled a long distance for the pur-pose of laying a certain matter before me.

You ask if there is any hope of my "doing anything for the restoration of the Constitutional Government of the Hawaiian Islands." I suppose that this question is largely prompted by the fact that soon after the over-turning of the late Government of the Queen, I investi-gated that transaction and was satisfied that there had been such an unjustifiable interference in aid of that movement, on the part of representatives of the Govern-ment of the United States in its Diplomatic and Naval service, as to call for correction, not only to rectify what seemed to be a wrong done to others, but also through that rectification to ward off what appeared to be a danger to American honor and probity.

"Fully appreciating the constitutional limitations of my Executive power and by no means unmindful of the hindrances that might arise, I undertook the task. Having failed in my plans, I committed the entire subject to the Congress of the United States, which had abundant power and authority in the premises. The Executive branch of the Government was thereby discharged from further duty and responsibility in the matter unless moved thereto by Congressional command. The Congress has, both by its action and its omission to act, signified that nothing need be done touching American interference with the overthrow of the Government of the Queen.

"Quite lately a government has been established in Hawaii which is in full force and operation in all parts of the Islands. It is maintaining its authority and discharging all ordinary governmental functions. Upon general principles and not losing sight of the special circumstances surrounding this case, the new government is clearly entitled to our recognition without regard to any of the incidents which accompanied or preceded its inauguration.

"This recognition and the attitude of the Congress concerning Hawaiian affairs of course lead to an absolute denial of the least present or future aid or encouragement on my part to an effort to restore any government heretofore existing in the Hawaiian Islands."

When the Republican platform of 1896 was sent broadcast over the country, it contained these words: "The Hawaiian Islands should be controlled by the

United States." No one could question the fact that Hawaii was now in a condition quite different from that of the days of the revolution. Her republic was firmly established, her Constitution in effective operation, and she had demonstrated her ability to preserve order at home and to fulfil her obligations abroad. Furthermore, the friends of annexation unhesitatingly urged two most effective arguments, and urged them through the medium of organized propaganda. These were first, commercial interest, and second, fear of Japan.

Almost ninety-three per cent of Hawaii's trade, declared one of their propaganda leaflets, is with the United States. China and Japan have only about two and a half per cent, although they number in the islands over forty thousand out of a total population of a hundred and ten thousand. "We can prevent Chinese occupying our beautiful country . . . but it is not so with Japan. . . . Japan wants colonies and possessions. From the Japanese press and from what her people say here, it is evident that Japan intends to possess Hawaii. . . . While you are maintaining your policy of 'hands off' and 'let Hawaii alone' . . . the Japanese will quietly and peacefully pour into Hawaii till they simply overwhelm us by their numbers. . . . When Hawaii is full of Japanese, of whom many will be educated and just as intelligent and capable of self-government as our present electors, can it be supposed that we can prevent them from voting? Never! and by a single election all will be changed. . . . In place of the beloved Stars and Stripes, our ports will be filled with ships carrying the bright field and proud sun flag of Japan."

In response to such appeals President McKinley, on June 16, 1897, submitted to the United States Senate a new treaty of annexation. And three days later Mr.

Cleveland wrote to Mr. Olney: "Did you ever see such a preposterous thing as the Hawaiian business? The papers I read are most strongly opposed to it and there ought to be soberness and decency enough in the Senate to save us from launching upon the dangerous policy which is foreshadowed by the pending treaty; but I am prepared for almost anything."

For a time the opposition in the Senate proved stronger than Mr. Cleveland had dared hope. The expected ratification failed to materialize, and on February 16, 1898, Mr. Cleveland, now a private citizen, wrote confidently to Olney: "All the influence of this administration appears unable thus far to bring to a successful issue the Hawaiian monstrosity." But the annexationists bided their time, which now was not far off. On April 25, 1898, came the declaration of war against Spain, and for a time it seemed that the annexation question would have to wait upon more pressing matters. "Hawaii," wrote Mr. Olney to Mr. Cleveland, with the intimacy of an old comrade in arms, "seems to be in the soup."

That "soup," however, offered unforeseen advantages to the cause of annexation, for the new government of Hawaii soon won further favor in the United States by openly violating international law in allowing American ships of war to coal in Honolulu and to use the islands as a sort of naval base, thus giving a graphic illustration of the vastly increased importance of annexation, now that American guns had made for us a Philippine problem.

About a month after Admiral Dewey's victory at Manila Bay (May 1, 1898), President McKinley remarked to Mr. Cortelyou: "We need Hawaii just as much and a good deal more than we did California. It is Manifest Destiny." Two months later he signed a joint resolution of both houses annexing the islands, and on August 12th, the very American flag which Grover Cleveland had caused to be hauled down was raised again in token of American sovereignty. "Manifest Destiny" had triumphed at last.

After reading the newspaper account of the closing scene in the long drama, Mr. Cleveland sadly wrote to Mr. Olney: "Hawaii is ours. As I look back upon the first steps in this miserable business and as I contemplate the means used to complete the outrage, I am ashamed of the whole affair."

The world's past struggles toward liberty and equality have had as their goal liberty and equality among those of the white race. Its struggles to come lie along the pathway that leads to liberty and equality among all peoples, whether white or black, red, brown, or yellow. In the Hawaiian affair Grover Cleveland made many minor mistakes, but in holding that far-off goal before the eyes of his fellow-citizens, he was, in a very real and a very heroic sense, a world-pioneer.

CHAPTER III

BREAKING THE ENDLESS CHAIN—THE FOUR BOND ISSUES

*"There is a vast difference between a standard of value and
a currency for monetary use."*
—GROVER CLEVELAND.

W HAT our nation needs—and sorely needs," Mr.
Cleveland said, when speaking in honor of the
great American, Carl Schurz, "is more patriotism that
is born of moral courage—the courage that attacks abuses
and struggles for civic reforms, single-handed, without
counting opposing numbers or measuring opposing
forces."

Had these words been written for Grover Cleveland
himself, they could not have better described his attitude
toward the duties which go with office. His public life
was a succession of such conflicts. Before one storm was
over, there always appeared on the political horizon
another cloud the size of a man's hand, prophesying
another deluge. When thinking of his public life, he
instinctively thought of conflict, and his writing regarding his two administrations deals wholly with the history
of major struggles in the interest of what he conceived to
be the honor of the Republic and the safety of its people.

Four years before his death, in outlining a course of
lectures regarding his second term, to be delivered at
Princeton University, he wrote: "The members of that
administration who still survive, in recalling the events
of this laborious service, cannot fail to fix upon the years
1894 and 1895 as the most troublous and anxious of their
incumbency." He enumerated as the chief incidents of

74

that testing time the following leading conflicts: (1) "Unhappy currency complications [which] compelled executive resort to heroic treatment for the preservation of our nation's financial integrity, and forced upon the administration a constant, unrelenting struggle for sound money." (2) "A long and persistent executive effort to accomplish beneficent and satisfactory tariff reform." (3) "A very determined labor disturbance [which] broke out in the City of Chicago." (4) "Executive insistence upon the Monroe Doctrine [which] culminated in a situation that gave birth to solemn thoughts of war."

The first and most pressing of these questions was but the recurrence, in a slightly different form, of the struggle which had resulted in the repeal of the Sherman Law, on November 1, 1893. Almost immediately after that repeal it became apparent that the President had won not a victory but an armistice, and that another trial of strength was inevitable. This was precipitated neither by Mr. Cleveland nor by his free silver opponents, but by the operation of economic law, menacing the country with the banishment of gold and the consequent establishment of a silver standard of value.

Despite the opposition which he offered to the free coinage of silver, President Cleveland never objected to the free use of silver as money. What he feared, and fought, was the substitution of a silver basis of value for our established gold standard, and the repeal of the Sherman Law had done little to quiet his fears. He was still responsible for the impossible task of keeping the two metals at a parity, which meant that still he must be ready to pay a gold dollar whenever a Treasury note, representing only a deposit of about sixty cents worth of silver, was presented with a demand for gold.

To do this it was essential that the gold reserve, designed to cover only greenbacks, be maintained at a strength sufficient for this added strain upon it. But, despite the fact that he had stopped the monthly increase of Treasury notes by repealing the Sherman Law, his gold reserve was melting away. The combined attack of the outstanding $450,000,000 of United States notes and greenbacks was working ruin, for, when redeemed for gold, they had to be reissued, only to return and draw out more gold.

Thus, in an endless chain, the paper money ran, dragging the gold reserve ever downward, and bringing the country ever nearer to the point where gold payment must be refused. Gold, furthermore, was being exported to an extent that added to the President's alarm. As the total amount of gold in the country was now only $597,697,865, it was not difficult to foresee the end.

The only available means of replenishing the gold reserve was through the issue of government bonds, as authorized by an act of January 14, 1875. But the practical value of this method was greatly lessened by the fact that such bonds could not be made payable in gold. To persuade the public to buy for gold five per cent ten-year bonds, four and a half per cent fifteen-year bonds, or four per cent thirty-year bonds "payable in coin," was certain to prove difficult, as the purchaser must take the chance of having them redeemed in depreciated silver at the end, should the Treasury Department so order.

In forcing the repeal of the Sherman Law, President Cleveland had, therefore, taken only the first step in his monetary reform, and he now prepared for the second, the issuing of bonds to secure the gold necessary to maintain the gold reserve.

At once the free silver men of both parties formed plans to block the program.

Congressman William Jennings Bryan was especially active in opposition. On January 5, 1894, Secretary Morton wrote to Henry T. Thurber, Private Secretary to the President:

"Find herewith enclosed a Washington dispatch taken from the Omaha *Daily Bee* of Tuesday, January 2. Mr. Heath, who signs it, is rather a careful and conservative man, and, I think, incapable of willing misrepresentation. Therefore, I send the article to you, that the President may see precisely how Mr. Bryan represents himself to his people in Nebraska, upon the issuance of bonds, which are vital to the good credit of our common country.

"Very truly yours,

"J. STERLING MORTON."

The enclosed clipping declared: "Bryan comes uppermost. . . . Fate of the bond issue in his hands. . . . Bryan, after all, appears to hold the whip hand upon the administration, and will be heard from and felt in such a way as to compel President Cleveland to respect if not fear him. He is a member of the Ways and Means Sub-committee having in charge the subject of the public debt. To this sub-committee, composed also of McMillin, of Tennessee, and Whiting, of Michigan, will be referred the bond question. The administration is very anxious for authority to issue $200,000,000 or more of bonds, with which to meet current expenses, fill the deficiency vacuum and replenish the gold reserve. Mr. Bryan is opposed to a bond issue for any purpose, and so are his two colleagues. . . . It looks as though a bond issue may be defeated."

A later paragraph throws light upon Mr. Bryan's political methods: "In view of Mr. Bryan's new accession of strength by virtue of the proposed bond issue, it will create no surprise if he hereafter gets his full share of the Nebraska federal patronage. He is now confident of being able to name the postmaster at Lincoln. . . . If the Morton-Castor combine cuts him out of this piece of local patronage, it can confidently be expected that Mr. Bryan will make the fur fly on the bond issue problem."

There is nothing to indicate that President Cleveland ever contemplated the issue of $200,000,000 of bonds at any one time, although the total amount of the bonds actually issued by him, in his fight to preserve the gold standard, greatly exceeded that amount, and the statement that he designed to employ the proceeds of the bond issue to meet current expenses was palpably untrue. The Treasury Department had no authority to issue bonds for such a purpose, and the President later assured Congress that "at no time . . . has there been any consideration of the question."

By January 17th, the gold reserve stood at $70,000,000, and the public was showing itself more and more distrustful of the government's will or ability to furnish gold upon demand. The same day Secretary Carlisle announced that $50,000,000 in ten-year five per cent bonds, redeemable in "coin," would be on sale for gold until the first of the following February. But he warned all prospective purchasers that no bid would be considered which did not offer a fraction over seventeen per cent premium, thus reducing the yield to three per cent.

The bond sale worked far less smoothly than did the endless chain. Buyers were so alarmingly few that the President, fearful lest the issue fail, despatched Mr. Carlisle to New York to confer with a number of well-known financiers, an unwelcome expedient for one who had often declared that "the government ought not, regardless of any public purpose, to identify itself with private business or speculation." The financiers, fully conscious of the danger, rallied to the support of the government, and "barely in time to prevent a disastrous failure of the sale," as Mr. Cleveland later explained. The gold realized from this sale amounted to $58,660,917.63, thus raising the reserve to $107,440,802, and the crisis was over for the moment.

The President knew, however, that it was only for the moment, and therefore toward the end of March he sent to Congress a message which urged "the desirability of granting to the Secretary of the Treasury a better power than now exists to issue bonds to protect the gold reserve." In view of the composition of that body, prudence demanded that, pending its answer, he should avoid any action likely to lead to conflict. But, unfortunately, such a course was impossible. The Seigniorage Bill which Congress had just passed was waiting his signature, and sign it he could not.

Seigniorage is the gain accruing to the government by the purchase of bullion at a price less than the value stamped on the metal when coined. It represents the difference between a silver dollar and a dollar's worth of silver. The Seigniorage Bill provided for an addition to the currency of approximately 50,000,000 silver dollars, coined from the Seigniorage in the Treasury, and worth intrinsically about fifty per cent. of their face value. Congressman Bland of Missouri—"Silver Dick," his admirers called him—was its sponsor, and it was the darling project of the free silver men, who regarded it as the test to determine whether or not the President was an irreconcilable enemy of silver.

The receipt of the Seigniorage Bill, therefore, placed

the President in serious embarrassment. Many of his sound money supporters assumed that he would veto it. Carl Schurz wrote: "Put your heel on this seigniorage humbug and save the country's honor."

On the other hand, many friends as ardently "sound money" as Mr. Schurz, urged him to sign the bill, arguing that the amount of silver was so small as to add little to the danger of the situation, and that the enmity which would be aroused by a veto would greatly weaken his chance of being given the power needed for an effective bond issue. Among these Secretary Gresham was conspicuous, and no one could question the fact that he was the soundest of sound money men. Still others urged him to sign the bill in the interest of party unity. "If you veto it," wrote David R. Francis, "the party will be so irreparably divided and demoralized that defeat will ensue."

But the latter argument only angered the President. He could not comprehend how sound money men could hope to purchase party unity by consenting to an increase of unsound money. By the terms of the bill, the seigniorage was to be coined "into legal tender standard dollars," the fiat of the government being substituted for real value.

William Elroy Curtis, then Washington correspondent for the Chicago *Record,* gives this account of an interview in which the President expressed his views upon the ethics of the situation:

"The president lost his temper yesterday while a party of western and southern congressmen were trying to persuade him to sign the silver bill. . . . After discussing the financial side of the question they brought up the political end of it, and one of them told the president that unless the bill became a law there was no hope for the democrats' getting a majority in the next congress. He added, by way of a clincher, that it would be scarcely possible for him and several others of the gentlemen present to be re-elected.

"Whereupon the president turned on him and remarked that he supposed that was the reason why the bill got so many votes in the house, and proceeded to give his opinion of members of congress who pandered to the delusions of the people and voted for all sorts of legislation in order to keep themselves in office. He said that the credit of the government and the condition of the national finances were too important to be treated from that point of view, and that he had a decided contempt for anyone who would ask him to aid in such legislation for such a reason."

Having considered the bill wholly upon its merits, and with reference to the public interest, Mr. Cleveland returned it to Congress with his veto, on March 29, 1894, the very day when he asked Congress for "a better power than now exists to issue bonds."

Had it been possible, the President would doubtless have swallowed his pride and his personal opinions and signed, in order to win support for the demand for power which he had just made upon Congress, but he considered the Seigniorage Bill a concession to dishonesty and as such he could no⁺ sign it. This his veto message made perfectly plain:

"My strong desire to avoid disagreement with those in both Houses of Congress who have supported this bill would lead me to approve it if I could believe that the public good would not be thereby endangered and that such action on my part would be a proper discharge of official duty. Inasmuch, however, as I am unable to satisfy myself that the proposed legislation is either wise or opportune, my conception of the obligations and responsibilities attached to the great office I hold forbids the indulgence of my personal desire and inexorably confines me to that course which is dictated by my reason and judgment, and pointed out by a sincere purpose to protect and promote the general interests of our people."

In the face of this veto Congress refused to grant the extra powers for which the President had pleaded, and the latter was forced to make shift to defend the gold standard with the powers already possessed. For this he saw no chance, save a succession of bond issues, likely to give only temporary relief.

So hopeless was the situation that he at times indulged the thought that he had made a mistake in consenting to return to office. "I do not mind confessing to you," he wrote to one of his former New York law partners, Howard Van Sinderen, on April 6th, "that my position at 15 Broad Street was an easier one than I now occupy, and I occasionally wonder if it was not quite as useful."

Within three months of the close of the first bond sales, the gold reserve stood at $78,693,267, and was still sinking, while domestic hoarding and exportation of gold were on the increase, and the customs revenues brought practically no gold into the Treasury. The time had come for another issue or a silver basis.

With state and congressional elections almost in sight, this was a hard alternative, but Mr. Cleveland showed no hesitation. "An obedient regard for official duty," he later explained, "made the right path exceedingly plain."

Unfortunately for the President, and for the party

which he led, this plain path of duty made plain also the path of opportunity for Hill, Sheehan, and Murphy, in New York, and for like-minded politicians throughout the land. So sinister was the interpretation given by his enemies to the bond issue and its approaching duplicate that many of the President's former supporters turned against such of the party candidates as remained his friends, and supported those who were openly antagonistic to him. The Democrats of New York assembled in a rollicking convention at Saratoga on Monday, September 24th, and staged an anti-Cleveland scene which recalls the description of Revolutionary Boston, as a place where the King's enemies went about in homespun and his friends in tar and feathers. They nominated David B. Hill for Governor and equally dear enemies for other important state offices.

The folly of this course was soon evident. The Reform Democrats, revolting from Hill, nominated Everett P. Wheeler for Governor, thus insuring the election of Levi P. Morton, candidate of the Republicans and Independent Republicans. William L. Strong, Republican and Union Anti-Tammany candidate for Mayor of New York, won an overwhelming victory, while, in the country at large, there was a veritable landslide toward Republicanism. "The latest returns," declared the New York *Tribune* of November 8, 1894, ". . . show that there have been elected to the next House of Representatives 234 Republicans, 117 Democrats and 5 Populists." Even the solid South was broken, not one but many Southern states returning Republican Congressmen in considerable numbers: West Virginia 4, Maryland 3, Kentucky 4, Virginia 2, North Carolina 3, Tennessee 4, Missouri 7, Delaware 1, and even Texas 1.

On November 14th, eight days after the elections, the second bond issue was announced, $50,000,000 of five per cent bonds being again the proposition presented to the public. But the public was no more disposed than formerly to part with gold in exchange for bonds. Once more bidding was dishearteningly slow and insultingly low.

At last came a bid "for all or none" from a combination of thirty-three banking institutions and financiers of New York. Their offer being more advantageous to the government than all previous bids, it was accepted, and the President had the satisfaction of seeing $58,538,500 added to the gold reserve.

In view of the unkind and ungenerous interpretation which has been so often put upon this transaction, it is only fair to quote the words of Mr. Cleveland, written ten years later: "The President . . . of the United States Trust Company . . . rendered most useful and patriotic service in making both this and the previous offer of bonds successful. . . . He afterward testified under oath that the accepted bid for 'all or none,' in which his company was a large participant, proved unprofitable to the bidders."

In calmer days even the New York *World* acknowledged that: "The first two bond issues by the Cleveland administration . . . were made with full publicity and entire propriety."

When on December 3, 1894, Congress heard the President's annual message, it listened to no vague generalities written to conciliate hostile factions, or disarm jubilant political opponents. He painted the financial situation in somber colors, and suggested the cure in specific terms. But neither his pleas, his arguments, nor his lucid explanations produced the slightest effect upon his enemies, who rejoiced at his discomfiture and declined to give him the authority which he demanded.

In January, 1895, the gold withdrawals amounted to $45,000,000, and again the end of gold payment was not far off unless Congress would consent to act or the President should for the third time issue bonds. On the 28th, he again appealed to Congress, but again his plea was disregarded, and by February 8th the gold reserve was less than fifty per cent of the traditional level of safety.

Meanwhile, many of his most trusted advisers were eagerly urging him to invoke expert aid from Wall Street again, but with little success. While bitterly resentful toward Congress, he was disposed to blame the bankers also, and declined to hold further conference with them. Finally, however, less in concession to friendly advice than because he had become convinced that the public would not purchase more government bonds, he agreed to see J. P. Morgan, though he was still firmly resolved that any new issue of bonds should be first offered to public subscription. In commenting upon this decision, a prominent banker declared: "If a man needs beef, he goes to a butcher; if he needs gold, he goes to a banker. If he needs a great deal of beef, he goes to a big butcher; if he requires a great deal of gold, he must go to a big banker and pay his price for it."

The story of the now famous interview between the President and Mr. Morgan was later thus related by Mr. Cleveland himself:

"On the evening of the seventh day of February, 1895, an interview was held at the White House with J. P. Morgan of New York. . . . Secretary Carlisle was present nearly or quite all the time; Attorney General Olney was there a portion of the time, and Mr. Morgan and a young man from his office and myself all the time.

"At the outset Mr. Morgan was inclined to complain of the treatment he had received from Treasury officials in the repudiation of the arrangement which he thought he had been encouraged to perfect in connection with the disposal of another issue of bonds. I said to Mr. Morgan [that] whatever there might be in all this, another offer of bonds for popular subscription, open to all bidders, had been determined upon, and that there were two questions I wanted to ask him which he ought to be able to answer: one was whether the bonds to be so offered would probably be taken at a good price on short notice; and the other was whether, in case there should be imminent danger of the disappearance of what remained of the gold reserve, during the time that must elapse between published notice and the opening of bids, a sufficient amount of gold could be temporarily obtained from financial institutions in the City of New York to bridge over the difficulty and save the reserve until the Government could realize upon the sale of its bonds.

"Mr. Morgan replied that he had no doubt bonds could be again sold on popular subscription at some price, but he could not say what the price would be; and to the second inquiry his answer was that, in his opinion, such an advance of gold as might be required could be accomplished if the gold could be kept in the country, but that there might be reluctance to make such an advance if it was to be immediately withdrawn for shipment abroad, leaving our financial condition substantially unimproved.

"After a little further discussion of the situation, he suddenly asked me why we did not buy $100,000,000 in gold at a fixed price and pay for it in bonds under Section 3700 of the Revised Statutes.

"This was a proposition entirely new to me. I turned to the Statutes and read the section he mentioned. Secretary Carlisle confirmed me in the opinion that this law abundantly authorized such a transaction, and agreed that it might be expedient if favorable terms could be made.

"The section of the Statute referred to reads as follows: 'Section 3700. The Secretary of the Treasury may purchase coin with any of the bonds or notes of the United States, authorized by law, at such rates and upon such terms as he may deem most advantageous to the public interest.'

"Mr. Morgan strongly urged that, if we proceeded under this law, the amount of gold purchased should not be less than $100,000,000; but he was at once informed that in no event would more bonds be then issued than would be sufficient to provide for adding to the reserve about $60,000,000, the amount necessary to raise the fund to $100,000,000. . . .

"The position of Mr. Morgan and other parties in interest whom he represented was such in the business world that they were abundantly able not only to furnish the gold we needed, but to protect us . . . against its immediate loss. Their willingness to undertake both these services was developed during the discussion of the plan proposed."

Mr. Morgan also announced that he and his associates would be glad to accept bonds bearing three per cent instead of four per cent if they were made payable in gold instead of in coin, but the power to authorize such a transaction lay wholly with Congress, and the House of Representatives had just declined to sanction such a change. Mr. Morgan then suggested that ten days be allowed in which to induce Congress to change its decision, as the government could thus save $16,000,000. But Mr. Cleveland knew that such a delay would avail nothing, and so, again to quote his words:

"After careful consideration of every detail until a late hour of the night, an agreement was made by which J. P. Morgan & Co., of New York, for themselves and for J. S. Morgan & Co., of London, August Belmont & Co., of New York, for themselves and for N. M. Rothschild & Sons, of London, were to sell and deliver to the Government 3,500,000 ounces of standard gold coin of the United States, to be paid for in bonds bearing annual interest at the rate of 4% per annum, and payable [in coin] at the pleasure of the Government after thirty years from their date, such bonds to be issued and delivered from time to time as the gold coin to be furnished was deposited by said parties in the Sub-Treasuries or other depositories of the United States.

"At least one half of the [gold] coin so delivered was to be obtained in Europe, and shipped from there in amounts not less than 300,000 ounces per month, at the expense and risk of the parties furnishing the same; and so far as was in their power they were to 'exert all financial influence and make all legitimate efforts to protect the Treasury of the United States against the withdrawals of gold pending the complete performance of the contract.'"

"The conference lasted some hours," writes John G. Milburn, "under conditions so tense as to be almost indescribable. I remember Mr. Morgan's describing how he held a large unlighted cigar in his hand, and at the end of the conference he found it was gone, having been unconsciously ground into powder under the excitement of the occasion."

But, despite this excitement, Mr. Morgan's outward appearance was quite calm, and Mr. Cleveland later commented upon his "quiet, masterly way of coming to the rescue."

The conference over, the President retired to prepare a message for the opening of the congressional session on the morrow, leaving to Secretary Carlisle, Attorney General Olney, and the bankers the task of reducing the agreement to writing.

The Morgan-Cleveland bond contract was a bold move; indeed it is doubtful whether a bolder could be found in our financial history, and the message sent to Congress the next day was not less bold. In barely one thousand words, Mr. Cleveland explained, not a plan, but an action. He informed Congress that, as they had failed to grant him the power needed to defend the public credit, he had acted "in pursuance of Section 3700 of the Revised Statutes" and concluded an agreement "with parties abundantly able to fulfill their undertaking."

Five days later the President wrote to his British Ambassador:

Executive Mansion, Washington.
Feby. 13, 1895.

My dear Mr. Bayard:

First of all I want to thank you, from the bottom of my heart, for several very kind and very comforting letters I have received from you. I have been dreadfully forlorn these many months and sorely perplexed and tried.

Think of it!! Not a man in the Senate with whom I can be on terms of absolute confidence. Our Wisconsin friend and former associate seems somehow to be cowed, and our Delaware friend has only spasmodic self-assertion and generally is in doubt as to the correctness of what I do or want to do. Not one of them comes to me on public business unless sent for and then full of reservations and doubt. We are very far apart in feeling and, it seems to me, in purposes. I am on the whole glad you are not among them. Your efforts to stem the tide would only hurt and grieve you. And yet I must not forget the opportunity you would have to add glory to your patriotic career and raise the hopes and inspire the faith of your Countrymen. I am sorry the malevolent change in our public life since you and I worked together here, has been made known to me. I am sure you cannot fully realize it.

I have at my side a Cabinet composed of pure-minded, patriotic and thoroughly loyal men. I sometimes feel guilty when I recall the troubles I have induced them to share with me. In our hand to hand conflict our triumphs are many but I am afraid as we triumph our party loses and the Country does not gain as it should; and yet what would the condition be without us?

You may be surprised to learn that in all the darkness I have never lost the feeling that the American people and I have a perfectly fair understanding.

I do not believe you will think me vain and foolish if I say to you that I ought to be and am profoundly grateful for a guidance which has thus far kept me from pitfalls. God knows I cannot bear mistakes now.

Our friends at the Capitol have blindly wandered into a close trap on the financial question. To-day the House Ways and Means Committee expect a bill for gold bonds, and the Senate is thrashing about in a way that is pitiable. In the meantime the administration is lightened from a heavy load by our last arrangement for the procurement of gold. I have not a doubt that we shall be free from anxiety on that score for a good long breathing spell.

That trouble over, another looms up. I do not see how I can make myself responsible for such a departure from our traditions as is involved in an appropriation in the Diplomatic bill, for building a cable by the Government to Hawaii. The Senate has thus amended the House bill. The House will stubbornly oppose and resist it and I hope it will be disposed of in conference and rejected. If it is not, another conflict will be forced upon me. I hear to-day that the claim is made that I have heretofore expressed myself favorably towards such a scheme. I suppose this claim is based upon references to the usefulness of telegraph communication between us and Hawaii in my annual messages of 1886 and 1888. Whatever inferences are attempted to be drawn from those expressions I do not believe we should in present circumstances boom the annexation craze by entering upon Government cable building.

I long for the 4th of March to come with no necessity in sight for a special session. We shall not need it for the purpose of making another effort to bridge or cure financial troubles.

I need not say to you that I shall be delighted at all times to hear from you. I am surprised to see how sensibly the English papers treat our situation as manifested by the clippings you sent me.

I trust you will be alert to discover any growing inclination in England to deal with the silver question internationally, and advise us if you see a propitious opening.

Mrs. Cleveland and the babies are well. God be praised for that! I often think that if things should go wrong in that end of the house, I should abandon the ship.

If she were not in bed and asleep, Mrs. Cleveland

would send her love to you and Mrs. Bayard. Mine goes anyway.

Yours very sincerely,

GROVER CLEVELAND.

HON. T. F. BAYARD,
U. S. Embassy,
London, England.

As the opposition studied the situation created by the Morgan contract and the President's message, it saw how cleverly Mr. Cleveland had chosen his position. There now appeared no hope of defeating his main purpose, for the bonds had been sold and $65,116,244.62 had been thereby secured for the gold reserve. But the presentation of a joint resolution, designed to make the new bonds specifically payable in gold, and known to be of executive origin, offered them a chance to present their views, and to balk him of complete success. Attack upon this joint resolution was rendered easier by the fact that Congress had rejected a similar proposition a few hours before the Morgan-Cleveland interview.

In describing the debate, the New York *Herald* correspondent wrote: "Mr. Bryan, of Nebraska, amused the House by offering himself as a martyr to the cause of free coinage and cheap dollars, declaring that he would willingly give up his life to secure the defeat of the pending resolution." He declared that the President's suggestion to make the bonds payable in gold was the first instance in which a bribe had been offered to our people by foreign money lenders. "They come to us," he said, "with the insolent proposition, 'We will give you $16,000,000, paying a proportionate amount each year, if the United States will change its financial policy to suit us.'"

In this opposition Mr. Bryan was joined not only by

silver Democrats, silver Republicans, and Populists, but also by some sound money men, who objected either to the terms of the Morgan-Belmont-Rothschild contract itself, or to the idea of such a contract, whatever its terms. When the vote came, therefore, it was a crushing defeat for the President's policy, 94 Democrats, 63 Republicans, and 10 Populists constituting the opposition in a vote of 167 to 120. In consequence, the bonds of the syndicate issue bore four per cent instead of three per cent interest; though the premium allowed under the contract made the interest, in effect, only three and three quarters per cent, and the United States paid $549,159 a year for thirty years, or a total of $16,474,770, as the price of William Jennings Bryan's first victory over Grover Cleveland.

After consultation together, the President and the Secretary of the Treasury decided not to insist upon the literal fulfilment of the Morgan promise, that "at least one half of the gold . . . be supplied from abroad"; "but the remainder of the contract," to quote Mr. Cleveland himself, was "so well carried out . . . that during its continuance the operation of 'the endless chain' . . . was interrupted. No gold was, during that period, taken from the Treasury to be used in the purchase of bonds, as had previously been the case, nor was any withdrawn for shipment abroad."

As soon as the bonds came into the possession of their purchasers, Morgan, Belmont, and the Rothschilds, the lack of confidence which had forced the United States Government to sell its second issue at a rate lower than its first disappeared. Indeed, the public, confident that the bonds were now secure of payment in gold, showed an astonishing eagerness to purchase them.

The original syndicate formed a second syndicate,

taking in certain other prominent banks, international bankers, and gold importers. This second syndicate took over the entire issue of bonds and, on February 20th, offered them for public sale, the bidding beginning in London and New York at the same hour. The scenes recall the one in Philadelphia, when shares of the first United States Bank were offered to the public by Secretary of the Treasury, Alexander Hamilton. Men crowded, cursed and struggled for a place in the line of those eager to pay 118½ for bonds which their indifference had forced their President to sell to the syndicate at 104½ only a few days before. Mr. Morgan personally supervised the bids at his office, and in twenty-two minutes gave the signal that the sale was over; but for hours thereafter men held their places in the hope that they might yet be able to purchase. In London a similar scene was enacted, Rothschild & Sons receiving fifteen times as many applications as they were able to fill. Thus the bankers, as a result of the confidence which their confidence had restored, reaped a full harvest.

These operations resulted, of course, in bitter denunciations of the President, who was assailed as the friend of robbers, enriching himself from the treasury of the nation over which he was called upon to rule, and opening its vaults to the sinister influence of the great unscrupulous banking concerns of the world. His enemies seized every item which could be distorted into a pretext for abuse. His friendship with Commodore Benedict, of the Chicago Gas Trust, was cited as a suspicious circumstance, and as wild tales spread throughout the land, Populism grew in the West in exact proportion as they were believed, Bryan's spiritual kinsfolk whispering the alarming rumor that Grover Cleveland was not a Democrat, but a Republican, a rich spoilsman dividing the spoil with the strong.

But the third issue of bonds could no more permanently save the financial situation than had the second, and soon the "endless chain" again began to work. In his third annual message (December 2, 1895), therefore, the President again pleaded with Congress for a law which would make the gold standard safe, but he pleaded in vain.

In his anxiety to find some way to restore public confidence, he suggested: "The only thorough and practicable remedy . . . is found in the retirement and cancellation of our United States notes, commonly called greenbacks, and the outstanding Treasury notes issued by the Government in payment of silver purchases under the [Sherman] Act of 1890. I believe this could be readily accomplished by the exchange of these notes for United States bonds, of small as well as large denominations, bearing a low rate of interest." He urged also that authority be "given to the Secretary of the Treasury to dispose of the bonds abroad for gold if necessary to complete the contemplated redemption and cancellation."

As the cancellation of so large an amount of currency would produce a dangerous financial stringency unless its place were immediately filled by some other kind of money, he suggested that "the currency withdrawn . . . might be supplied by such gold as would be used on their retirement or by an increase in the circulation of our national banks." And he added a suggestion, which shows how little he objected to silver dollars as currency or to the coining of the seigniorage under safe conditions: "I do not overlook the fact that the cancellation of the Treasury notes . . . would leave the Treasury in the actual ownership of sufficient silver, including seigniorage, to coin nearly $178,000,000 in standard dollars. It is worthy of consideration whether this might not from time to time be converted into dollars or fractional coin and slowly put into circulation."

The moment another bond issue was suggested, the campaign of misrepresentation and recrimination began again. Not satisfied with the vast proceeds of deals already made with the robber barons, his opponents declared, he is now planning again to open the people's treasury to their exploitation. At this critical moment the situation was suddenly rendered far more critical by the Venezuelan crisis. On December 17, 1895, President Cleveland's startling Venezuelan message went to Congress, and the menace of war accelerated the flight of gold.

In view of the situation thus complicated almost beyond precedent, the President urged Congress not to take a Christmas recess until they had done something to put the country upon a solid financial basis. But the hour for recess was at hand and, as Mr. Cleveland later scornfully commented, "it should not have been expected that members of Congress would permit troublesome thoughts of the Government's financial difficulties to disturb the pleasant anticipations of their holiday recess." Without giving the least heed to the President's plea, Congress dispersed for its brief Christmas recess, leaving him to cope with the situation as best he could.

But Wall Street, less eager for vacation, worked while Congress celebrated. On Monday, December 23d, Robert Bacon, of the firm of J. P. Morgan & Co., made a trip to Washington, accompanied by the President's late law partner, Francis Lynde Stetson, to be joined within a few hours by Mr. Morgan himself.

"During my visit," Mr. Morgan later explained,

". . . no negotiations for a loan were commenced or even suggested, nor was there then or since any agreement or request that I should take any steps preparatory to making a contract. The result of my visit was that I came to the following conclusions:

"First.—That the President and Secretary of the Treasury were determined to use every power at their command to restore and maintain the gold reserve.

"Second.—That no steps would be taken or even any preparatory negotiations commenced until it was ascertained what action, if any, Congress would be likely to take in response to the appeal of the President for adequate and improved means for making such restoration.

"Third.—That the Executive Department would prefer, if possible, to secure $200,000,000 of gold in order to avoid any probable necessity for similar negotiations before the meeting of the new Congress in 1897.

"Fourth.—That it was absolutely certain that no adequate relief could be obtained from Congress, and that no bill could be passed through the Senate for the improvement of the monetary system of the country.

"Upon my return, appreciating to the full the gravity of the situation, and keenly alive to the fact that early action was essential, and in order that I might be prepared, if called upon to act promptly, I took steps to ascertain to what extent it would be possible to secure the co-operation of capitalists, institutions, and others in forming a syndicate which would agree to sell to the United States Government $200,000,000 of gold coin.

"In my efforts, while far from sanguine as to the result, the ready acquiescence of James Stillman, Esq., President of the National City Bank, New York, Edward D. Adams, Esq., with full power representing the Deutsche Bank of Berlin, Germany; John A. Stewart,

Esq., President [of the] United States Trust Company, Pliny Fisk, Esq., of Messrs. Harvey Fisk & Sons, and others . . . encouraged me to proceed.

"The contract, as prepared and signed by the participants, did not stipulate whether the purchase should be by private contract or by public offer. The only proviso (in addition to the important one that no gold should be withdrawn from the Treasury) was that the minimum amount of the contract should be $100,000,000 and the maximum . . . not exceeding $200,000,000. . . . At the end of three or four days the total of $200,000,000 was reached, and I had in my hands full authority which would enable me, whenever and however the Executive might decide to act, to secure that amount of gold for the Treasury reserve in exchange for United States Bonds. . . .

"The formation of the syndicate being completed, I commenced negotiations for the permanent placing of a portion of the loan by public issue in Europe, should a contract with the Government be made."

News of Mr. Morgan's negotiations was soon abroad, and was wrongly interpreted by many of the papers of the country as evidence of a secret agreement between the President and Wall Street.

The New York *World* of January 3, 1896, under the heading, "Grover Cleveland's Golden Opportunity, Smash the Ring," declared: "This bargain has been made with a suspicious secrecy which has been guarded by a picket line of falsehoods put forth for the misleading of the people. It is a bargain between yourself in your official capacity and your near friends. It promises to give princely millions of the people's money to those friends, and that without any need. . . . You must see, Mr. Cleveland, that secrecy of negotiation under such circumstances is bound to excite suspicion. You must realize that men are already saying things which the newspapers as yet hesitate to print."

The editorial further announced the *World's* readiness to purchase one million of the bonds on a three per cent basis, and ventured to assure the President that there were thousands of others willing to take a similar course, if given the opportunity. "Trust the People, Mr. Cleveland! Appeal to them! Smash the gold ring!" it urged.

This attitude of the *World,* far from helping matters, made more difficult the task of accomplishing the purposes of the Government, and the next day Mr. Morgan addressed to the President the following letter, which shows how far the *World* was from a knowledge of the facts:

New York, 219 Madison Avenue.
January 4, 1896.

To the President,
    Washington, D. C.
Sir:

It is with great hesitation that I venture to address you in relation to the present financial situation.

As you are doubtless aware financial affairs are approaching a serious crisis, and the tension today is extreme, and, whilst no outward evidences have developed, we are likely at any moment to reach the point, and consequences, which it will then be too late to remedy. The gravity of the situation must be my excuse.

The most important step at the moment is the restoration of Government credit, by placing the amount of the gold reserve in the Treasury beyond question. This once accomplished confidence both at home and abroad in the stability of our currency will be restored.

After my recent visit to Washington I became convinced that any legislative action to improve the methods at the disposal of the Executive was unlikely, in fact impossible. I therefore took steps to ascertain whether it would be possible to obtain the coöperation of parties at home and abroad to an extent that would enable me to negotiate a contract with the Government for the sale of 11,500,000 ounces of gold approximating 200,000,000 of Dollars on about the basis of the contract of February 8th, 1895. In this effort I have been successful and am now in a position to make such a contract for the full amount.

I do not hesitate to affirm, in fact to urge, that such a contract would in every way be for the best interests of the Government and the people, and would be followed by less derangement of the money market, of trade, in fact of all interests, including foreign exchanges, which until recently were in such an increasingly prosperous condition, and I urge your serious consideration of such a contract.

At the same time I recognize the effect of legislation which has been proposed and the discussions thereupon in both houses of Congress, all of which might lead you to hesitate to make a private contract, and, consequently, in view of the gravity of the situation, I feel bound to say, that if after a conference, in which I can more fully lay the matter before you, and without expressing any confidence in such a mode of procedure in face of previous failures of similar attempts, but recognizing as I do that the responsibility of decision lies with you, I pledge to you every influence and effort in my power to assist the Government in its endeavor to make successful a negotiation by public advertisement which shall result in the sale to the Treasury of 11,500,000 ounces United States gold coin ($200,000,000), and further, I will so far as I possibly can, take such steps as will enable the Syndicate which I represent to join in making the negotiation successful to its full amount.

Awaiting the indication of your pleasure, I remain,

Respectfully yours,

J. PIERPONT MORGAN.

Meanwhile, the Christmas recess over, Congressmen and Senators returned to their seats, armed with copies of the *World's* attack upon the President, and there began a strange debate, a strife of words with a sensational newspaper article as the chief arsenal from which was drawn ammunition for both offense and defense. Senator Sherman declared that "while Congress has, perhaps too hastily, but with entire unanimity, supported the President in maintaining the interests and honor of our country in the field of diplomacy, it has not and will not approve his recommendations on the more important subject of our financial policy, and especially of our currency. It will not approve his secret bond syndicate contract." Senator Elkins, of West Virginia, introduced a resolution "directing the disposal of bonds by public sale to the highest bidder," his speech in defense of this insult being frankly based upon hearsay and newspaper history. Senator Hill, in defense of what he supposed to be the intentions of the administration, questioned whether the public would purchase the bonds if offered to them. "There have been assertions," he cried, "but assertions are not backed with proof. Let these people who want bonds come forward and say so. Where are they? The sole person to come forward so far is Mr. Pulitzer of the *World*. So far so good. Where are the persons to take the other $49,000,000 of a loan?" This defense was gravely answered by Senator Henry Cabot Lodge, who spoke *World* in hand, and without the thorough knowledge of the facts which the country was entitled to expect from this scholar-statesman.

After reading with astonishment the debates concerning his reputed intentions, Mr. Cleveland sent to Senator Caffery the following statement:

Executive Mansion, Washington.
Jan. 5, 1896.

My dear Senator:

I have read to-day in the Congressional Record the debate in the Senate on Friday concerning the financial situation and the bond issue. I am amazed at the intolerance that leads even excited partisanship to adopt as a basis of attack the unfounded accusations and assertions of a maliciously mendacious and sensational newspaper.

No banker or financier, nor any other human being, has been invited to Washington for the purpose of arranging in any way or manner for the disposition of bonds to meet the present or future needs of the gold reserve. No arrangement of any kind has been made for the disposition of such bonds to any syndicate or through the agency of any syndicate. No assurance of such a disposal of bonds has been directly or indirectly given to any person. In point of fact, a decided leaning toward a popular loan and advertising for bids has been plainly exhibited on the part of the administration at all times when the subject was under discussion.

Those charged with the responsibility of maintaining our gold reserve, so far as legislation renders it possible, have anxiously conferred with each other, and, as occasion permitted, with those having knowledge of financial affairs and present monetary conditions as to the best and most favorable means of selling bonds for gold. The unusual importance of a successful result, if the attempt is again made, ought to be apparent to every American citizen who bestows upon the subject a moment's patriotic thought.

The Secretary of the Treasury, from the first moment that a necessity for the sale of another issue of bonds seemed to be approaching, desired to offer them, if issued, to the people, by public advertisement, if they could thus be successfully disposed of. After full consideration he came to the conclusion, with which I fully agree, that the amount of gold in reserve, being now $20,000,000 more than it was in February last, when a sale of bonds was made to a syndicate, and other conditions differing from those then existing, justify us in offering the bonds now about to be issued for sale by popular subscription. This is the entire matter, and all these particulars could have been easily obtained by any member of the Senate by simply inquiring.

If Mr. Morgan, or anyone else, reasoning from his own standpoint, brought himself to the belief that the government would at length be constrained to again sell bonds to a syndicate, I suppose he would have a perfect right, if he chose, to take such steps as seemed to him prudent to put himself in condition to negotiate.

I expect an issue of bonds will be advertised for sale to-morrow, and that bids will be invited, not only for those now allowed by law, but for such other and different bonds as Congress may authorize during the pendency of the advertisement.

Not having had an opportunity to confer with you in person since the present session of Congress began, and noticing your participation in the debate of last Friday,

I have thought it not amiss to put you in possession of the facts and information herein contained.

Yours very truly,

GROVER CLEVELAND.

That same day the New York *World* sent 10,370 telegrams to leading bankers of America, asking whether they would buy if the loan were thrown open to popular subscription, and 5,300 replies were received, ranging in length from 300 to 600 words each. They filled three full pages of the *World,* printed in the finest type. Some answered yes, some answered no, but the question remained: Who will pay the highest price? And even the New York *World* could not answer.

On January 6, 1896, Secretary Carlisle announced a new thirty-year four per cent loan, not for $200,000,000 as Mr. Morgan expected, but for $100,000,000. This made the syndicate contract available only to bid for all or none, owing to the minimum therein set. Therefore Mr. Morgan, "unwilling to make such a bid under present circumstances," as he told his associates, decided to dissolve the syndicate. Feeling, however, that the knowledge of its existence would tend to make this popular loan a success, he did not actually effect the dissolution until January 14th, when, as he informed the bankers concerned, "the subscriptions by individuals and others, including many of the syndicate whom I have encouraged to subscribe, from present indications, will insure the complete success of the issue."

The test of public faith came, however, with the bidding. A month was allowed for the process, during which 4635 bids were received from forty-seven states and territories. As the advertisements had promised, the bonds were awarded to the highest bidders, but only 827 proved higher than J. Pierpont Morgan and Co. To these accordingly was awarded $62,321,150 worth of bonds. The rest of the issue went to Mr. Morgan and his associates, not by the will of the President, but by the will of the people who had failed to display the faith in the nation's bonds which the bankers displayed. Nor were the gains of the bankers excessive, especially as, had the gold standard failed, their bonds would have been paid in silver, worth only fifty cents on the dollar. In subsequent hearings before a Congressional Committee, it was shown that they made five per cent upon their actual investment.

This transaction successfully ended one of the most remarkable experiments in the history of finance. Had the run on the Treasury continued one month longer, the possibility of gold payments would have ceased. On the last day of January, 1896, the gold reserve had dropped below $50,000,000. At the end of February it stood at $124,000,000. By a single issue of bonds $111,000,000 had been added to the gold reserve.

Thus, during that second term, which Senator Stewart, to the delight of his Populist friends, pronounced probably the worst that ever occurred in this or any other country, President Cleveland accomplished what he himself and most of his countrymen later considered his greatest service to the American people, and the credit belongs almost exclusively to him. Congress had refused help, the Democratic and Populist parties had withheld sympathy, and the Republicans had cynically avoided responsibility. But by an ingenious interpretation of executive power based upon laws which could not be repudiated, Mr. Cleveland had, within two years, added all told $293,000,000 of gold to the reserve fund by the creation of a debt of only $262,000,000.

The fourth bond issue was the last ever made in time of peace, for so thoroughly was the work accomplished that even the panic which swept over the country during the political crisis of the following summer could not again drag the gold reserve to the danger point. The endless chain was broken.

CHAPTER IV

THE WILSON-GORMAN TARIFF

"A tariff for any other purpose than public revenue is public robbery."
—GROVER CLEVELAND.

THOUGH forced by circumstances to fight the first great battle of his second administration in the interest of sound money, Mr. Cleveland had not for a moment lost sight of the fact that he had been restored to power upon the basis of a definite pledge to overthrow the McKinley tariff and substitute one built upon the opposite principle. The very platform upon which he had won his second term denounced protection as fraud, and the McKinley tariff as "the culminating atrocity of class legislation." That this tariff had brought not prosperity but hard times, the President, in his first annual message (December 4, 1893) attempted to prove, citing the estimates of the Secretary of the Treasury which forecast a deficit of $28,000,000.

The Republicans, on the other hand, pointed with pride to a surplus of over two and a quarter millions for the year ending June 30, 1893, and attributed the failing revenue and hard times to a general distrust of Democratic rule. They felt it wise also to await the results of the repeal of the Sherman Law before complicating the situation by "tinkering with the tariff." Their pleas for further delay, however, were discounted by the President as selfish attempts to continue the McKinley system of special favors, despite the recent verdict of the people, and in this same first annual message he squarely faced the new Congress with a statement of its duty:

"If there is anything in the theory of a representa-tion in public places," he declared, ". . . if public offi-cers are really the servants of the people . . . our failure to give the relief so long awaited will be sheer recreancy. Nothing should intervene to distract our attention or dis-turb our effort until this reform is accomplished."

Mr. Cleveland was confident that sufficient revenue could be collected under a tariff allowing free raw ma-terials to American factories, and only the necessity of revenue justified the imposition of tariff duties, according to his economic creed. He argued that free raw materials would mean cheaper necessities, greater regularity of em-ployment, a wider market, and a settled prosperity, thus enabling the people easily to supply the revenue needed for an economical administration of the government.

"Even if the oft disproven assertion could be made good that a lower rate of wages would result from free raw materials and low tariff duties," he said, "the intelli-gence of our workmen leads them quickly to discover that their steady employment, permitted by free raw ma-terials, is the most important factor in their relation to tariff legislation." With his customary care for the strict fulfillment of all governmental obligations, by whomso-ever incurred, he warned Congress against such a revision of the tariff as would suddenly endanger interests built upon faith that protection would remain, and begged that "unselfish counsel" and a "willingness to subordinate personal desires and ambitions to the general good" might prevail.

A tariff bill, designed to embody these ideas, and later famous as the Wilson Bill, had been already prepared, in consultation with the President, and was ready to be presented to Congress when the President's message of December 4th was read. It was not a free trade measure, but it was a step in that direction. Lumber, coal, iron, and wool were placed on the free list, and sugar, both raw and refined. The duty was cut down on woolens, linens, and cottons, in the shape of manufactured goods. This bill the President commended to the favorable attention of Congress, declaring that it dealt with the subject of tariff "consistently and as thoroughly as existing conditions permit." To the clause providing for "a small tax upon incomes derived from certain corporate investments," he had, however, given only a reluctant assent, as necessary to provide against temporary deficiencies.

Forty-nine days after the repeal of the Sherman Law, this bill was presented to the House of Representatives by William L. Wilson, chairman of the Ways and Means Committee, and, as he had expected, Mr. Cleveland found himself facing another major conflict. The free wool item alienated the farmers, as it materially reduced their profits from flocks of sheep. Free iron ore offended the mine owners. Free refined sugar was a blow at the sugar trust, to which the McKinley Bill gave a subsidy, and which desired to keep the duty upon refined sugar, while admitting raw sugar free. On the other hand, the growers clamored for a duty on raw sugar to protect their crops from the cheap products of foreign countries, and so, by placing both classes of sugar on the free list, the bill added both the sugar trust and the sugar growers to the enemies created by the income tax clause and other specific provisions.

As the discussion in the lower house proceeded, however, it became evident that even such a combination of opponents could not defeat the Wilson Bill. Richard Croker instructed the Tammany Congressmen to stand by the President's policy, and to fight aggressively for the bill. The President's more regular supporters urged upon their colleagues in Congress the expediency of keeping the party's pre-election pledges, and warned them of the inevitable consequences incident to their betrayal. On February 1, 1894, the House passed the Wilson Bill by a vote of 182 to 106, sixty-one Congressmen being absent or otherwise avoiding the record, and cheers from the Democratic side indicated the belief that victory for tariff reform was in sight.

But the Senate was yet to act, and Mr. Cleveland knew that there his plea for a "willingness to subordinate personal desires and ambitions to the general good" would fall upon many deaf ears. There, as the President had learned to his sorrow, the interests stood intrenched. There, the administration majority was in effect non-existent, and there was little in the Wilson Bill likely to win supporters.

When the Populist Senators voted with the Democrats, they could together muster a majority of nine. When the Populist support went with the Republicans, the Democrats were left with a bare majority of three. But upon questions directly interesting the President, as did this, there were certain to be serious Democratic defections. The free silver Senators were still smarting under their defeat in the repeal of the Sherman Law. The spoilsmen hated him as the President who refused to "divide the spoils," and the Senators of special interests saw in him only a difficult person who could not appreciate their arguments.

What the President saw in the Senate is indicated by a story which went the rounds, doubtless invention but fairly representing his opinion: One night Mr. Cleveland was roused from a heavy sleep by his wife, who whis-

pered, "Wake up, Mr. Cleveland, wake up, there are robbers in the house." "Oh, no, my dear," replied the President, turning heavily, "I think you are mistaken. There
are no robbers in the House, but there are lots in the
Senate."

To the Senate, indeed, the President's plea for unselfish counsel was like a whisper in the teeth of a north
wind. Protection they understood; free trade they feared;
but unselfish counsel they ridiculed. Louisiana Senators
saw their duty through the sugar house; Maryland, West
Virginia, Alabama, and Pennsylvania Senators looked at
theirs from the mouth of the mine; Senator Hill felt that
his line of greatest political usefulness was in the defeat
of the income tax clause, which touched his constituency
most closely; while his colleague, Senator Murphy, despite Tammany's instructions, indulged in an enthusiasm
for high duties on collars and cuffs, the chief desire of the
leading political manipulators of his senatorial district.
Senators Gorman and Brice were open to conviction regarding the President's tariff bill; but conviction waited
upon the assurance that the measure would be kind to
certain interests which had been kind to them.

"The truth is," later declared the Republican Senator
Cullom, "we were all—Democrats as well as Republicans
—trying to get in amendments in the interest of protecting
the industries of our respective states."

Thus did the United States Senate, whose glorious history had justified the claim that it was "the most august
deliberative body in the world," approach the task of tariff
revision, not to subordinate personal desires and ambitions
to the general good, but to subordinate the general good
to personal desires and ambitions. In a spirit of live and
let live, each Senator was allowed his slice, and as a result

the Wilson Bill lost its character so shamelessly as to become almost unrecognizable.

The President watched, with consternation, the process by which the Senate was writing "private" upon a public measure, designed to fulfill a public pledge.

"When I came here," he wrote to L. Clarke Davis on February 25th, "I knew perfectly well that there were schemes, ideas, policies, and men with which and with whom I should be obliged to do battle, and hard and trying battle. I thought the right must win and perhaps I relied too sentimentally upon the right to win. I thought the men who professed to be willing to fight with me were sincere and earnest.

"I still believe that right will win but I do not now believe that all the men who loudly proclaimed their desire for better things were in earnest.

"At any rate not a few of them are doing excellent service in the cause of the worst possible political methods and are aiding in bringing about the worst and most dangerous political situation."

When at last on July 3d, the Wilson Bill passed the Senate, by a vote of thirty-nine to thirty-four, with twelve Senators silent, it carried back to the House and to its indignant sponsors, 634 alterations, many of them fundamental in character. The free raw material idea, the very essence of the President's plan, had been well nigh annihilated. Coal, sugar, and iron ore had been removed from the free list, while wool, lumber, and copper were left to grace alone.

There followed the usual Committee of Conference which, however, failed to agree; and when, on July 19th, Mr. Wilson rose to report and repudiate that which he had proudly called his own, he presented to Congress a letter which the President had sent him just as he was entering the conference, and which he requested the clerk to read to the House. In it Mr. Cleveland boldly denounced the Senate amendments, the basis of the conference, as indicative of party perfidy and party dishonor. "Every true Democrat and every sincere tariff reformer," he declared, "knows that this bill in its present form and as it will be submitted to the conference, falls far short of the consummation for which we have long labored, and for which we have suffered defeat without discouragement." And he warned the conferees of the dangers which lay in the pathway of those guilty of "the abandonment of Democratic principles."

There can be no doubt that by this letter Mr. Cleveland designed to aid the defeat of the Senate's amendments. Although his whole political philosophy was opposed to executive interference in pending legislation, he felt that his party in the Senate had entered into a conspiracy to violate a promise, made to the people, and that it was his duty to thwart them, or at least to let the people know that he had not connived with them. His disclaimer was answered by Senators Gorman, Jones, and Vest, who insisted in open Senate that the President had approved the changes which the Senate had made in the bill.

In commenting on Senator Gorman's defense of the amendments, Mr. Dickinson wrote to the President on July 23d:

"My dear Mr. President:
"The Gorman defense will carry the hangers-on . . . but will not impress the strong men. . . . Summing it up, it is a clever confession that the Senate bill is a sacrifice of principle and a surrender of everything we fought for in 1892. He avoids [responsibility] by urging that a compromise was necessary to pass *any* bill; but the

country knows that, with the votes of his coterie, a bill in
entire harmony with the platform would have met with
the approval of the Senate months ago. A compromise
was only necessary because *he* stood in the way, and *he* is
the man who demanded the concessions which he deplores
in his argument. His witnesses on the other point—that
they did this thing because you approved it—remind one
of Tony Weller's 'halibi.' Unspeakably weak, and unspeakably infamous is his appeal to the lawless and the
unreflective on your action in the late labor troubles.

"Whatever the outcome at present, it remains that for
the sake of your supporters and friends, for the cause you
have led since 1884, for your own place in history, and
for your own fame, it was absolutely necessary for you
to make the record that you have made on the pending
measure."

The outcome was far from satisfactory to Mr. Cleveland, however. The will of the Senate prevailed upon
every disputed point, the House yielding after long and
stubborn resistance.

As soon as the Wilson-Gorman Tariff Act, as it was
now called, reached the President's desk, advice was
offered him from every side. The soundness of the bill,
its unspeakable unsoundness, and a hundred other contra-
dictory points were urged, and as he gave no public indication of his intentions regarding it, human ingenuity was
soon taxed to the utmost in an effort to show contempt.
Among other insults, he received ninety-odd letters suggesting that he sign the tariff bill with the quill of a crow.

On August 23d Senator Palmer warned him:

"Your message of 1887 made Tariff reform the leading issue. . . . The present Tariff bill contains all that

your true friends in Congress were able to obtain. . . .
If you . . . conclude to veto the bill, they can defend
you. . . . If you sign the bill, you thereby retain the
leadership of the Democratic party. The party can defend you and itself by comparing the measure with the
McKinley Bill. They can point to free wool, free lumber, and the large reductions upon the woolen, cotton and
other schedules, and to the abolition of the sugar
bounty. . . .

"If you allow the bill to become a law without your
signature, you abdicate the leadership of the Democratic
party on the issue that made you President. . . . The
commander of an army and the leader of a party must
alike share the fortunes of their followers. The present
Tariff bill is a Democratic measure."

The President, however, did not agree with Mr.
Palmer. The day before the expiration of the ten days
allowed him by law for consideration of the bill, he sent
to Congressman Catchings the following analysis of the
problem as it appeared to him:

Executive Mansion, Washington,
August 27th, 1894.

Hon. T. C. Catchings,
My dear sir:—
Since the conversation I had with you and Mr. Clark
of Alabama a few days ago, in regard to my action upon
the tariff bill now before me, I have given the subject
further and most serious consideration. The result is I
am more settled than ever in the determination to allow
the bill to become a law without my signature.

When the formulation of legislation which it was
hoped would embody Democratic ideas of tariff reform

was lately entered upon by Congress, nothing was further from my anticipation than a result which I could not promptly and enthusiastically endorse.

It is therefore with a feeling of the utmost disappointment that I submit to a denial of this privilege.

I do not claim to be better than the masses of my party, nor do I wish to avoid any responsibility which, on account of the passage of this law, I ought to bear as a member of the Democratic organization. Neither will I permit myself to be separated from my party to such an extent as might be implied by my veto of tariff legislation, which though disappointing, is still chargeable to Democratic effort. But there are provisions in this bill which are not in line with honest tariff reform, and it contains inconsistencies and crudities which ought not to appear in tariff laws or laws of any kind.

Besides, there were, as you and I well know, incidents accompanying the passage of the bill through the Congress, which made every sincere tariff reformer unhappy, while influences surrounded it in its latter stages and interfered with its final construction, which ought not to be recognized or tolerated in Democratic tariff reform counsels.

And yet, notwithstanding all its vicissitudes and all the bad treatment it received at the hands of pretended friends, it presents a vast improvement to existing conditions. It will certainly lighten many tariff burdens that now rest heavily upon the people. It is not only a barrier against the return of mad protection, but it furnishes a vantage ground from which must be waged further aggressive operations against protected monopoly and governmental favoritism.

I take my place with the rank and file of the Democratic party who believe in tariff reform and who know what it is, who refuse to accept the results embodied in this bill as the close of the war, who are not blinded to the fact that the livery of Democratic tariff reform has been stolen and worn in the service of Republican protection, and who have marked the places where the deadly blight of treason has blasted the counsels of the brave in their hour of might.

The trusts and combinations—the communism of pelf —whose machinations have prevented us from reaching the success we deserved, should not be forgotten nor forgiven. We shall recover from our astonishment at their exhibition of power, and if then the question is forced upon us whether they shall submit to the free legislative will of the people's representatives, or shall dictate the laws which the people must obey, we will accept and settle that issue as one involving the integrity and safety of American institutions.

I love the principles of true Democracy because they are founded in patriotism and upon justice and fairness toward all interests. I am proud of my party organization because it is conservatively sturdy and persistent in the enforcement of its principles. Therefore I do not despair of the efforts made by the House of Representatives to supplement the bill already passed by further legislation, and to have engrafted upon it such modifications as will more nearly meet Democratic hopes and aspirations.

I cannot be mistaken as to the necessity of free raw materials as the foundation of logical and sensible tariff reform. The extent to which this is recognized in the legislation already secured is one of its encouraging and redeeming features; but it is vexatious to recall that while free coal and iron ore have been denied us, a recent letter of the Secretary of the Treasury discloses the fact

that both might have been made free by the annual surrender of only about seven hundred thousand dollars of
unnecessary revenue.

I am sure that there is a common habit of underesti-
mating the importance of free raw materials in tariff
legislation, and of regarding them as only related to concessions to be made to our manufacturers. The truth is,
their influence is so far-reaching that if disregarded, a
complete and beneficent scheme of tariff reform cannot be
successfully inaugurated.

When we give to our manufacturers free raw materials we unshackle American enterprise and ingenuity,
and these will open the doors of foreign markets to the
reception of our wares and give opportunity for the continuous and remunerative employment of American labor.

With materials cheapened by their freedom from
tariff charges, the cost of their product must be corre-
spondingly cheapened. Thereupon justice and fairness
to the consumer would demand that the manufacturers be
obliged to submit to such a readjustment and modification
of the tariff upon their finished goods as would secure to
the people the benefit of the reduced cost of their manufacture, and shield the consumer against the exaction of
inordinate profits.

It will thus be seen that free raw materials and a just
and fearless regulation and reduction of the tariff to meet
the changed conditions, would carry to every humble
home in the land the blessings of increased comfort and
cheaper living.

The millions of our countrymen who have fought
bravely and well for tariff reform should be exhorted to
continue the struggle, boldly challenging to open warfare and constantly guarding against treachery and half-
heartedness in their camp.

Tariff reform will not be settled until it is honestly and fairly settled in the interest and to the benefit of a patient and long suffering people.

Yours very truly,
GROVER CLEVELAND.

Within twenty-four hours after this letter was written, the Wilson-Gorman Bill became a law (August 28, 1894), but without the signature of Grover Cleveland.

Writing in commendation of the President's stand in this matter, Wayne MacVeagh, formerly a member of the Garfield-Arthur Cabinet, and a frequent critic of Mr. Cleveland, said:

Personal   Embassy of the United States, Rome.

September 10, 1894.

My dear Sir:

I have just received your letter to Mr. Catchings by today's mail and I must at once thank you *for every word of it.*

I sometimes wonder if you have any true conception of the services you have been enabled to render to your country. You have made, no doubt, many mistakes— some perhaps grievous ones. You know how I regretted the "Higgins" appointment in your former term, and how I regretted your decision not to call the extra session as soon as you were inaugurated this last time and postpone as far as possible all questions of office until the tariff was revised and the Sherman bill repealed. No doubt I failed to see the arguments on the other side in both instances and I only recall these differences of opinion now as evidence that I have not been in the habit of giving indiscriminate approval to whatever you did.

But I do wish you to appreciate, to some extent at

least, what you have done for the country as a whole in the last eighteen months—in spite of wholly unequaled and wholly undeserved opposition in your own party— and what is far more weighty to my mind, in spite of the inevitable opposition your ideas and standards of public duty encounter in the Senate without regard to party. There many men of *both* parties have persuaded themselves that they are at liberty to serve themselves before their party, and their party before their country—while you reverse this order. Then a good many Democrats in the Senate—a great many indeed—had had their pride as "practical politicians" sorely wounded by your re-nomination and re-election against their well-known predictions and wishes.

Yet what have you not accomplished? You have put the nation's foreign affairs upon the sound basis of respect for the rights of others while exacting from others respect for our own—and criticism on that subject has absolutely disappeared.

You have made every dollar circulating in the United States as good as a gold dollar and, whoever may "fret or fume," that great work will never be undone.

You suppressed at almost no cost of blood and not much in money, a hideous outbreak of lawlessness which threatened to unsettle men's minds as to the respect due to law. Consider the value of that precedent alone in the immediate future.

And now for the first time in an entire generation— since 1861—you have turned a revision of the tariff away from higher to lower duties. For the first time in that long period trade is to be freer and the people's burdens less heavy.

And to crown all, you have written this last letter— *the bravest and best thing it seems to me you have yet done.* Those who were willing to misrepresent, were able to distort the plain meaning of your allusions to the sugar schedule in the letter to Mr. Wilson—but these last words are incapable of such abuse.

And then it summons both the party and the country to continue the inevitable struggle for still greater commercial freedom and still fewer and less heavy taxes to be levied by the protected interests upon their less favored fellow citizens. In the long run—nay, even in a short run—*free wool means all raw materials free.*

I know what discouragements you have encountered and how dark and hopeless the path before you must often have seemed; but if ever man did, you have served your country not only well but *effectively* since March 4, 1893.

Don't on any account answer this—get all the rest you can.

Sincerely yours,
WAYNE MACVEAGH.

To
HON. GROVER CLEVELAND.

A few weeks later Mr. Carnegie wrote:

New York, N. Y.,
5 West 51st St.,
December 14, 1894.

To HIS EXCELLENCY,
THE PRESIDENT of the
UNITED STATES.
Dear Sir:

I venture to address you, because a letter to the highest official will attract most attention, and also because of my respect for you personally.

There is great trouble in regard to the national

finances owing to a serious falling off in the Government's revenues. Permit me to lay a suggestion before you, which has nothing whatever to do with Free Trade or Protection, and is not in any possible sense a party question since neither party has ever acted upon the policy I am now about to suggest.

In 1892 the tariff duties were collected from foreign imports of the luxuries of the rich as follows:

Wool manufactures	$34,293,609
Silk manufactures	16,965,637
Cotton manufactures	16,436,733
Flax manufactures	10,066,636
Glass and china manufactures	10,339,000
Wines, liquors, etc.	8,935,000
Tobacco, cigars	11,882,557

Here are $108,000,000 of revenues from seven classes of luxuries; and here are a few others which netted over six millions more—jewelry, artificial flowers, clocks, brushes, paper, perfumeries, musical instruments, making 114 millions, or two thirds of the total collected from imports—174 millions.

Now Mr. President, you have only to enquire to find that the masses of the people use none of these articles to speak of. As far as silk and woolen cloths are concerned, the home manufacturer supplies the masses. In regard to linens, common grade tablecloths are imported, but even in regard to these the poorer classes use cotton tablecloths of domestic manufacture.

Under the present tariff law these articles have been greatly reduced, and the main work of the Wilson Bill is this reduction of the luxuries of the rich, which yield two thirds of all the revenue collected. That the originators of the present tariff intended any such result, is not to be believed. The movement against the tariff, begun by you, was to meet the question of a surplus when reductions were required to limit the exactions of revenue from the people to the actual wants of the Government.

When the "condition and not the theory which confronts you" has changed, the statesman who regarded the condition and not the theory, may be expected to leave the theory to-day and deal with the new conditions. Such would be consistency in the highest sense, although genius cares little for consistency and is only concerned to do what is best at the time.

My suggestion therefore is that a short bill be passed increasing for two years the duties upon these articles de luxe, used only by the extravagant few, at least 50 per cent. I should go even beyond this, but this increase would yield, say fifty millions of additional revenue, and not one workingman or his family, nor a man upon a small salary would be affected to the extent of one dollar.

It is a mistake to suppose that foreign imported articles, which are really articles de luxe used by the rich, can be either greatly diminished or greatly increased by a change in duties, because cost is not the first consideration with the purchasers, taste, fashion, being potent. But to guard against the belief that these imported articles were used to any extent by the masses, the proposed additional duty should be placed upon cloths of certain grades and value. This would allow the masses to use these articles upon as favorable terms as now, but believe me Sir, they do not use imported articles at all.

You no doubt have it within your power to ascertain whether this be true or not, may I beg you so to ascertain. I believe you will agree with me that if this be true, you have here the best remedy possible, and the easiest to carry, for our present trouble.

This is neither free Trade nor Protection, neither party has ever treated these luxuries simply from a revenue point of view, the Republican bills have been protective, and the Democratic bills in the direction of lower duties. This is neither, but simply the best means of raising more revenue, and I submit for your consideration that if this can be raised upon the extravagances of the pleasure-loving luxurious-living few, and it is for the best interests of the masses of the people that this should be done. The Income Tax could readily be abandoned, and yet the increased duties proposed would come as exclusively as the Income Tax will from the few having more than four-thousand dollars income per annum, and require no increase of officials or entail additional cost; besides these duties would yield double any estimate made of the Income Tax revenue.

It is a new policy Mr. President, and I cannot but think one worthy of you, and one which requires just such a man to propose and establish. I am Mr. President, with great respect

Very sincerely yours,

ANDREW CARNEGIE.

HIS EXCELLENCY, GROVER CLEVELAND, PRESIDENT.

Executive Mansion,
Washington, D. C.

P. S.

People generally do not quite understand to what extent foreign textile articles are for the rich only. Take wool, for instance: In 1890 the value of the home manufactured article was $338,000,000. The high-priced foreign fine woolens were imported to the value of only $35,500,000, their value per yard being much greater than that of the ordinary qualities produced at home; the number of yards probably was not beyond six or seven per cent of the total consumption. We have a similar result with cotton: The value of the home-manufactured product in 1890 was $268,000,000, and the total amount imported was valued at only $28,000,000. Even in regard to silks imported, the manufactured product of American mills in 1890 was valued at $69,000,000, the total imported silk manufactures $31,000,000 only. These are also of much higher value per yard than the home product. Since 1890 the silk manufacturers of America have gained greatly, and are constantly filling the home demands more completely.

If the foreign woolens, silks, and linens were classified as to fineness and value, it would be seen that goods of common grades, such as the people generally use, were no longer imported to any considerable extent, nor can they be under the present bill.

By limiting the bill to two years and confining the increased duties to the higher qualities, it could not be said that the measure was framed in the interests of the home manufacturer, because the finer qualities could not be successfully produced to any great extent in the short space of two years, and manufacturers would not invest capital for the necessary special machinery, etc.

The increased revenues thus obtainable with the decrease in pensions, and the natural increase of revenues from increase of wealth and population would give the last year of the Administration a splendid record, and the President would pass into history as a Statesman who met an emergency by a heroic and original measure. At the same time, its close would be graced by a reduction of duties by the expiration of the temporary act.

The Republican party, of course, could be relied upon

to favor this measure, and surely a sufficient number of the Democratic party would see its wisdom.

A. C.

Disappointed as they were in the final form of their tariff bill, the Democrats were somewhat comforted by the presence of the income tax clause, but their satisfaction was of short duration, for Senator Hill of New York promptly attacked the constitutionality of the latter, denouncing it as a direct tax not based on population, and quite beyond the power of the Federal Government. He denounced it also as continuing in a period of peace measures which had been accepted by the people only as a stern war necessity.

In 1861 a three per cent tax had been imposed on incomes over eight hundred dollars. In 1862 the rate had been increased to five per cent on incomes between six hundred and five thousand dollars, and to seven and a half per cent on incomes between five thousand and ten thousand dollars. Incomes over ten thousand a year had been taxed ten per cent. In 1864 another change was made, providing for the taxing at five per cent of all incomes between six hundred and five thousand dollars, all over five thousand being called upon to pay ten per cent. But these war taxes had expired in 1872, and Senator Hill protested against their re-enactment in time of peace. He also denounced the exemption of four thousand dollars as making the measure class legislation and therefore contrary to the spirit of free government. He pointed out indignantly that it was unjust and sectional in its provisions, bearing more heavily upon the East than upon the West and South. Despite protests, however, the Treasury sent out blanks and got ready for the collection of the tax, while its opponents selected cases which were sent to the Supreme Court, in order that the question of constitutionality might be judicially determined.

Pending a decision, Mr. Cleveland, while by no means an enthusiastic supporter of the income tax, prepared to meet the requirements of the law in his own case. "The President," reported a Washington dispatch, "has filed his income tax returns and has included his salary, although the law expressly stipulates that no act of Congress shall increase or decrease the compensation of the President of the United States during his term of office, and the income tax certainly does decrease his salary to the extent of $920 a year. There would be no question concerning its application to the salary of his successor in office, but he seems to have desired to set a good example to the people by construing a doubtful question in the law against himself and in favor of the government." He was, however, not called upon to pay the $920, as by a decision of the Supreme Court on May 20th, the income tax clause of the Wilson-Gorman bill was declared unconstitutional.

This opinion was the more remarkable in view of the fact that fifteen years earlier the Supreme Court had rendered the opposite decision by unanimous consent. It now reversed that decision by the narrow majority of one vote, Associate-Justices Harlan, Brown, Jackson, and White voting to uphold the law, Associate-Justices Brewer, Field, Gray, Shiras, and Chief Justice Fuller voting to declare it unconstitutional.

As a sequel to the defeat of Mr. Cleveland's efforts to keep faith with the people over tariff reform, we find two incidents showing his breadth of vision and unusual magnanimity of spirit. When the Wilson Bill left the House, sugar, both raw and refined, was upon the free list. In the Senate, however, the sugar Senators secured protective rates satisfactory to the Trust, and the question had been not inappropriately raised as to how this protection of an industry certainly in no sense "infant" was secured. Recriminations followed, and an investigation.

The investigating committee, composed of two Democratic Senators, two Republican Senators, and one Populist, unearthed scandal enough to justify even the most radical preachers against the trust evil. Henry O. Havemeyer, President of the Sugar Trust, admitted on the stand that the Trust regularly contributed to the campaign chest of the party most likely to serve their interests in any particular state, and concealed these under the head of "expenses" on their books. He also admitted that sugar lobbyists had been kept in Washington when the Wilson Bill was pending, to influence the people's representatives in the interest of sugar. Senator Quay defiantly admitted that while deliberating on the tariff on sugar, he had been buying and selling sugar stock, and boldly proclaimed his intention to continue to do so.

The Committee's report, signed by every member, deprecated the "pressure to which Congress and its members are subjected by the representatives of great industrial combinations whose enormous wealth tends to suggest undue influence."

Had there been anything vindictive in the President's nature, he would have been disposed to interpret every subsequent case in a manner unfavorable to these sugar barons. Instead, he was as scrupulously fair in interpreting the law when touching them as he was with reference to any other citizen, as is shown by the following letter to Attorney-General Harmon:

Gray Gables,
Buzzard's Bay, Mass.
July 31, 1895.

My dear Mr. Attorney General

. . . I am a good deal annoyed by the situation of the sugar bounty question and Comptroller Bowler's position in relation to it.

I have always expressed the opinion that in view of the fact that the McKinley law provided that the bounty should be paid for a certain number of years—in so many words or in effect—that sugar producers had more than an ordinary right to rely upon the payment of the bounty during that time. Having relied upon the permanency, of the bounty to the extent provided by the limit fixed in the law, it has always seemed to me that when the bounty was swept away in the midst of the producing season and after expense had been incurred on the faith of the promised bounty, equity and justice dictated some reimbursement of the loss sustained by reliance upon the promise of the Government. I don't call this a bounty but a *reimbursement.* I hold the belief that the money appropriated by way of such indemnification should be paid, and I am very earnest in this belief and I think I am perfectly consistent in claiming at the same time to be one of the strongest opponents of bounties in the Country.

I have no idea that there is any constitutional objection in the way of the Government's doing a thing so clearly in the line of equity and good conscience, as is this indemnification to the sugar producers who have incurred expense they would not have incurred except for the Government's invitation.

I thought the question all out before approving the appropriation; and while I esteem Mr. Bowler as an excellent and careful officer, I do not think that in this case he is called on to override the Congress and the President on a question so entirely judicial as the constitutionality of this provision.

Even if he should think it his duty to take up the judicial question of constitutionality, I am by no means certain that he would find in the decision of the District Court of Appeals justification for deciding against the appropriation. Before he assumes such a responsibility (if in any case he should assume it) he should have, it seems to me, the judgment of the highest court upon the exact point. He certainly has not the former and I do not believe the judgment of the Court of Appeals covers the phase of the bounty question now presented.

I cannot but feel the greatest anxiety on this subject; for I have been an openly avowed advocate of this measure of restitution; and until I get new light, shall continue my efforts to bring it about whoever withstands.

I am not at all adverse to Mr. Bowler's knowing my views.

Yours sincerely,

GROVER CLEVELAND.

HON. JUDSON HARMON,
    Attorney General,
        Washington.

Even more surprising was his selection, in the heat of the sugar conflict, of one of his strongest opponents, Senator White, of Louisiana, to a vacant place upon the Supreme Bench. That vacancy, caused by the death of Associate Justice Samuel Blatchford, had already brought the President much trouble, and not a little humiliation. Soon after Mr. Blatchford's death, Mr. Cleveland had nominated William B. Hornblower, of New York, a man admirably equipped for the post, but unfortunately possessed of powerful political enemies, chief among whom was the New York Senator, David B. Hill.

Hill had not forgotten that Hornblower had been one of the committee of nine, appointed by the Association of the Bar of the City of New York to investigate the conduct of Isaac H. Maynard, attorney and counsel for the Board of State Canvassers, and accused of illegal action in the senatorial count of 1891. At that time, Maynard had been Deputy Attorney General of New York State, acting under the general direction of Governor Hill. The committee had reported that Maynard had committed one of the gravest offenses known to the law, that of falsifying election returns, and had recommended, by unanimous consent of its nine members, Frederic R. Coudert, James C. Carter, John E. Parsons, Clifford A. Hand, Edmund Randolph Robinson, John L. Cadwalader, William B. Hornblower, Elihu Root, and Albert Stickney, that: "A copy of this report be transmitted to the Senate and Assembly, and that those bodies be respectfully requested to consider whether the conduct of Judge Isaac H. Maynard therein mentioned does not demand an exercise of the power to remove judges vested by the Constitution in the Legislature." Hill's resentment against the committee was great, and against Hornblower it was especially bitter, as the latter had been appointed on the committee at the suggestion of Judge Maynard's counsel, and was therefore, according to Hill, Maynard's representative. His acquiescence in the verdict Hill therefore regarded as treason.

When Mr. Hornblower's nomination to the Supreme Bench came before the Judiciary Committee of the United States Senate, Hill, now a Senator from New York and a member of the committee, marked it for

slaughter. He managed to delay action until the end of
the extra session during which the President had made the
nomination, and let it be understood that he would fight it
if presented during the regular session. Conscious of
Mr. Hill's powerful opposition, and unwilling to em-
barrass the administration, Mr. Hornblower made known
his willingness to withdraw his name. Mr. Cleveland's
reply was characteristic: "Tell Hornblower that his
name will go into the Senate the first day of the regular
session of Congress and will stay there until confirmed."

Confirmation, however, proved impossible. The
Judiciary Committee reported the nomination to the
Senate, where it met determined opposition. Some of the
Senators resented the fact that Mr. Hornblower had
been nominated without previous consultation with the
Judiciary Committee; some felt that well established custom had been slighted by the President's failure to discuss the question with the Senators from New York before presenting a New York man for so important a
position; some were eager to express their antagonism
against Mr. Cleveland in order to show their loyalty to
the Silverites. Others, but not enough, echoed the statement of Senator Morgan: "I hate the ground that man
[Cleveland] walks on, but I do not believe in turning
down a good man for the Supreme Court for the purpose
of rebuking Cleveland." When at last the vote was taken,
Mr. Hornblower failed to secure the majority necessary
for confirmation.

After the defeat of Mr. Hornblower, the President
nominated Judge Wheeler H. Peckham, against whom
also Senator Hill turned his poisoned arrows. In his
eagerness to secure Peckham's confirmation, Mr. Cleveland sent the following appeal to Joseph H. Choate,
recognized leader of the New York bar:

Executive Mansion, Washington.

January 27, 1894.

My dear Mr. Choate,

You can do what I deem to be a great service to the Country and add very much to the prospect of a high honor coming to the Bar of New York if you will immediately write a letter to Senator Hoar representing to him the good things you know concerning Wheeler H. Peckham's fitness for a place on the bench of the Supreme Court.

You can hardly conceive what little and mean things have been and will be resorted to in an effort to defeat him. One pretext is that he has an infernally bad temper, and there is an inclination in certain quarters to hide behind this pretext. I suppose, of course, there is nothing in this allegation. If I am right in this supposition I wish you would negative the charges and speak of Mr. P's ability in such a way as your knowledge of the man justifies.

Let me suggest that it would be very well indeed if you could convey to Senator Hoar, or have presented to him, Mr. Evarts' good opinion of Mr. Peckham, as well as your own. I wish Mr. Carter would also write.

I desire Mr. Peckham's confirmation,

1st On account of his merits and fitness, and

2nd Because I want the appointee to come from the New York Bar *and I have no names in reserve which represent it.*

Yours very sincerely,

GROVER CLEVELAND.

JOSEPH H. CHOATE, ESQ.,

New York City.

But nothing could save Mr. Peckham, in view of the curse, called senatorial courtesy, which "Dave" Hill

wielded against him, and in view of the number of Mr.
Cleveland's own senatorial enemies. The President next
urged Mr. Frederic R. Coudert to allow his name to be
sent in, but the latter declined on the grounds of personal
obligations to clients. Thus, long before the conflict over
the Wilson Bill was ended, the opposition Senators
boasted that President Cleveland could nominate no man
whom the Senate would confirm as Associate Justice. A
mocking phrase to that effect, by Senator Chandler of
New Hampshire, coming to Mr. Cleveland's ears when
the debate upon the sugar sections of the Wilson Bill was
at its hottest, the latter remarked: "I'll name a man
to-morrow whom the Senate will unanimously confirm,
and for whom that pestiferous wasp will himself be compelled to vote."

To those who watched the sugar debate in the Senate,
few names would have seemed less likely to be thus employed than that of Edward Douglas White, Senator from
Louisiana. Mr. White was a member of the Gorman-
Brice alliance, and through it was seeking to restore
duties upon sugar, iron ore, coal, and other raw materials
which the House had put on the free list. His standing
before the country, however, was not shaken by his
activities in the interest of his constituency, and it would
have been hard to find a representative man in any party
ready to credit against him the charge, so effective against
others, of being "Senator from Havemeyer."

Although, of course, conscious of the high regard in
which he was held, Senator White did not suspect that the
President, whose cherished plans he was so effectively
opposing, was considering him in connection with the
much-discussed vacant Associate-Justiceship. Indeed it
is said that when he received a request to call at the White
House he remarked to a friend that this would probably

be his last call upon President Cleveland. To his astonishment, instead of reproaches for his anti-administration activities, he was offered the vacant seat on the Supreme Bench, and at once accepted. The Senate unanimously confirmed the appointment, on February 19, 1894, without even the formality of a reference to a committee, and America witnessed the remarkable sight of a soldier of the lost cause, a man who had raised his hand against the Stars and Stripes, first sitting with the Court in whose hands lies the interpretation of the Constitution, and later presiding over it as the universally loved, honored, and trusted Chief Justice.

It is characteristic of Mr. Cleveland that when, eighteen months later, Mr. Justice Jackson died, he again contemplated a trial of strength with the Senate by the nomination of Mr. Hornblower, but the following letter rendered such a course impossible:

875 Madison Avenue, New York.
Nov. 9/ 95.

Dear Mr. President,

I observe that the newspapers are again mentioning my name as a possible nominee to succeed Mr. Justice Jackson. I have been meaning for some time past to write you, asking you to leave me out of the question, as I have definitely made up my mind that in justice to my family I ought not to make the pecuniary sacrifice involved in giving up my professional income for a judicial salary, and that I should therefore feel constrained to decline a nomination, if tendered me, even if confirmation by the Senate were certain to follow and without protracted delay.

I have hesitated to write, however, lest I should seem

to assume—as of course I had no reason to assume—that you were considering the possibility of my nomination.

When you named me two years ago to succeed Mr. Justice Blatchford, I allowed the high honor of the appointment and the congeniality of judicial work to outweigh the consideration of pecuniary sacrifice; but further reflection has led me to look upon the matter differently.

With best regards, I remain,
Yrs very sincerely,
WM. B. HORNBLOWER.
To the
HON. GROVER CLEVELAND,
Pres. of the U. S.

The President then turned again to Mr. Coudert, who again refusing, he named Rufus W. Peckham, brother of Wheeler H. Peckham and, in order to forestall hostile action on the part of Senator Hill, sent the following letter:

Executive Mansion, Washington.
Nov. 18, 1895.

My dear Senator:
Secretary Lamont has shown me your letter to him, and I appreciate your willingness to come to Washington to confer with me if thought desirable. There is only one matter which I desired to talk with you about that I think, to save you the trip here, and especially in view of your expected absence from the opening of Congress, I ought to write you about. All other things will as you say "keep" until you arrive here.

I have been a good deal bothered about a nomination to the U. S. Supreme Court—not because I have had much personal doubt as to the best selection under all the circumstances, but on account of other considerations outside of absolute fitness.

Of course I want to nominate a New Yorker; and my mind has been constantly drawn to Judge Peckham as the best choice. It seemed to me a short time ago that I ought to know whether or not he would accept the plan, and I wrote to him asking the question. After some reflection he replied in the affirmative. So you see I am committed to the nomination. I think the place should be filled by a confirmed nominee as early as practicable and I want to send in the name as soon as the Senate meets.

I suppose in your absence and with a lack of knowledge on the part of the Committee as to your feeling in the matter, it might and would be laid over until your arrival.

Have you any desire as to the time of sending in the nomination?

I think the court needs him and I would be glad to have him qualified very early if you could find it consistent and agreeable to pave the way for it in your absence.

I need hardly say to you that this is entirely confidential except as you may see fit to confer with Judge Peckham himself.

Yours very truly,
GROVER CLEVELAND.

HON. DAVID B. HILL,
Albany, N. Y.

This time Senator Hill proved amenable, possibly owing to the fact that another presidential year was at hand, with Grover Cleveland at last out of the running. The opposition was called off, and Mr. Peckham was confirmed.

CHAPTER V

THE PULLMAN STRIKE OF 1894

"The real interests of labor are not promoted by a resort to threats and violent manifestations."
—GROVER CLEVELAND.

IF some ingenious mind could invent a process by which labor would instantly recognize its friends, the problems of the world would be immeasurably simplified. No President was ever more vilified by labor than was Grover Cleveland, and yet, in view of his public acts and private papers, it is fair to say that no President ever sympathized more sincerely with its every just and honorable ambition. On the other hand, no President ever saw more clearly the duties and obligations which belong to labor, and the supreme necessity, in the interest of capital and labor alike, of maintaining law and order as the only basis of society.

To reconcile opposing positions, not to take sides with one or the other of opposing factions, he felt to be the line of promise in labor disputes. He therefore refused to become the partisan of labor in order to conciliate the labor vote, and was equally careful not to allow himself to be branded with the mark of capital. In this way he stood free to act for the nation when these two contended, and, in consequence, he was especially loved by neither. To-day, however, as we review his career from the vantage point of a generation freed from the passions engendered by his many conflicts, it is clear that his paramount sympathy was for those who depend upon their physical labor for the necessities of life, and that, while fully conceding and loyally defending the legal

138

rights of capital, he felt himself, in a more special sense, the champion of the majority. "The capitalist can protect himself," he often declared, "but the wage earner is practically defenseless."

That reconciliation was necessary between these two genii of the lantern, he attributed more to the sins of capital than to the sins of labor, although he saw with clear eyes the many sins of both. Communism, he said, is "a hateful thing and a menace to peace and organized government"; but he added, "The Communism of combined wealth and capital, the outgrowth of overweening cupidity and selfishness which assiduously undermines the justice and integrity of free institutions, is not less dangerous than the Communism of oppressed poverty and toil which, exasperated by injustice and discontent, attacks with wild disorder the citadel of misrule."

He eagerly welcomed every suggestion which offered a prospect of bridging the chasm between employer and employee; and one of the reasons for his great admiration for Andrew Carnegie was that the steel magnate showed a zeal equal to his own in the search for the germ of reconciliation.

In acknowledging an autograph copy of Mr. Carnegie's volume, *The Gospel of Wealth,* Mr. Cleveland said: "I am by no means in a despairing mood; but I am afraid that there is danger in the fact that you are nearly the only man, able experimentally to preach the 'Gospel of Wealth,' who is attempting to lessen a gulf by going nearer to those who cannot hope to climb nearer to him." And in commenting upon a manuscript received from the same friend, he wrote:

"I have thought for a long time that there must be a way to so weld capital and labor together that the distressing result of their quarrels and misunderstandings would be prevented; and now I am wondering if your address does not point that way.

"Perhaps a plan could now be evolved from the theories and facts you suggest, that would adjust itself to all conditions; but you state the rule which must underlie any effective remedy, when you say: 'You must capture and keep the heart of the original and supremely able man before his brain can do its best'—but I am sure your own experience justifies you in further saying: 'You must capture and keep the heart of any *working man* before his *hands* will do their best.' "

This idea of reconciliation runs through his labor discussions of every period. In accepting the nomination as Governor of New York, and the first nomination as President, in his first inaugural address, and in his earlier presidential utterances, it appears and reappears. And with it is seen, with ever increasing definiteness, his conviction that arbitration is the only sane method of reconciliation.

"The proper theory upon which to proceed," declared his special message of April 22, 1886, "is that of voluntary arbitration as a means of settling these difficulties. But I suggest that instead of arbitrators chosen in the heat of conflicting claims, and after each dispute shall arise, for the purpose of determining the same, there shall be created a Commission of Labor, consisting of three members, who shall be regular officers of the Government, charged among other duties with the consideration and settlement, when possible, of all controversies between labor and capital. . . . In July, 1884, by a law of Congress, a Bureau of Labor was established and placed in charge of a Commissioner of Labor. . . . The Commission which I suggest could easily be engrafted upon the bureau thus already organized." Out of this suggestion grew the

Springer Bill, which President Cleveland approved on October 1, 1888, and which provided special federal machinery for the arbitration of labor disputes.

Reconciliation, however, was not his supreme theory. That place of honor belonged to the idea of enforcement of law; and its testing was not far off.

Labor troubles had been brewing since the beginning of Mr. Cleveland's second term, due, he believed, chiefly to the effects of the McKinley tariff and free silver legislation. In the summer of 1893 the situation was rendered more acute by the Columbian Exposition, which brought 12,000,000 people to Chicago, and tested to the utmost the extraordinary railroad facilities of the country.

When the great event was over and the well-to-do sightseers had departed, Chicago was left to deal with the derelicts of many lands and of many tongues, who had drifted to the scene of the world's interest, and had not been able to drift out again. Caught by the panic of 1893, their plight was rendered far more desperate than it would normally have been. Soup kitchens and charity organizations of all kinds did their futile best to relieve the distress; but such are only weak anæsthetics, able to deaden pain for but a moment, and discontent grew apace.

Moreover, Chicago was but one center of a disease which reached from ocean to ocean. A party rendered careless by long power had sown the wind and another party was called upon to reap the whirlwind. Such at least was the President's interpretation. Throughout the country an army of discontent, the unemployed of a nation, victims of circumstance, and products of vicious habits, were facing that hard winter with a feeling that government had failed.

By spring, discontent had hardened into purpose. Dreaming of wealth by the operation of government printing presses, shouting for an issue of five hundred million dollars of unreal, inconvertible paper money, with which to relieve their very real needs, Coxey, Kelly, and Frye, generals of a horde gathered from all parts of the country, marched on Washington.

On April 28th the "Army of the Commonwealth of Christ," led by Coxey, reached the city, a depleted, bedraggled retinue of tramps, and, straggling across the lawns of the Capitol, ended their glorious march in the lock-up for having disregarded the sign: "Keep off the grass." But though the project ended ridiculously, it indicated a dangerous failure of free government in America. If jest, this great uprising was a solemn jest, for so vast an army of unemployed is a real problem in any age and in any land. There was, moreover, another army, the greater army of the employed, preparing to exhibit a similar spirit of discontent and protest against a free government that had failed of full success.

The history of organized labor has been a short history, though sporadic attempts to combine in self-defense have marked many ages in the world's progress. Capital, on the other hand, has long understood the art of combination for class protection. Indeed, it has usually contemplated far more than mere protection, effecting in addition plans for the exploitation of labor. Thus these two, twin brethren by nature, have too commonly faced one another as enemies—alert, suspicious, and at frequent intervals openly hostile.

Expedients labeled "welfare work," "employer's generosity," or what not, have at times been used in the hope of keeping labor content with an unfair division of the common gains, but labor, though it has generally taken what was offered, has done so sullenly, desiring not gratuities, but partnership.

The Pullman Palace Car Company had gone the full distance in its attempt to make labor physically comfortable. Its magnates had provided a village near Chicago, with good cottages, well paved streets, excellent sanitary arrangements, and beautiful parks. They had acted with uncommon generosity, and they looked for gratitude and contentment in the village.

But they looked in vain. "Happy Pullman Town" was neither grateful nor satisfied; it was a seething mass of discontent. And why? Partly, no doubt, because the comforts which men's hands had earned were handed out to them as though they were gratuities, partly because their rents were from twenty to twenty-five per cent higher than corresponding rents in Chicago. Moreover, the ears of employers were keen. Whispers of discontent or criticism seemed in some mysterious way to connect with the distant chambers where sat the owners of the company, in whose eyes criticism was ingratitude and when discovered meant for the workman the dusty road and the black list.

During the spring of 1894, four thousand of the Pullman village residents joined the American Railway Union, which had been organized the year before to protect railway workers against the General Managers' Association, an organization representing forty-two railroads, and aiming to control labor. The growth of this union had been phenomenal. Between August, 1893, and June, 1894, it had enrolled 150,000 members from all classes of railway employees, and was, as Mr. Cleveland later expressed it, "the most compact and effective organization of the kind ever attempted."

In May, 1894, the Pullman Company declared a reduction of twenty per cent in the wages of their employees, the denizens of the lovely village, and dismissed a number of them as being no longer necessary in view of the state of the market. At once a committee of the villagers called on President Pullman, and requested that the wages be restored to their original standard. This request was refused, and soon after, three of the committee were discharged, contrary to the promise given by Mr. Pullman. At this point five sixths of the inhabitants of the village struck, and they, too, were discharged, and with them the one sixth who had not joined the strikers.

Had the lowering of wages been accompanied by a corresponding lowering of dividends and of officers' salaries, the men would have had little cause for resentment; but salaries and dividends remained unchanged, and, as the Company refused to arbitrate, the cause of the strikers was taken up by the Railway Union, which forbade its members to operate trains with Pullman cars attached.

How far the leaders of the Union were from plans of violence when the strike started is shown by the following proclamation issued by Eugene V. Debs, its President:

"To all striking employees:

"In view of the report of disturbances in various localities, I deem it my duty to caution you against being a party to any violation of law—municipal, State or national—during the existing difficulties. We have repeatedly declared that we respect law and order, and our conduct must conform to our profession. A man who commits violence in any form, whether a member of our order or not, should be promptly arrested and punished, and we should be the first to apprehend the miscreant and bring him to justice.

"We must triumph as law-abiding citizens or not at all. Those who engage in force and violence are our real enemies. We have it upon reliable authority that thugs and toughs have been employed to create trouble, so as to prejudice the public against our cause. The scoundrels should be made in every case to pay the full penalty of the law.

"I appeal to you to be men, orderly and law-abiding. Our cause is just. The great public is with us, and we have nothing to fear. Let it be borne in mind that if the railroad companies can secure men to handle their trains, they have that right. Our men have the right to quit, but their right ends there. Other men have the right to take their places, whatever the propriety of so doing may be. Keep away from railroad yards or rights of way, or other places where large crowds congregate. A safe plan is to remain away entirely from places where there is any likelihood of being an outbreak.

"The railroad managers have sought to make it appear that their trains do not move because of the interference of the strikers. The statement is an unqualified falsehood, and no one knows this better than the managers themselves. They make this falsehood serve their purpose of calling out the troops. Respect the law, conduct yourselves as becomes men, and our cause shall be crowned with success."

It was not long, however, before the strikers were openly boasting that they would, if necessary, "tie up and paralyze the operations of every railway in the United States, and the business and industries dependent thereon," and were emphasizing their meaning by intimidation and violence. Just when and at whose instigation violence was begun, it is not easy to determine. Some writers have concluded that the change was due to secret machinations of the railway managers, who realized that thus would the strikers weaken their own cause. Others have traced it to the human driftwood whom the World's Fair had left stranded in Chicago, while many have laid the blame at the door of President Debs himself. But there can be no doubt that almost from the first the strikers were guilty of what the courts later described as a "conspiracy to prevent the railroad companies . . . from performing their duties as common carriers," and that, early in the strike, they succeeded in many sections of the country.

As early as June 28th, news reached Mr. Cleveland that on the Southern Pacific system the mails were completely obstructed, and similar complaints poured in from other sections of the West and South. To each in turn, at his direction, the Attorney-General wired the message: "See that the passage of the regular trains, carrying United States mails in the usual and ordinary way . . . is not obstructed." On June 30th the Superintendent of the Railway Mail Service at Chicago telegraphed to his chief at Washington: "No mails have accumulated at Chicago so far. All regular mail·trains are running nearly on time with a few slight exceptions." But on the same day the District Attorney for the Chicago District warned the President that violent interference with transportation was imminent, and urged that the marshal be instructed to place special deputies upon all mail trains, with orders to protect the mails.

The desired order was sent at once, with the addition, "Action ought to be prompt and vigorous"; and the 'Attorney-General followed it the next day by the appointment of Edwin Walker as special counsel for the United States, and by the suggestion that an injunction be secured from the Circuit Court of the District forbidding in advance those acts of violence which the government had reason to fear. As yet, if we may accept the testimony of Mr. Debs, later given under oath, there was no actual violence anywhere; but Mr. Olney was convinced that violence was at hand and the injunction was intended to prevent it.

Such an injunction was clearly within the competency of the Federal Courts under general principles of law, and, in addition, the Constitution specifically places the United States mails and Interstate Commerce under the exclusive care of the federal government. Moreover, by an act of July 2, 1890, Congress had provided that conspiracies in restraint of trade or commerce among the several states were illegal, and had instructed the Circuit Courts of the United States to prevent and restrain such conspiracies. Furthermore, the law left no doubt of the President's power in the premises, section 5298 of the Revised Statutes of the United States containing these words: "Whenever by reason of unlawful obstructions, combinations or assemblages of persons, or rebellion against the authority of the United States, it shall become impracticable in the judgment of the President to enforce, by the ordinary course of judicial proceedings, the laws of the United States within any State or Territory, it shall be lawful for the President to call forth the militia of any or all of the States, and to employ such parts of the land or naval forces of the United States as he may deem necessary."

Whether, however, it was wise, at such a time, to invoke so unrestrained a power as a blanket injunction which meant, if effective, the immediate end of the strike, was even then questioned by farsighted men, some of whom had themselves handled this two-edged sword to their regret. On July 14, 1894, Henry M. Shepard, Presiding Justice of the First District of the Illinois Appellate Court, wrote to Judge Gresham:

"I don't remember, if I ever knew, how you have, when on the bench, ruled with reference to operating the

Government through a writ of injunction . . . but I do think some of the Judges have run wild over the question. I did once, and I guess about the first, undertake to execute all the functions of government—Executive, Judicial, and perhaps Legislative—in putting down a switchman's strike on the Lake Shore road, some eight or ten years ago, by an injunction writ, and I am now pretty certain I ought to have been impeached. I would have given a hundred dollars to a fund for the employment of a lawyer for the switchmen to present a motion to dissolve the injunction within a week after I granted it (*ex parte*), but no one came and I sent two poor devils to jail on the theory in my own mind that so long as the order stood it must be obeyed. It broke up the strike, or had a tendency to do so, but I concluded I was exercising very dangerous powers."

The idea of an injunction was naturally resented by the strikers, who saw that it would force them either to abandon the strike or defy the court, and they regarded the appointment of Walker as indicating that the federal government was on the side of the railroads. Governor Altgeld later summed up the objections to Walker in these words: He was "one of the most prominent corporation lawyers in the country . . . the hired attorney of one of the railroads involved in the strike, and . . . at the time personally engaged in fighting strikers, and therefore had an interest in the outcome. Yet this man was clothed with all the powers of the government and he brought to the use of himself and his clients, without expense to them, the service of over 4,000 United States marshals, of a specially picked United States Grand Jury, of several United States judges, and of the United States army. Never before were the United States government and the corporations of the country so completely blended, all the powers of the one being at the service of the other, and never before was the goddess of justice made a mere hand-maid for one of the combatants."

The injunction was promptly prepared by the court, to be ready for use when needed. It commanded "all persons . . . absolutely to desist and refrain from in any way or manner interfering with, hindering, obstructing, or stopping any of the business of any of the following named railroads [a list of which was inserted] as common carriers of passengers and freight between or among any States . . . and from in any way or manner interfering with, hindering, obstructing or stopping any trains carry-ing the mail."

To ask Mr. Debs and his fellow leaders to bow to so drastic an injunction at a moment when blood was hot, and when victory seemed to them assured, was a stern test of their sweet reasonableness. "The railway managers were completely defeated," Debs later explained. "Their immediate resources were exhausted, their properties were paralyzed, and they were unable to operate their trains." But to expect Grover Cleveland to demand less than complete obedience to law was to ask the impossible, in view of his oath of office, and of his conviction that he must act in the interest of the public, which belonged neither to the General Managers' Association nor to the American Railway Union. Their mail and their com-merce were being hindered in lawful transit. Their lives and their property were being jeopardized. Their Presi-dent must interfere, cost what it might, offend whom it might.

On July 2nd news reached the White House that the injunction had been issued to restrain Debs and his fellow officials, together with parties of names unknown, and that the writs would be served that same afternoon. The President was, furthermore, warned that the temper of the strikers was such as to indicate that troops might be required, "if the United States mails were to be kept moving and the injunction respected."

"IF the United States mails were to be kept moving" was a proposition which Mr. Cleveland never harbored. His method of reasoning on such a subject was not in conditional clauses. There were no "ifs" or "buts" in his attitude toward lawlessness. The United States mails *would* be kept moving. Interstate commerce *would* be kept open, whoever opposed. His special council had appealed for troops, and troops he should have. Accordingly General Nelson A. Miles, Commandant of the Department of Missouri, was warned to "expect orders at any time."

This dispatch had scarcely touched the wires, when startling news arrived: "When the injunction was granted . . . a mob of from two to three thousand held possession of a point in the city near the crossing of the Rock Island by other roads, where they had already ditched a mail train, and prevented the passing of any train, whether mail or otherwise. . . . I . . . believe that no force less than the regular troops of the United States can procure the passage of mail trains, or enforce the orders of the courts." The dispatch bore the signatures of Edwin Walker, Thomas E. Milchrist, and Judge P. S. Grosscup.

In reply District Attorney Milchrist was informed that "While action should be prompt and decisive, it should of course be kept within the limits provided by the Constitution and laws," and orders were issued through the War Department which brought Colonel Crofton's regiment to Chicago, where General Miles himself assumed command. The day, as it chanced, was July 4th. The outlook was so alarming that before the day closed Miles requested more troops for Fort Sheridan, and in reply the War Department authorized him to draw six companies from Fort Leavenworth and two from Fort Brady.

When Benjamin Franklin was informed of George III's intention of sending redcoats to Boston to put down rebellion, he replied, "If sent they will not find a rebellion, but they will create one." This was a true prediction, and a similar one might have been made regarding the immediate effect of the arrival of federal troops in Chicago. For the time at least, they bred not peace but war. Governor Altgeld interpreted their presence as a threat against local self-government, and his indiscreet utterances deepened the resentment of the strikers and their friends. General Miles reported an increase in the size of the sullen mobs, a bolder series of lawless attacks upon trains, mingled with occasional instances of outrages upon persons or property. "The injunction of the United States Court," he declared, "is openly defied, and unless the mobs are dispersed . . . more serious trouble may be expected."

Such was the state of affairs when Governor Altgeld addressed to President Cleveland the following telegram of protest:

Executive Office, State of Illinois.
July 5, 1894.

The HON. GROVER CLEVELAND,
President of the United States,
Washington, D. C.
Dear Sir:

I am advised that you have ordered federal troops to go into service in the State of Illinois. Surely the facts have not been correctly presented to you in this case or you would not have taken the step, for it is entirely unnecessary and, as it seems to me, unjustifiable. Waiving all questions of courtesy, I will say that the State of Illinois is not only able to take care of itself, but it stands ready to-day to furnish the Federal Government any assistance it may need elsewhere. Our military force is ample and consists of as good soldiers as can be found in the country. They have been ordered promptly whenever and wherever they were needed. We have stationed in Chicago alone three regiments of infantry, one battery and one troop of cavalry, and no better soldiers can be found. They have been ready every moment to go on duty and have been and are now eager to go into service. But they have not been ordered out because nobody in Cook County, whether official or private citizen, asked to have their assistance, or even intimated in any way that their assistance was desired or necessary.

So far as I have been advised, the local officials have been able to handle the situation. But if any assistance were needed the State stood ready to furnish one hundred men for every one man required, and stood ready to do so at a moment's notice. Notwithstanding these facts, the Federal Government has been applied to by men who had political and selfish motives for wanting to ignore the State government. We have just gone through a long coal strike, more extensive here than in any other state, because our soft-coal field is larger than that of any other state. We have now had ten days of the railroad strike, and we have promptly furnished military aid wherever the local officials needed it.

In two instances the United States Marshal for the southern district of Illinois applied for assistance to enable him to enforce the processes of the United States courts, and troops were promptly furnished him, and he was assisted in every way he desired. The law has been thoroughly executed and every man guilty of violating it during the strike has been brought to justice. If the Marshal for the northern district of Illinois or the authorities of Cook County needed military assistance they had but to ask for it in order to get it from the State.

At present some of our railroads are paralyzed, not by reason of obstructions, but because they cannot get men to operate their trains. For some reason they are anxious to keep this fact from the public, and for this purpose are making an outcry about obstructions in order to divert attention. Now, I will cite to you two examples which illustrate the situation: Some days ago I was advised that the business of one of our railroads was obstructed at two railroad centers, that there was a condition bordering on anarchy there; and I was asked to furnish protection so as to enable the employees of the road to operate the trains. Troops were promptly ordered to both points. Then it transpired that the company had not sufficient men on its line to operate one train. All the old hands were orderly, but refused to go. The company had large shops in which work a number of men who did not belong to the railway union and who could run an engine. They were appealed to to run the train, but flatly refused. We were obliged to hunt up soldiers who could run an engine and operate a train.

Again, two days ago, appeals which were almost frantic came from officials of another road, stating that at an important point on their lines trains were forcibly obstructed, and that there was a reign of anarchy at that place; and they asked for protection so that they could move their trains. Troops were put on the ground in a few hours' time, when the officer in command telegraphed me that there was no trouble and had been none at that point, but that the road seemed to have no men to run trains; and the sheriff telegraphed that he did not need troops, but would himself move every train if the company would only furnish an engineer. The result was that the troops were there over twelve hours before a single train was moved, although there was no attempt at interference by anybody. It is true that in several instances a road made efforts to work a few green men, and a crowd standing around insulted them and tried to drive them away; and in a few other places they cut off Pullman sleepers from trains. But all these troubles were local in character and could easily be handled by the State authorities. Illinois has more railroad men than any other state in the Union, but as a rule they are orderly and well behaved. This is shown by the fact that so very little actual violence has been committed. Only a very small per cent of these men have been guilty of any infractions of the law. The newspaper accounts have in many cases been pure fabrications, and in others, wild exaggerations.

I have gone thus into details to show that it is not soldiers that the railroads need so much as it is men to operate trains, and that the conditions do not exist here which bring the cause within the Federal statutes, a statute that was passed in 1881, and was in reality a war measure. This statute authorized the use of Federal troops in a state whenever it shall be impracticable to enforce the laws of the United States within such states by the ordinary judicial proceedings. Such a condition does not exist in Illinois. There have been a few local disturbances, but nothing that seriously interfered with the administration of justice, or that could not be easily controlled by the local or state authorities, for the Federal troops can do nothing that the state troops cannot do.

I repeat that you have been imposed upon in this matter, but even if by a forced construction it was held that the condition here came within the letter of the statute, then I submit that local self-government is a fundamental principle of our Constitution. Each community shall govern itself so long as it can and is ready and able to enforce the law, and it is in harmony with this fundamental principle that the statute authorizing the President to send troops into states must be construed. Especially is this so in matters relating to the exercise of police power and the preservation of law and order. To absolutely ignore a local government in matters of this kind, when the local government is ready to furnish assistance needed and is amply able to enforce the law, not only insults the people of this state by imputing to them an inability to govern themselves or an unwillingness to enforce the law, but is in violation of a basic principle of our institutions. The question of Federal supremacy is in no way involved —no one disputes it for a moment—but under our Constitution Federal supremacy and local self-government must go hand in hand, and to ignore the latter is to do violence to the Constitution.

As Governor of the State of Illinois, I protest against this and ask immediate withdrawal of the Federal troops from active duty in this State. Should the situation at any time get so serious that we cannot control it with the State forces, we will promptly and freely ask for Federal assistance; but until such time I protest with all due deference against this uncalled for reflection upon our people, and again ask the immediate withdrawal of these troops.

I have the honor to be,

Yours respectfully,

JOHN P. ALTGELD, Governor of Illinois.

This lengthy statement, Mr. Cleveland later declared, "so far missed the actual condition as to appear irrelevant and, in some parts, absolutely frivolous." "It was probably a very fortunate circumstance that the presence of United States soldiers in Chicago at that time did not depend upon the request or desire of Governor Altgeld."

The President's reply was immediate and definite, but its sure, unargumentative tone was calculated, though not designed, to exasperate the Governor still more:

Washington,
July 5, 1894.

Hon. John P. Altgeld,
Governor of Illinois,
Springfield, Illinois.

Federal troops were sent to Chicago in strict accordance with the Constitution and laws of the United States upon the demand of the Post Office Department that obstruction of the mails should be removed, and upon the representations of the judicial officers of the United States that process of the Federal courts could not be executed through the ordinary means, and upon abundant proof that conspiracies existed against commerce between the states. To meet these conditions, which are clearly within the province of Federal authority, the presence of Federal troops in the city of Chicago was deemed not only proper but necessary, and there has been no intention of thereby interfering with the plain duty of the local authorities to preserve the peace of the city.

Grover Cleveland.

As printed in the Chicago *Times,* the letter closed at this point. An autograph copy found among the Lamont papers, however, adds this postscript, which clearly shows how far Mr. Cleveland was from serving the cause of the railway management:

"Mr. McNaught should be informed that whatever arrangement is made by the Company with its employees must positively be made without relying upon the Government for any guarantee whatever. The Military power of the Government refuses to be drawn into any relation with the details of railroad management.   *G. C.*"

That Mr. Debs was even yet determined to avoid violence is evident from the following paragraph from his pen, printed in an anti-Debs Chicago newspaper on July 5th: "We hold the position that we can win without even the semblance of violence, and if we cannot I prefer to lose rather than tolerate violence. Let me repeat: There is but one well-defined estimate of the situation, and that is, we hold the railroads cannot get men sufficient to run their trains. On that proposition we win or lose. We shall not interfere with any man who wants to work. We have not done so and shall not. A man has a legal right to quit work, and it is not the part of the troops or the civil officers of the law to arrest them for so doing, though I am informed such an arrest was made today. The American Railway Union will protect its men from the penalties of such arrests."

It is only fair to add that Governor Altgeld sent out many orders directing the sheriffs of the various counties of Illinois to see that the traveling public was protected and that trains were kept moving. It is also true that he insisted that "the reports . . . as to actual conditions in Chicago during the strike were malicious libels upon the city." But he later admitted that from July 4th to July 14th $355,612 worth of property was destroyed.

It was clearly the duty of both President Debs and Governor Altgeld to continue to preach peace and obedience to law, even in the face of the injunction; unfortunately, however, they chose another course, and one which compelled the hand that still held the olive branch to change it for the sword. Debs now defiantly resisted the injunction, and encouraged others to do likewise, while Altgeld flayed it in the words: "A Federal judge, not content with deciding controversies brought into his Court . . . proceeds to legislate and then administer. He issues a ukase which he calls an injunction forbidding whatever he pleases . . . and he deprives men of the right of trial by jury when the law guarantees this right, and he then enforces this ukase in a summary and arbitrary manner by imprisonment, throwing men into prison not for violating a law, but for being guilty of a contempt of court in disregarding one of these injunctions." In the following open telegram he added further fuel to the flame of lawlessness:

[*July 6, 1894*]

The HON. GROVER CLEVELAND,
    President of the United States,
        Washington, D. C.
Sir:
    Your answer to my protest involves some startling conclusions, and ignores and evades the question at issue, that is, that the principle of local self-government is just as fundamental in our institutions as is that of Federal supremacy.

    1. You calmly assume that the Executive has the legal right to order Federal troops into any community of the United States, in the first instance, whenever there is the slightest disturbance, and that he can do this without any

regard to the question as to whether that community is able to and ready to enforce the law itself. And inasmuch as the Executive is the sole judge of the question as to whether any disturbance exists or not in any part of the country, this assumption means that the Executive can send Federal troops into any community in the United States at his pleasure and keep them there as long as he chooses.

If this is the law, then the principle of local self-government either never did exist in this country or else has been destroyed, for no community can be said to possess local self-government if the Executive can at his pleasure send military forces to patrol its streets under pretense of enforcing some law. The kind of local self-government that could exist under these circumstances can be found in any of the monarchies of Europe and is not in harmony with the spirit of our institutions.

2. It is also a fundamental principle in our government that except in times of war the military shall be subordinate to the civil authority. In harmony with this provision the state troops when ordered out act under and with the civil authorities. The Federal troops you have ordered to Chicago are not under the civil authorities, and are in no way responsible to them for their conduct. They are not even acting under the United States Marshal, or under any Federal officer of the State, but are acting directly under military orders issued from military headquarters at Washington, and in so far as these troops act at all it is military government.

3. The statute authorizing Federal troops to be sent into states in certain cases contemplates that the state troops shall be taken first. This provision has been ignored, and it is assumed that the Executive is not bound by it. Federal interference with industrial disturbances

in the various states is certainly a new departure, and opens up so large a field that it will require a very little stretch of authority to absorb to itself all the details of local government.

4. You say that the troops were ordered into Illinois upon the demand of the Post Office Department and upon representations of the judicial officers of the United States that process of the courts could not be served and upon proof that conspiracies existed. We will not discuss the facts, but look for a moment at the principle involved in your statement. All of these officers are appointed by the Executive. Most of them can be removed by him at his will. They are not only obliged to do his bidding, but they are, in fact, a part of the Executive. If several of them can apply for troops one alone can, so that under the law, as you assume it to be, an Executive, through any one of his appointees, can apply to himself to have the military sent into any city or number of cities, and base his application on such representations or showing as he sees fit to make. In fact, it will be immaterial whether he makes any showing or not, for the Executive is the sole judge and nobody else has any right to interfere or even inquire about it. Then the Executive can pass on his own application. His will being the sole guide, he can hold the application to be sufficient and order troops to as many places as he wishes, and put them in command of any one he chooses and have them act, not under the civil officers, either Federal or State, but act directly under military orders from Washington, and there is not in the Constitution or laws of the land, whether written or unwritten, any limitation or restraint upon his power. His judgment, that is, his will, is the sole guide, and it being purely a matter of discretion, his decision can never be examined or questioned.

This assumption as to the power of the Executive is certainly new, and I respectfully submit that it is not the law of the land.

The jurists have told us that this is a government of law, and not a government by the caprice of individuals; and, further, instead of being autocratic, it was a government of limited power. Yet the autocratic Russia could certainly not possess nor claim to possess greater power than is possessed by the Executive of the United States, if your assumption is correct.

5. The Executive has the command not only of the regular forces of the United States, but of the military forces of all the states, and can order them to any place he sees fit, and as there are always more or less local disturbances over the country, it would be an easy matter, under your construction of the law, for an ambitious Executive to order out the military forces of all the states and establish at once a military government. The only chance of failure in such a movement could come from rebellion, and with such a vast military power at command this could be readily crushed, for, as a rule, soldiers will obey orders. As for the situation in Illinois, that is of no consequence now, when compared with the far-reaching principle involved. True, according to my advices, Federal troops have now been on duty for over two days and, although the men were brave and the officers valiant and able, yet their very presence proved to be an irritant because it aroused the indignation of a large class of people who, while upholding law and order, had been taught to believe in local self-government and therefore resented what they regarded as an unwarranted interference.

Inasmuch as the Federal troops can do nothing but what the state troops can do there, and believing that the state is amply able to take care of the situation and to enforce the law, and believing that the ordering out of the Federal troops was unwarranted, I again ask their withdrawal.

JOHN P. ALTGELD.

At the same time, General Miles and other officers and officials reported riotous assemblies, violent mobs, and stealthy dealings in arson and murder. One of General Miles's telegrams declared: "Of the twenty-three roads centering in Chicago only six are unobstructed in freight, passenger and mail transportation. . . . Large numbers of trains moving in and out of the city have been stoned and fired upon by mobs, and one engineer killed. There was a secret meeting to-day of Debs and the representatives of labor unions considering the advisability of a general strike of all labor unions. About one hundred men were present at that meeting." Miles later telegraphed: "Men who were in secret meeting last night say that all labor union men will be called out Monday. In meantime all labor men have been advised to get Winchester rifles and pistols. They hope to have one hundred thousand men in this city. They decided to support . . . strike in every way. . . . I recommend immediate concentration of troops near Chicago . . . to be ready any emergency Monday."

In view of such facts, and they were but representative of many, the Governor's "rather dreary discussion of the importance of preserving the rights of the States," as Mr. Cleveland later described his lengthy telegram, only exasperated the President. "I confess," he declared, "that my patience was somewhat strained, when I quickly sent the following dispatch . . .":

Washington,
July 6, 1894.

HON. JOHN P. ALTGELD,
Governor of Illinois,
Springfield, Ills.

While I am still persuaded that I have neither transcended my authority or duty, in the emergency that confronts us, it seems to me that in this hour of danger and public distress discussion may well give way to active effort on the part of all in authority to restore obedience to law and to protect life and property.

GROVER CLEVELAND.

Attorney-General Olney was equally contemptuous. To the Washington *Post* he said:

"It is hardly worth while to discuss at length the false premise and the illogical *non-sequiturs* of the Altgeld manifesto. As a campaign platform, it is a safe prediction that the author will be found to be the only person to stand upon it.

"The soil of Illinois is the soil of the United States and, for all United States purposes, the United States is there with its courts, its marshals, and its troops, not by license or comity, but as of right. The paramount duty of the President of the United States is to see that the laws of the United States are faithfully executed, and in the discharge of that duty he is not hampered or crippled by the necessity of consulting chief of police, Mayor, or even Governor. In the present instance nothing has been done and nothing ordered which the most captious critic can condemn as any invasion of State rights.

"The action of the national executive has been simply and exclusively directed to the enforcement of the United

States laws, the execution of the orders and processes of the United States courts, and the prevention of any obstruction of the United States mails.

"The notion that the territory of any State is too sacred to permit the exercise thereon, by the United States government, of any of its legitimate functions never had any legal existence, and, as a rule of conduct, became practically extinct with the close of the civil war."

Two days later, the President issued his famous Proclamation of July 8, 1894:

"Proclamation
"By the President of the United States
"Whereas, by reason of unlawful obstructions, combinations and assemblages of persons, it has become impracticable in the judgment of the President to enforce, by the ordinary course of judicial proceedings, the laws of the United States within the State of Illinois and especially in the city of Chicago within said state; and,

"Whereas, for the purpose of enforcing the faithful execution of the laws of the United States and protecting its property and removing obstructions to the United States mails in the state and city aforesaid, the President has employed a part of the military forces of the United States:

"Now, therefore, I, Grover Cleveland, President of the United States, do hereby admonish all good citizens and all persons who may be or may come within the city and state aforesaid, against aiding, countenancing, encouraging or taking any part in such unlawful obstructions, combinations and assemblages; and I hereby warn all persons engaged in or in any way connected with such unlawful obstructions, combinations and assemblages to disperse and retire peaceably to their respective abodes on or before twelve o'clock noon on the ninth day of July instant.

"Those who disregard this warning and persist in taking part with a riotous mob in forcibly resisting and obstructing the execution of the laws of the United States or interfering with the functions of the Government and destroying or attempting to destroy the property belonging to the United States or under its protection cannot be regarded otherwise than as public enemies.

"Troops employed against such a riotous mob, will act with all the moderation and forbearance consistent with the accomplishment of the desired end; but the stern necessities that confront them will not certainly permit discrimination between guilty participants and those who are mingled with them from curiosity and without criminal intent. The only safe course therefore for those not actually unlawfully participating is to abide at their homes, or at least not to be found in the neighborhood of riotous assemblages.

"While there will be no hesitation or vacillation in the decisive treatment of the guilty, this warning is especially intended to protect and save the innocent.

"In Testimony Whereof I have hereunto set my hand and caused the seal of the United States to be hereto affixed.

"Done at the city of Washington this eighth day of July, A.D., in the year of our Lord One Thousand Eight Hundred and Ninety-four, and of the Independence of the United States of America the One Hundred and Eighteenth."

Upon reading this proclamation, Mr. Debs declared it "a plot to place Chicago under martial law at the instiga-

tion of the railway companies in furtherance of the latter's plan to destroy public sympathy. This cannot be
done. This meeting to-night will in all probability last
until daylight. I am certain that every union represented,
numbering over 100,000 laborers, will vote to strike to-
morrow."

With the coming of the morrow, however, came new
evidence of the President's determination. He issued a
second proclamation which recognized the conflict as
nation-wide, and warned the good people "at certain
points and places within the States of North Dakota,
Montana, Idaho, Washington, Wyoming, Colorado, and
California, and the Territories of Utah and New Mexico,
and especially along the lines of such railways traversing
said States and Territories as are military roads and post
routes and are engaged in Interstate commerce and in
carrying United States mails," to "retire peaceably to
their respective abodes on or before 3 o'clock in the afternoon on the 10th day of July instant."

These proclamations had the desired effect, though
indirectly. Debs and his associates having failed to "retire peaceably," at the command of the Court, were "in
contempt." They were accordingly arrested on July 10th,
and their arrest ended the strike.

But Mr. Cleveland was not yet entirely satisfied.
Having carried into effect his primary policy—the enforcement of law—he announced the intention of appoint-
ing a commission to investigate the questions which had
caused the strike. Of this announcement Mr. Debs declared: "We have no doubt that the board will be composed of men of high character and ability, and that they
will be able to locate the right or wrong involved in the
existing controversy, by virtue of which a satisfactory
settlement will be reached. It is to be hoped that the

board will be promptly appointed and organized, that its work will be prosecuted vigorously to the end of a speedy settlement of the existing conflict. We are of course for arbitration, and have been from the very beginning, and had this principle been recognized this strike would have been avoided."

The next day, he and his fellow prisoners sent the President the following telegram:

July 13, 1894.

The HON. GROVER CLEVELAND,
   President of the United States,
      Washington, D. C.
Dear Sir:
   We the undersigned beg to advise you that we have just submitted the following proposition to the Railway Managers, and if it meets with your approval we respectfully request that you take such action as you may deem proper to influence its acceptance:—

Chicago, Ill., *July 13, 1894.*

To the Railway Managers
Gentlemen:
   The existing troubles growing out of the Pullman strike having assumed continental proportions, and there being no indication of relief from the widespread business demoralization and distress incident thereto, the Railway employees, through the Board of Directors of the American Railway Union, respectfully make the following proposition as basis of settlement: They agree to return to work in a body at once, provided they shall be restored to their former positions without prejudice except in cases, if any there be, where they have been convicted of crime —this proposition looking to an immediate settle-

ment of the existing strike on all lines of railway is inspired by a purpose to subserve the public good. The strike, small and comparatively unimportant in its inception, has kindled in every direction until now it involves or threatens not only every public interest but the peace, security and prosperity of our common country. The contest has waged fiercely. It has extended far beyond the limits of interest originally involved and has laid hold of a vast number of industries and enterprises in no wise responsible for the differences and disagreements that led to the trouble. Factory, mill, mine, and shop have been silenced. Widespread demoralization has sway. The interests of multiplied thousands of innocent people are suffering. The common welfare is seriously menaced. The public peace and tranquillity are in peril. Grave apprehension for the future prevails. This being true, and the statement will *not* be *controverted,* we conceive it to be our duty as citizens and as men to make extraordinary efforts to end the existing strife and avert approaching calamities whose shadows are even now upon us. If ended now the contest, however serious in some of its consequences, will not have been in vain. Sacrifices have been made but they will have their compensations. Indeed, if lessons shall be taught by experience the troubles now so widely deplored will prove a blessing of inestimable value in the months and years to come. The differences that led up to the present complications need not now be discussed. At this supreme juncture every consideration of duty and patriotism demands that a remedy for existing troubles be found and applied. The employees propose to do their part by meeting their employers half-way. Let it be stated that they do not impose any condition of settlement except that they be returned to their former positions. They do not ask the recognition of their organization or of any organization. Believing this proposition to be fair, reasonable and just, it is respectfully submitted with the belief that its acceptance will result in the prompt resumption of traffic, the revival of industry, and the restoration of peace and order.

Respectfully,

EUGENE V. DEBS, President

GEO. W. HOWARD, Vice-President

SYLVESTER KOLIHER, Secty.,

American Railway Union.

But Mr. Debs no longer had anything to offer. The strike was over, and all that remained was for the courts to decide upon the penalty. He and his associates refused to give bail, scorning to wear the martyr's crown without bearing also the martyr's cross, as their admirers claimed; or, perhaps, as Mr. Cleveland less charitably suggested, "intending by such an act of martyrdom either to revive a waning cause, or to gain a plausible and justifying excuse for the collapse of their already foredoomed movement."

By July 22d Mr. Debs seems to have entirely changed his attitude. From Cook County jail, Chicago, contemptuously christened by the pro-Pullman press "Headquarters of the American Railway Union," he sent out the following declaration:

"We propose to continue this strike against the Pullman Company through good and evil report and without regard to consequences, until justice shall be done. We will use every available means to press the contest. Dungeons shall not daunt us. The struggle is for humanity and against the most cruel tyranny, and, unless we are dead to every impulse of mercy and fellow-feeling, must be crowned with success."

On July 26th, Mr. Cleveland announced his commission, Carroll D. Wright, John D. Kernan, and Nicholas E. Worthington, and directed them to "visit the State of Illinois and the city of Chicago and such other places in the United States as may appear proper . . . make careful inquiry into the causes of any pending dispute or existing controversy, and hear all persons interested therein."

While Mr. Debs and his fellow prisoners awaited trial, this commission carried forward its investigations, examining all told one hundred and nine witnesses. According to the testimony, the railroads lost in property destroyed, hire of United States Deputy Marshals, and incidental expenses, at least $685,308. The loss of earnings to these roads was estimated at $4,672,916. As estimated also, the 3,100 employees at Pullman lost $350,000 in wages, and the 100,000 employees upon the twenty-four railroads centering in Chicago paid at least $1,389,143 for their part in the strike. The Commission found also that during the strike the number shot and fatally wounded was 12, number arrested by police, 515; number arrested under United States statutes and against whom indictments were found, 71. The arrests made by the police were for murder, arson, burglary, assault, intimidation, riot, and lesser crimes. The cases passed upon by the United States Grand Jury were for obstruction of the mail, conspiracy in restraint of trade, and conspiracy to injure, oppress, threaten, or intimidate. It further found that, "The conditions created at Pullman enable the management at all times to assert with great vigor its assumed right to fix wages and rents absolutely, and to repress that sort of independence which leads to labor organizations and their attempts at mediation, arbitration, strikes, etc."

On December 10, 1894, the President transmitted the full report to Congress. Four days later the Illinois Circuit Court decided that these facts did not justify Mr. Debs and his companions in their course of resistance to organized authority and defiance of a federal injunction. It sentenced Mr. Debs to six months' imprisonment, and his associates to three months each, "for contempt of court." The decision was based upon the Sherman Anti-Trust Law of 1890, "an act to protect trade and commerce against unlawful restraint and monopolies"—an interesting development in view of the fact that the controversy had proceeded from a strike of laboring men against the unjust exactions of the Pullman Palace Car Company, one of the most perfect monopolies ever devised, which Mr. Debs hyperbolically characterized as "remorseless as a man-eating tiger."

An appeal was taken to the Supreme Court, President Debs and his fellows applying for a writ of habeas corpus on the ground that the facts found by the Circuit Court did not constitute disobedience to the writs of injunction served upon them. The case was argued on March 25 and 26, 1895, and on May 27th a decision was handed down, sustaining the verdict of the Circuit Court and completely vindicating the legality of President Cleveland's course. The decision declared:

"The United States may remove everything put upon highways, natural or artificial, to obstruct the passage of interstate commerce, or the carrying of the mails. . . . It is equally within its competency to appeal to the civil courts for an inquiry and determination as to the existence and the character of any of them, and if such are found to exist or threaten to occur, to invoke the powers of those courts to remove or restrain them, the jurisdiction of the courts to interfere in such matters by injunction being recognized from ancient times and by indubitable authority. . . .

"The complaint filed in this case clearly shows an existing obstruction of the artificial highways for the passage of interstate commerce and the transmission of the mails, not only temporarily existing, but threatening to continue, and under it the Circuit Court had power to issue its process of injunction.

"Such an injunction having been issued and served upon the defendants, the Circuit Court had authority to inquire whether its orders had been disobeyed, and when it found that they had been disobeyed, to proceed under Rev. Stat. § 725, and to enter the order of punishment complained of."

By this prompt and determined course, Mr. Cleveland had made it clear, not only that law must be obeyed, but that the nation is paramount and state lines only geographical expressions when the welfare of the country is at stake. He prized the decision of the court, not because it vindicated his dignity, but because, to quote his own words, it established "in an absolutely authoritative manner, and for all time, the power of the national government to protect itself in the exercise of its functions."

CHAPTER VI

THE VENEZUELAN AFFAIR

"The rules of conduct governing individual relations are equally applicable as between enlightened nations."
—GROVER CLEVELAND.

WHEN Grover Cleveland became President, few of his contemporaries would have classed among the most important of the great outstanding questions which confronted him a boundary dispute which for almost three quarters of a century had periodically caused friction between Venezuela and Great Britain. Yet such was the case.

In 1814, Great Britain, by her treaty with the Netherlands, acquired the provinces of Essequibo, Demerara, and Berbice, which under her rule came to be known as British Guiana. In 1840 Mr. (later Sir) Robert Schomburgk, an English engineer, was sent by England to survey and delimit its boundaries, as a preliminary measure, and report to the British Government. He took particular care to fortify himself with the history of the case, from actual exploration and information obtained from the Indians and from the evidence of local remains, and on such data he based his report.

At Point Barima, where the remains of a Dutch fort still existed, and at the mouth of the Amacura, he placed two boundary posts. At the urgent entreaty of the Venezuelan government these two posts were afterwards removed, but the concession was made with the distinct understanding that Great Britain did not thereby in any way abandon her claim to that position. In fact the Schomburgk line, as finally drawn, was a great reduction of the boundary claimed by Great Britain as her right and its proposal originated in a desire on her part to come to a friendly arrangement with a weaker power with whom she desired to remain in cordial relations.

As soon as Schomburgk's report was submitted to the Venezuelan government, the latter objected, with a statement of her own claims—claims starting in such obsolete grounds as the original discovery by Spain of the American continent, and supported by quotations more or less vague from the writing of travelers and geographers. She adduced no substantial evidence of actual conquest or occupation of the territory claimed.

Lord Aberdeen, then Secretary of State for Foreign Affairs, pointed out that it would be impossible to arrive at any agreement if both sides brought forward pretensions of so extreme a character, and announced certain concessions which Great Britain was prepared to make "out of friendly regard to Venezuela," on condition that the Venezuelan government would agree that no part of the territory proposed to be ceded should be alienated at any time to a foreign power, and that the Indian tribes residing in it should be protected from oppression. No answer to this note was ever received from the Venezuelan government, and in 1850 Her Majesty's Government informed the British Chargé d'Affaires at Carácas that as the proposal had remained for more than six years unaccepted, it must be considered as having lapsed, and instructed him to make a communication to the Venezuelan government to that effect.

Venezuela subsequently permitted projects to be set on foot for the occupation of Point Barima and certain other disputed positions, and the British Chargé d'Affaires was instructed to inform the government of Venezuela "that, whilst on the one hand Great Britain had no intention of occupying or encroaching upon the disputed territory, she would not, on the other hand, view with indifference aggressions on that territory by Venezuela." To which the Venezuelan government replied that Venezuela had no intention of occupying or encroaching upon any part of the territory in dispute, and that orders would be issued to the authorities in Guiana to abstain from taking any steps contrary to this engagement.

For a generation thereafter the question received little consideration, Venezuela being the victim of absorbing revolutions; and when at the end of that time it began again to be discussed, it had grown more difficult, owing to the value of the gold fields lying between the admitted dominions of the two contestants and claimed by both. Venezuela protested that Great Britain had moved the line of her pretensions westward, appropriating some 33,000 square miles of Venezuelan territory; and British statesmen indignantly denied the accusation.

In 1876 Venezuela requested American intervention in her behalf, and a few months later suggested to Great Britain that the justice of the respective claims of the two nations might readily be determined by the discussion of historical proofs, or, if Great Britain preferred, that "a conventional line fixed by mutual accord" might be agreed upon. Neither idea, however, secured the desired results. Our Secretary of State did not intervene; and Venezuela refused to accept the line suggested by Lord Salisbury.

After various other proposals, Venezuela requested that the question be submitted to arbitration, but the reply of Lord Granville, now Secretary of State for Foreign Affairs, wholly disregarded the request, and further insistence met curt refusal at the hands of the British ministry.

Early in the year 1885, it seemed that a settlement had been provided by the negotiation of a general treaty between Great Britain and Venezuela, which specified that all differences should be arbitrated, should the method of friendly negotiation fail. But Lord Salisbury, who had succeeded Lord Granville in the Foreign Office, repudiated the treaty in a note of July 27, 1885.

In December of the following year, Secretary Bayard offered the co-operation of our government to England, to the end that the question might be decided by arbitration, but Lord Salisbury refused the offer. By February, 1887, the controversy had become so heated that Venezuela, in protest against what she termed "acts of spoliation," suspended diplomatic relations with Great Britain. Secretary Bayard, during the following year, called attention to the fact that Great Britain had apparently enlarged her boundary claims, thus committing the United States to a position of sympathy with Venezuela; but no action was taken. And so the affair stood until 1890, when Lord Salisbury, to the astonishment of the Venezuelan government, declared that, while Great Britain would not waive her title to any of the territory comprised within the Schomburgk line which, despite the objections of Venezuela, she still believed to be correct, and within which many English had now long been established, she would be willing to refer to arbitration her claims to certain territory west of that line.

Here matters rested for the remainder of President Harrison's term. Fifty-two years of intermittent controversy had done nothing to settle the question. The United States, when she had ventured to touch the matter at all, had done so with so uncertain a hand as to produce results negligible or worse. Fish, Evarts, Blaine, Frelinghuysen, and Bayard, all able Secretaries of State, had considered the subject. All had commented upon its relationship to the Monroe Doctrine; but, with the exception of Secretary Bayard's offer of arbitration, no one of them had made any definite contribution toward its solution.

England's position, as later defined by Lord Kimberley, was that the negotiations between the two countries had led to no results because "Venezuela has insisted on maintaining a claim extending beyond the River Essequibo and including a large portion of long settled districts of the Colony of British Guiana. On the other hand, Great Britain has throughout been prepared to make large abatements from her extreme claim although Her Majesty's Government has been continually accumulating stronger documentary proofs of the correctness of that extreme claim as being their inheritance from their Dutch predecessors."

Upon his return to power in 1893, Mr. Cleveland faced the question in a new spirit, conscious that if further neglected it might prove serious, in view of the tendency of the nations of Europe to seek an extension of their territory at the expense of weak and backward peoples, and of the equally apparent tendency of South American countries to use the name of the United States as a shield against Europe in times of danger, while insisting upon absolute freedom of action when no danger threatened.

Mr. Cleveland was by nature disposed to suspect strong nations of designs against weaker ones, a tendency which his experiences with Germany in Samoa and the United States in Hawaii had not lessened. He was also a firm believer in arbitration as a means of settling international disputes; but, in the case of Venezuela, England had shown little disposition to consider that method, and he felt that the time had come when the question must be settled, peacefully if possible, but settled. Secretary Gresham was also an enthusiast for arbitration, while Thomas F. Bayard, now Ambassador to the Court of St. James, felt that America and Great Britain were committed to this principle. In the hands of these three men rested the decision of America's course regarding the Venezuelan boundary. All three believed that powerless nations are entitled to the same rights as are powerful nations, and that it is the duty of the latter to see that these rights are respected. All three believed in the special responsibility of the United States to see that the American continent be left in the freest enjoyment of the right of self-determination as guaranteed by the Monroe Doctrine. If it were true, as Secretary Bayard had said, that the United States had a moral right to protect the sovereign independence of the distant, dark-skinned peoples of the far Pacific, then was it more than a moral right, it was a moral duty, to see that nations covered by the Monroe Doctrine were similarly protected.

Shortly after Ambassador Bayard took up his post in London, he wrote to Secretary Gresham that the time was ripe for a settlement of the Venezuelan boundary dispute: "Great Britain has just now her hands very full in other quarters of the globe. The United States is the last nation on earth with whom the British people or their rulers desire to quarrel, and of this I have new proofs every day in my intercourse with them. The other European nations are watching each other like pugilists in the ring." To the diplomatic mind of our Ambassador, England's necessity was America's opportunity, and the determination to force arbitration upon a hard-pressed, friendly nation at a moment when she was considered not free to refuse, was both ungenerous and unfair, especially in view of the fact that Great Britain had as her Ambassador at Washington Sir Julian Pauncefote, a man whom Secretary Gresham himself described as candid, fair, and an open fighter, although "a firm supporter of British interests."

On December 1, 1894, Gresham instructed Bayard to open the question by pointing out to the British government that "England and America are fully committed to the principle of arbitration and this Government will gladly do what it can do to further a determination in that sense." As Bayard proceeded, the old difficulties reappeared. In a confidential dispatch of April 5, 1895, he reported that Lord Kimberley had shown him a map of the disputed territory "on which were delineated, in different colors, the three lines of delimitation. The line coloured in pink was the Schomburgk line, one of the terminal points of which was a short distance inside the mouth of the Orinoco, and which His Lordship stated was conclusively proven and established as a British possession, and would not be submitted to arbitration, but that the ownership of the territory intersected by the other two lines, they would be willing to submit to arbitration."

Upon the receipt of this dispatch, Gresham began the preparation of a report for the guidance of the government during the negotiations, but before the work was completed, death intervened. His loss was a severe blow to Mr. Cleveland, both personally and officially. On the train in which the remains were taken to the widow's home in Chicago, he showed the depth of his grief. He sat for a long time absorbed in thought. At length he asked one of the members of his Cabinet to escort him forward to the baggage car where the coffin was carried, and, arriving there, indicated a wish to be left alone. An hour or so later, as he had not returned to his stateroom, two members of the Cabinet went forward to the funeral car, fearing that he had been overcome by the heat or that some accident had happened. They found the President on his knees by the bier of the dead Secretary, his arms resting upon the coffin, his eyes full of tears. Apparently he had no notion of the flight of time. He was assisted to rise to his feet, and was then escorted back to his state-room. In this apartment he remained during the remainder of the journey, and a servant who went to take the President's orders found him lying in his berth, his face buried in the pillows.

Ten days later, Attorney-General Olney was made Secretary of State. He spent the remainder of the month in Washington, studying the documents upon which Secretary Gresham had been intent at the time of his death. As a result, early in July, he went to Gray Gables, and left with the President the draft of a letter written to Ambassador Bayard regarding the Venezuelan question. It was a statement of startling boldness, which, after careful consideration, Mr. Cleveland approved, conditionally, in the following letter:

Gray Gables,
Buzzards Bay, Mass.,
July 7, 1895.

My dear Mr. Olney,

About five hours ago our family was augmented by the addition of a strong plump loud voiced little girl. Mother and daughter doing well—also the "old man."

I want to thank you for the rubber gloves which came last night. If the blue fish will hang around here a little while longer I will test their effectiveness.

I read your deliverance on Venezuelan affairs the day you left it with me. It's the best thing of the kind I have ever read and it leads to a conclusion that one cannot escape if he tries—that is if there is anything of the Monroe Doctrine at all. You show there is a great deal of that and place it I think on better and more defensible ground than any of your predecessors—*or mine.*

Of course I have some suggestions to make. I always have. Some of them are not of much account and some of them propose a little more softened verbiage here and there.

What day after Wednesday of this week can you come and spend a few hours with me so that we can go over it together? Mrs. Cleveland sends love to Mrs. Olney.

Yours sincerely,
GROVER CLEVELAND.

HON. RICHARD OLNEY,
    Falmouth, Mass.

After a conference between Olney, Herbert, Carlisle, Harmon and Lamont, the letter was again revised, put on official State Department paper, was dated the 20th, and forwarded. The "verbiage" had been somewhat softened, but was still far from soft. Indeed, so strong were its terse paragraphs that Mr. Cleveland later christened it "Olney's twenty-inch gun."

It followed the line of facts which Secretary Gresham had worked out, but it did not follow his views regarding procedure. To Isidore Straus, who suggested, "Mr. Olney has stolen your husband's thunder," Mrs. Gresham replied: "No, there was to be no ultimatum as my husband had prepared it, and Mr. Olney and President Cleveland are entitled to all the credit for such a state paper." That the credit was, or should be real, Mr. Cleveland never doubted. Seven years before his death, speaking in Princeton, he declared: "In no event will the American principle [the Monroe Doctrine] ever be better defined, better defended, or more bravely asserted than was done by Mr. Olney in this dispatch."

For several months, the British Foreign Office remained silent, and when the time came for Mr. Cleveland's third annual message, he had nothing new to report. He, therefore, contented himself with the statement that the general conclusions of the Olney dispatch "are in substance that the traditional and established policy of this Government is firmly opposed to a forcible increase by any European power of its territorial possessions on this Continent . . . ; that as a consequence the United States is bound to protest against the enlargement of the area of British Guiana in derogation of the rights and against the will of Venezuela; that considering the disparity in strength of Great Britain and Venezuela, the territorial dispute between them can be reasonably settled only by friendly and impartial arbitration." In view of these facts, he informed Congress, "the dispatch in question called upon Great Britain for a definite answer to the question, whether it would or would not submit the territorial controversy . . . in its entirety to impartial arbitration."

Clearly he did not regard his action as involving any new principle. He was merely preparing to protect another impotent sovereign power, menaced, he believed, as had been Samoa and Hawaii, by a nation strong enough to work her will if left unchallenged. Moreover, unlike Samoa and Hawaii, Venezuela was within the area covered by the Monroe Doctrine, and he felt that any European nation, suspected of an attempt to control the destinies of an American state, either by forcible invasion or by the no less effective method of extending boundary lines, should submit her course to the investigation of impartial arbiters. He felt also that it was entirely proper to call upon her to do so. Whether or not she would consent, he made no attempt to predict.

The message off his mind, he decided to pay a visit to the wilderness where, free from the exactions of official routine, he might think out alone a course of conduct to be pursued when Lord Salisbury's long delayed answer should arrive. He therefore wrote to Olney:

Executive Mansion, Washington.
Dec. 3, 1895.

Dear Mr. Olney,

I want very much to go away this week Thursday and stay until next week—say Friday or some such matter.

Can I do so? I will have all the nominations to go in signed and they can be sent in by instalments during my absence.

The only thing I am hesitating about is the state of some things in your Department.

You cannot receive anything from Bayard or Sir Julian before the early part of next week. Why can you not put the thing in your pocket, so that no one will know you have heard it read or at least that you have it in possession, until I return? In the meantime if its transmission should be accompanied by any particular message you can, if you have time, be blocking it out.

If I were here I would not be hurried in the matter even if the Congress should begin grinding again the resolution-of-inquiry mill.

Yours very sincerely,
GROVER CLEVELAND.

HON. RICHARD OLNEY,
Secretary of State.

A few days later John Bassett Moore, a loyal supporter of Mr. Cleveland's, sent to Postmaster General

Wilson a twelve-page letter of protest against the President's position.

"I am apprehensive," he said, "that, unless great judgment is exercised, the President's announcement will prove to have started us on a course that involves not only the abandonment of all our traditions, but also our participation in numberless quarrels.

"The statement that the question can be reasonably settled only by such arbitration as Venezuela proposes, certainly was not based on any examination of the merits of the subject.

"The whole system of arbitration presupposes that. nations will be reasonable in their claims. The claim of Venezuela to all territory west of the Essequibo is not a scrupulous claim. . . . Instead of asserting that arbitration is the only reasonable way of settling the question, I should say that it would be a very unsatisfactory way of attempting it; and in so saying I do not forget that Lord Granville once consented to lump boundary and all other questions in a general arbitration.

"We have arbitrated boundary disputes and so has Great Britain, but never, so far as I am informed, where a line had not previously been agreed upon by direct negotiation. Governments are not in the habit of resigning their functions so completely into the hands of arbitrators as to say, 'We have no boundaries; make some for us.' . . . It would be at least unusual to leave it to arbitrators to make a boundary. . . .

". . . Boundaries in South America have almost universally been settled on the basis of the *uti possidetis,* as the only practicable basis of peaceful adjustment."

The opinion of Mr. Moore (and his is an opinion

which all nations will be disposed to treat with consideration), was extremely unfavorable to Venezuela.

"For twenty years," he continued, "Venezuela, instead of settling her boundary dispute, has in various ways, some of them obviously dishonest, been trying to drag the United States into the dispute, and the United States has progressed good-naturedly step by step, without examining the merits of the case, till at length with a sudden impulse it leaps over the precipice blindly. And what is the position we now hold? It is substantially this: 'When a weak American republic asserts a claim to territory in America as against a strong European occupant, and offers to submit its claim to arbitration, the European power, if it refuses the offer, is to be considered as holding the territory by force, and as infringing the Monroe Doctrine.' This is the sum and substance of our position. . . .

"We now address Venezuela substantially thus: 'You are an American republic, and in your claims against European powers we back you. True you settled your southern boundary directly, on the basis of the *uti possidetis,* but this principle, though applicable everywhere else in South America, is inapplicable to your eastern boundary. Even the great doctrine of prescription, recognized by every publicist from the time of Grotius, and the very foundation of the peace of nations, is not applicable to that boundary. Claim what you will, and propose arbitration of it, and I will step in and say that it shall be settled in no other way. I know nothing of the merits of the controversy. I am simply backing you. This is according to the Monroe Doctrine.' Of course, the President never intended to say any such thing, but when we examine the facts, we find that it is precisely what he has said."

In concluding his letter, Mr. Moore expressed the

belief that President Cleveland would "not be willing to launch his country on a career as mad and as fatal as that on which France was started by Louis XIV."

But the President had definitely decided, before sending the Olney dispatch, that light must be thrown upon the British claims. Should the British Foreign Office refuse to throw the light, he would be compelled to have it thrown for her by the United States. This decided, he "cut bait," and waited.

While Mr. Cleveland pondered, Mr. Olney studied two dispatches from Lord Salisbury, dated November 26, 1895, which Sir Julian Pauncefote had delivered soon after the President's departure. In the first, while declaring that the Monroe Doctrine had "received the entire sympathy of the English Government," his Lordship frankly declined to accept Mr. Olney's interpretation of that doctrine as applicable to the boundary dispute between Great Britain and Venezuela, "a controversy with which the United States have no apparent practical concern." He emphatically denied our right to demand, "that when a European power has a frontier difference with a South American community, the European power shall consent to refer that controversy to arbitration," and insisted that Secretary Olney had misapprehended the meaning of America's historic policy.

His second dispatch was an historical brief in justification of England's course with reference to the Venezuelan boundary line, from the conquest and military occupation of the Dutch settlements in 1796. In general terms he designated the territory to which her Majesty's government was entitled as being embraced within the lines of the claim which she had presented from the first, and added: "A portion of that claim, however, they have always been willing to waive altogether; in regard to another portion they have been and continue to be perfectly ready to submit the question of their title to arbitration. As regards the rest, that which lies within the so-called Schomburgk line, they do not consider that the rights of Great Britain are open to question. Even within that line they have on various occasions offered to Venezuela considerable concessions as a matter of friendship and conciliation and for the purpose of securing an amicable settlement of the dispute. If, as time has gone on, the concessions thus offered have been withdrawn, this has been the necessary consequence of the gradual spread over the country of British settlements, which Her Majesty's Government cannot in justice to the inhabitants offer to surrender to foreign rule."

In conclusion Lord Salisbury asserted that his government had "repeatedly expressed their readiness to submit to arbitration the conflicting claims of Great Britain and Venezuela to large tracts of territory which from their auriferous nature are known to be of almost untold value. But they cannot consent to entertain, or to submit to the arbitration of another power or of foreign jurists however eminent, claims based on the extravagant pretensions of Spanish officials in the last century and involving the transfer of large numbers of British subjects, who have for many years enjoyed the settled rule of a British colony, to a nation of different race and language, whose political system is subject to frequent disturbance, and whose institutions as yet too often afford very inadequate protection to life and property."

In commenting on these dispatches, Mr. Bayard wrote to the President on December 4th: "The replies of Lord Salisbury to your Venezuelan instructions are in good temper and moderate in tone. Our difficulty lies in the wholly unreliable character of the Venezuelan rulers and

people, and results in an almost undefinable, and therefore dangerous, responsibility for the conduct by them of
their own affairs. I believe, however, that your interpretation of this boundary dispute will check efficiently the
tendency to 'land grabbing' in South America, which is
rather an Anglo-Saxon disposition everywhere."

To Secretary Olney, however, Lord Salisbury's dispatches were far from satisfactory, and by the time the
President returned to Washington Mr. Olney had formed
definite ideas as to the reply which should be sent and had
embodied them in a set of suggestions for a special message to Congress as strong and unyielding as had been his
"twenty-inch gun." He advised the President to ask for
an appropriation to meet the expenses of a commission to
determine what the true line between Venezuela and British Guiana should be, and added significantly: "When
such report is made and accepted, it will be the duty of
this Government to communicate to Great Britain the
boundary line thus ascertained and to give notice that any
appropriation of territory or exercise of jurisdiction by
Great Britain beyond that line (except with the consent
of Venezuela) will be regarded by this Government as a
wilful aggression upon the rights and interests of the
United States which this Government cannot suffer to go
undefended."

Armed with this document, Mr. Olney met the returning President, was closeted with him for a few hours,
and retired. Mr. Cleveland spent the remainder of the
night at his desk, and by dawn had the draft of a message
ready for the copyist. At ten o'clock he received a fair
copy, which he revised, and by noon his most famous
state paper was ready.

In the message as finally sent to Congress on December
17, 1895, about ninety per cent of Mr. Olney's sentences

were discarded; but his most menacing phrases were retained, and explain the later contention that the Venezuela Message was "a New England document, written by a New Englander." It was, however, Cleveland's in the same sense in which Monroe's most famous message was Monroe's, although drafted by John Quincy Adams, and as Washington's Neutrality Proclamation was Washington's, although showing traces of the pens of more than one eminent man of the time. In each case the responsibility rested upon the President, and upon him alone.

The message itself was brief. It is summed up in the words:

"The answer of the British Government . . . claims that . . . a new and strange extension and development of this [the Monroe] doctrine is insisted on by the United States; . . . that the reasons justifying an appeal to the doctrine . . . are inapplicable. . . .

"If a European power by an extension of its boundaries takes possession of the territory of one of our neighboring republics against its will and in derogation of its rights . . . this is the precise action which President Monroe declared to be 'dangerous to our peace and safety,' and it can make no difference whether the European system is extended by an advance of frontier or otherwise. . . .

"The dispute has reached such a stage as to make it now incumbent on the United States to take measures to determine . . . the true division line between the Republic of Venezuela and British Guiana. . . . When such report is made . . . it will . . . be the duty of the United States to resist by every means in its power . . . the appropriation by Great Britain of any lands . . .

which after investigation we have determined of right belong to Venezuela.

"In making these recommendations I am fully alive to the responsibility incurred and keenly realize all the consequences that may follow. . . . There is no calamity which a great nation can invite which equals that which follows a supine submission to wrong. . . ."

With the text of the message, the press received also the texts of Secretary Olney's note and of Lord Salisbury's two replies. There was no attempt to conceal from the people the extreme gravity of the situation.

Thus was the issue squarely drawn between the United States and Great Britain, and for once the President had the practically unanimous approval of the members of both houses of Congress, regardless of politics.

In his account of the reception of the message by Congress, the New York *Herald's* Washington correspondent telegraphed: "All the traditions of the Senate were cast to the winds when the message was read in that body, for the chamber rang with applause, in which the Republicans seemed to take even a more hearty part than the Democrats. In the House, the President's vigorous expressions were cheered to the echo . . . Republicans . . . as enthusiastic . . . as their political opponents. It is long since any President's message has had such a reception."

The first British mail brought an anxious letter to the President:

Personal

Embassy of the United States, London

Dec. 18, 1895.

Dear Mr. President:

With this note I send you the *Times* of this morning—in order that you may perceive the tone of *average*

British comment on your message to Congress and position in relation to the Venezuelan-Guiana boundary dispute and claim of right and duty under American policy as laid down by President Monroe to insist upon a submission of questions, touching the territorial jurisdiction of South American states to international arbitration—

I send to the Secretary of State fuller—or rather more numerous—public expressions on the subject—which while varying in phrase and tone—are entirely at one on the main point, i.e., of opposition to the propositions laid down in your message, and the instructions of the State Department conveyed to this Embassy—

In my correspondence while I was Secretary of State —also with Judge Gresham since I came here—and personally with you—my opinions have been genuinely stated—and as the Venezuelan transactions and history are unfolded I am not able to shake off a grave sense of apprehension in allowing the interests and welfare of our Country to be imperilled or complicated by such a government and people as those of Venezuela.

It is not needful that I should repeat these views—and I now wish to study carefully and deliberately the situation as it exhibits itself under the light suddenly cast upon this profoundly important question—which includes in its principles and treatment every European claim of ownership and control of soil in the western hemisphere—

May peace, happiness and health dwell in your home —and throughout the country you have served so unselfishly and faithfully—

Sincerely yours

The President   T. F. BAYARD.
of the United States.

Mr. Bayard's letter showed that he was mystified and uncertain regarding the exact position of the President, whose views he was to interpret to the British government and to the British people. Mr. Cleveland therefore sent the following reply:

Executive Mansion, Washington.
December 29, 1895.

My dear Mr. Bayard:

I thank you sincerely for the hunting stool you kindly sent me, and I hope I may have abundant occasion to recall by its use your thoughtfulness.

I am very sorry indeed that I cannot fully understand your very apparent thought and feeling on the Venezuelan question; and you must believe me to be entirely sincere when I say that I think my want of understanding on the subject is somehow my own fault.

You cannot fail to remember my inclination, during my former incumbency of this office, to avoid a doctrine which I knew to be troublesome and upon which I had nothing like your clear conception and information. I knew that your predecessors for many years, and you as well, regarded the Monroe doctrine as important, and I supposed that when it was frequently quoted by you and them in treating of this very question of Venezuelan boundary, it was so quoted because it was deemed to have relation to that question. Not being able to perceive how a doctrine could have any life or could do any good or harm, unless it was applicable to a condition of facts that might arise, and unless when applied all consequences must be appreciated and awaited, I was quite willing if possible within the limits of inexorable duty, to escape its serious contemplation.

I remember too how kindly and considerately you used to speak of and treat the people and the governments of South America, though fully understanding their weaknesses and faults, and how much, through your treatment of them these countries became attached to the Administration. Very few incidents attended my last coming to Washington, more pleasing than the heartiness with which the representatives of Central and South America welcomed me. These considerations are not, however, of importance since in an application of the Monroe doctrine, though another country may give the *occasion,* we are I suppose not looking after *its* interests but *our own.*

Events accompanying the growth of this Venezuelan question have recently forced a fuller examination of this question upon me and have also compelled us to assume a position in regard to it.

I am entirely clear that the doctrine is not obsolete, and it should be defended and maintained for its value and importance *to our government and welfare,* and that its defense and maintenance involve its application when a state of facts arises requiring it.

In this state of mind I am positive that I can never be made to see why the extension of European systems, territory, and jurisdiction, on our continent, may not be effected as surely and as unwarrantably under the guise of boundary claims as by invasion or any other means. In 1888 you called Mr. Phelps' attention to the apparent enlargement of Great Britain's boundary claims between the years 1877 and 1887, and I think within a year you have referred us to the same or other enlargements. I have not failed to notice the stress laid by Lord Salisbury upon the fact that settlements have been made by British subjects whose allegiance might be disturbed if England's insistence was found to be incorrect.

We do not say, either that Great Britain's boundary claim is false, nor that the enlargement of her claims toward the centre of Venezuela as now known, is unjustifiable beyond a doubt, nor that the settlements upon the territory claimed by Venezuela, have been brought about or encouraged while delay in settling the boundary has been prompted or permitted; nor do we attach too much prejudicial importance to other facts and considerations within our view, but we do say that these things and others furnished a controversy in which we were interested, that this controversy was complicated by facts so disputed that it presented a case which of all cases that can be imagined should be subjected to the sifting and examination which impartial arbitration affords.

The refusal to refer the question to such determination was intensely disappointing.

It was disappointing because we cannot see the force of the reasons given for refusal.

After a little hesitation, just here, I shall mention another reason for disappointment and chagrin, which I believe to be entirely irrelevant to the case and which has had absolutely nothing to do with any action I have taken. It would have been exceedingly gratifying and a very handsome thing for Great Britain to do, if, in the midst of all this Administration has had to do in attempts to stem the tide of "jingoism," she had yielded or rather conceded something (if she called it so, which I do not) for our sake. In our relations with her we have been open, honest and fair, except as to settling or providing for the adjustment of claims for Behring Sea seizures. I am ashamed of the conduct of Congress in that matter but it is understood everywhere how persistent the Administration has been in efforts to have the right thing done.

The insistence upon a principle or the assertion of a right should be the same in the case of England as Chili; and I do not see, the necessity actually arising, that former relations or anything of that sort should prevent action or change the course of action, except that good relations, etc., might induce a nation to acquiesce in arbitration when not obliged to do so, in aid of the ascertainment of facts which a friendly power felt should be developed to relieve it from embarrassment.

Great Britain says she has a flawless case. Our interest in the question led us to ask her to exhibit that case in a tribunal above all others recognized as a proper one for that purpose; and this was done to avoid a wrong procedure on our part in a matter we could not pass by.

Great Britain has refused our request. What is to be done? We certainly ought not, we certainly cannot abandon the case because she says she is right, nor because she refuses arbitration. We do not threaten nor invite war because she refuses—far from it. We do not propose to proceed to extremities, leaving open any chance that can be guarded against, of a mistake on our part as to the facts. So instead of threatening war for nor arbitrating, we simply say inasmuch as Great Britain will not aid us in fixing the facts, we will not go to war but do the best we can to discover the true state of facts for ourselves, with all the facilities at our command. When with all this, we become as certain as we can be, in default of Great Britain's co-operation, that she has seized the territory and superseded the jurisdiction of Venezuela—that is a different matter.

I feel that I would like you to know precisely what is in my mind and therefore I have hastily written you, without the least hint of it to any person whatever and without the least consultation.

It seems as if all the troubles and perplexities that can

gather about the office I hold, were just at this time, making a combined assault.

As ever

Your sincere friend,

GROVER CLEVELAND.

HON. T. F. BAYARD,
    Ambassador, &c., &c.,
        London.

The President's message fell like a crash of thunder upon English ears, attuned to the precision of diplomatic language, and made familiar by the history of "thin red lines of heroes" with the meaning of war. The *Annual Register* summed up its opinion in the following words: "The President's extraordinary proposal was believed to have been made in view of the approaching Presidential election, in which the American-Irish vote would be an important factor; and this belief was strengthened by the eagerness of Republicans and Democrats alike to associate themselves with a policy which affected to appeal to a sentiment of patriotism. For several days politicians in the United States, with a few exceptions, gave themselves up to a delirium of jingoism, and had that feeling continued and been reciprocated by the English press and the English people, the two countries might really have drifted into war."

Englishmen of whatever party, however, restrained their language, and hoped for an adjustment. In a speech at Bristol, two days after the publication of the message, the Chancellor of the Exchequer, as spokesman for the British Cabinet, confidently and courteously predicted that when the "case of Great Britain . . . was laid before the people, either on this side of the Atlantic or on the other, the result would be happy, peaceful, and honorable to both parties."

In contrast to such expressions from British statesmen, the manners displayed in the American Congress left much to be desired, needlessly complicating an already delicate situation by language as uncalled for as it was unparliamentary. Outside, in the street, the theater, and the market place, men of even lesser minds caught the infection. Jingoes shrieked for war; American yellow journals fanned the flame, and one gallant orator, climbing to the giddy peak of exaggerated patriotism, toppled over with the impious prayer that he might live to "guide center forward" against "my ancient enemy."

In opposition to this senseless war clamor, the New York *World* stood out conspicuously, earning the right to public gratitude by cabling to certain leading men of England for "a word of peace" with which to stem the tide of war.

Mr. Gladstone replied: "I dare not interfere. Common sense only required. I cannot say more with advantage."

The Prince of Wales, disregarding the convention which normally kept his name out of international disputes, answered that both he and the Duke of York "earnestly trust, and cannot but believe, that the present crisis will be arranged in a manner satisfactory to both countries, and will be succeeded by the same warm feeling of friendship which has existed between them for so many years."

John Redmond, on the other hand, sent a reply calculated to fan the war flame, and to encourage his Irish kinsmen across the sea: "You ask for an expression of opinion from me, on the war crisis, as a representative of British thought. In this, as in all other matters, I can speak only as a representative of Irish opinion. If war results from the reassertion of the Monroe Doctrine, Irish national sentiment will be solid on the side of America. With Home Rule rejected, Ireland can have no feeling of friendliness for Great Britain."

Congress having authorized the appointment of the commission "to determine . . . the true division line between the Republic of Venezuela and British Guiana," Mr. Cleveland selected the following distinguished citizens to act as that commission: David J. Brewer, Associate Justice of the Supreme Court of the United States, Richard H. Alvey, Chief Justice of the Court of Appeals of the District of Columbia, Andrew D. White, ex-President of Cornell University and ex-Minister to Russia, Frederic R. Coudert, one of the counsel for the United States in the Behring Sea Arbitration, and Daniel C. Gilman, President of Johns Hopkins University.

Their appointment apparently had the effect of arousing Great Britain to the need of a less dangerous method of settlement, for a few days later Ambassador Bayard sent the following cipher telegram to Secretary Olney, containing the plan for an adjustment by which neither Great Britain nor Venezuela would be called upon to abandon long established settlements:

Translation of cipher telegram sent from the Embassy *January 13, 1896.*
Olney, Secretary, Washington.

Lord Playfair, lately Liberal Cabinet Minister, came confidentially yesterday to my residence, at the request of Lord Salisbury and Secretary of State for Colonies, expressing earnest desire of both political parties here Venezuela dispute should not be allowed to drift, but be promptly settled by friendly co-operation. Suggests as solution, United States should propose conference with United States of European countries now having Colonies in American Hemisphere—Great Britain, France, Spain, Holland, to proclaim the Monroe Doctrine—that European Powers having interests in America, should not seem to extend their influence in that Hemisphere. If the United States would propose this, Great Britain would accept Monroe Doctrine, and it would become international law between countries named. Assuming from the President's Message, that any settlement of boundary satisfactory to Venezuela, would be unobjectionable to United States, friendly arbitration is suggested. There being no Venezuelan settlements inside Schomburgk line, and no British settlements beyond that line; therefore, irrespective of that line, mutual condition be accepted, that all British and all Venezuelan settlements be excluded from arbitration, but all country between the settlements be settled by a Court of Arbitration drawing a boundary line, which should be accepted by both countries. Such Court of Arbitration to consist of two or three Commissioners from England, two or three from Venezuela, and two or three from present United States Commission, to represent knowledge they have acquired. Under this principle, districts already settled by Venezuela or British Government or people, would not be referred to by arbitration, and there would be no difficulty in settling line by friendly arbitration. I will write you fully next Wednesday mail. But desire to express positive judgment, that proclaimed recognition of Monroe Doctrine as international law between Powers named would make it binding, not only on them, but practically on all other European Powers, and would end all contemplated plans of future conquest, or intermeddling alliances, in the Western Hemisphere, by European Powers, under any pretext.

BAYARD.

After carefully considering these suggestions, Mr. Cleveland and Mr. Olney decided against calling a conference of European powers to pass judgment on the Monroe Doctrine, declaring that they preferred to deal with Great Britain alone. To this Lord Salisbury readily consented.

Meanwhile the American Commissioners continued the work for which the President had appointed them. Confident of the British sense of fair play, they applied to the British government for aid, and on February 11th, the Honorable A. J. Balfour, First Lord of the Treasury, and Conservative Leader of the House of Commons, reported to Parliament: "We have promised to give them all the information we are able to give at the earliest possible moment." (Cheers.) "No false pride or diplomatic punctilio will be allowed to stand in the way of a settlement, as far as we are concerned. Whatever other conclusions the Commission may arrive it, it will most assuredly reach the conclusion that no desire to push beyond the due limit of the frontier of this empire has ever been the animating cause which moved British diplomacy in this long-drawn-out controversy." Lord Salisbury followed with the conciliatory announcement: "I do not think that the invoking of the Monroe Doctrine was, controversially, quite unnecessary," and admitted that satisfactory results would have come less rapidly had not the United States interfered. "I have had an increasing belief during the past few weeks that we shall . . . find some satisfactory settlement, and all danger of a rupture of relations between the two nations be entirely removed." (Cheers.)

By the middle of May both countries were intent upon the preparation of plans, and on the 22nd Lord Salisbury sent a definite proposal for the substance and form of a treaty for the creation of the joint arbitration committee. Seven weeks later Mr. Olney, acting in accordance with England's own suggestion to that effect, as expressed in Bayard's dispatch of January 13th, asked whether Great Britain would consent to unrestricted arbitration of the whole matter, "provided it were made the rule of the arbitration that territory which had been in the exclusive, notorious, and actual use and occupation of either party for sixty years should be held to belong to such party." This suggestion, differing from that of the British proposal only in that it specified the period of sixty years as the term of occupancy, was accepted by Lord Salisbury.

And so, in his fourth annual message, Mr. Cleveland was able to announce: "The Venezuelan boundary question has ceased to be a matter of difference between Great Britain and the United States, their respective Governments having agreed upon the substantial provisions of a treaty between Great Britain and Venezuela submitting the whole controversy to arbitration. The provisions of the treaty are so eminently just and fair that the assent of Venezuela thereto may confidently be anticipated."

On February 2, 1897, one month before President Cleveland's retirement, such a treaty between Great Britain and Venezuela was signed at the State Department in Washington. It was a strange, if not a unique instance of treaty making, American State Department officials having taken the leading part in the negotiations, although Great Britain and Venezuela were the signatories. Articles I and II provided for an arbitral tribunal to consist of five jurists, two on the part of Great Britain, two on the part of Venezuela (one named by President Cleveland and one by the Justices of the United States Supreme Court), and the fifth to be selected by these four. Article III empowered the tribunal to "determine the boundary line between the Colony of British Guiana and the United States of Venezuela"; while Article XIII bound the signatory powers "to consider the result of the proceedings of the tribunal of arbitration as a full, perfect, and final settlement of all the questions referred to the arbitrators." On October 3, 1899, the award was presented to the British Parliament, and the controversy was at an end.

That an adjustment, honorable alike to both England and America, was reached is to the credit of both; but the biographers of Lord Salisbury may safely add to his many achievements the fact that it was his proposal, transmitted through Ambassador Bayard's dispatch of January 13, 1895, which enabled America to abandon her independent study of the Venezuela boundary and opened the way to a peaceful settlement.

CHAPTER VII

THE WARWICK OF 1896

*"Our fealty to party rests upon something higher and
better than an instinct to blindly follow adventurous leader-
ership, regardless of consequences."*
                                            —GROVER CLEVELAND.

SOME time before the assembling of the National
Conventions of 1896, Mr. Euclid Martin, Chairman of the Nebraska State Central Committee, wrote to
President Cleveland from Omaha: "We held our pri-
maries day before yesterday in this city for the purpose of
selecting delegates to a Democratic State Convention.
The issues were many. Upon one side was Democracy
and the administration. Upon the other was Free Silver,
Populism, Bryanism, Strikism and a very large
sprinkling of Church. The ambition of those who oppose
the administration seemed to be to combine all of the
elements, and they were apparently successful. . . . The
Populists who wanted a Populist Governor were willing
to play upon the prejudices of the Catholic Church because the Republican nominee is supposed to be a member of a secret organization antagonistic to their church,
and the Honorable William Jennings Bryan was in it for
all there was in sight for himself. . . . *Circumstances*
and *treachery* of those who should *owe* you allegiance,
without calling names further, played an important part
in the result. Add to this a craze for which I cannot account, and which I am pleased to say is abating to some
extent, for Mr. Bryan, and the results are before you."

At the same time William Lynde Stetson warned him that the New York Democracy was in the hands of its worst enemies, and that the silver men "are making plans for 1896, when the silver party shall have swallowed the Populists, as the Republicans did free silver." Evidently, despite Mr. Cleveland's many battles in its behalf, the gold standard was not yet safe and could be permanently decided only by a national referendum in a presidential election. To educate the people upon this question before it was too late, therefore, appeared to the President the imperative need of the hour, and he began to urge upon those still in sympathy with his views the necessity of informing the public upon the dangers inherent in an unsound currency. With this in mind he wrote to a group of Chicago business men:

"If the sound money sentiment abroad in the land is to save us from mischief and disaster, it must be crystallized and combined and made immediately active. It is dangerous to overlook the fact that a vast number of our people, with scant opportunity thus far to examine the question in all its aspects, have nevertheless been ingeniously pressed with specious suggestions, which in this time of misfortune and depression find willing listeners, prepared to give credence to any scheme which is plausibly presented as a remedy for their unfortunate condition.

"What is now needed more than anything else is a plain and simple representation of the argument in favor of sound money. In other words, it is time for the American people to reason together as members of a great nation, which can promise them a continuance of protection and safety only so long as its solvency is unsuspected, its honor unsullied, and the soundness of its money un-questioned. These things are ill-exchanged for the illu-sions of a debased currency and groundless hope of advantages to be gained by a disregard of our financial credit and commercial standing among the nations of the world.

"If our people were isolated from all others and if the question of our currency could be treated without regard to our relations to other countries, its character would be a matter of comparatively little importance. If the American people were only concerned in the maintenance of their physical life among themselves they might return to the old days of barter, and in this primi-tive manner acquire from each other the materials to supply the wants of their existence. But if American civilization were satisfied with this, it would abjectly fail in its high and noble mission.

"In these restless days the farmer is tempted by the assurance that though our currency may be debased, redundant, and uncertain, such a situation will improve the price of his products. Let us remind him that he must buy as well as sell; that his dreams of plenty are shaded by the certainty that if the price of the things he has to sell is nominally enhanced, the cost of the things he must buy will not remain stationary. . . .

"It ought not to be difficult to convince the wage earner that if there were benefits arising from a degen-erated currency they would reach him least of all and last of all. In an unhealthy stimulation of prices an increased cost of all the needs of his home must long be his portion, while he is at the same time vexed with the vanishing visions of increased wages and an easier lot. The pages of history and experience are full of this lesson.

"An insidious attempt is made to create a prejudice against the advocates of a safe and sound currency by the insinuation, more or less directly made, that they belong to financial and business classes, and are therefore not only out of sympathy with the common people of the land, but for selfish and wicked purposes are willing to sacrifice the interests of those outside their circle.

"I believe that capital and wealth, through combination and other means, sometimes gain an undue advantage, and it must be conceded that the maintenance of a sound currency may, in a sense, be invested with a greater or less importance to individuals according to their condition and circumstances. It is, however, only a difference in degree, since it is utterly impossible that anyone in our broad land, rich or poor, whatever may be his occupation, and whether dwelling in a center of finance and commerce or in a remote corner of our domain, can be really benefited by a financial scheme not alike beneficial to all our people, or that anyone should be excluded from a common and universal interest in the safe character and stable value of the currency of the country. . . .

"If reckless discontent and wild experiment should sweep our currency from its safe support, the most defenseless of all who suffer in that time of distress and national discredit will be the poor, as they reckon the loss in their scanty support, and the laborer or workingman as he sees the money he has received for his toil shrink and shrivel in his hand when he tenders it for the necessaries to supply the humble home. Disguise it as we may, the line of battle is drawn between the forces of safe currency and those of silver monometalism."

Two weeks later, he wrote to Governor Stone of Mississippi:

Executive Mansion, Washington, D.C.
April 26, 1895.

HONORABLE J. M. STONE, Governor
My dear Sir:

. . . .

If we, who profess fealty to the Democratic party, are sincere in our devotion to its principles, and if we are right in believing that the ascendency of those principles is a guarantee of personal liberty, universal care for the rights of all, non-sectional, American brotherhood and manly trust in American citizenship in any part of our land, we should study the effects upon our party and consequently upon our country of a committal of the national democracy to this silver aberration.

If there are Democrats who suppose that our party can succeed upon a platform embodying such a doctrine, either through its affirmative strength or through the perplexity of our opponents upon the same proposition, or if there are Democrats who are willing to turn their backs upon their party associations in the hope that free, unlimited and independent coinage of silver can win a victory without the aid of either party organization, they should deceive themselves no longer, nor longer refuse to look in the face the results that will follow the defeat, if not the disintegration of the Democratic party upon the issue which tempts them from their allegiance. If we should be forced away from our traditional doctrine of sound and safe money our old antagonists will take the field on the platform which we abandon, and neither the votes of reckless Democrats nor reckless Republicans will avail to stay their easy march to power. . . .

Yours very truly,
GROVER CLEVELAND.

From that time until the assembling of the Democratic Convention, the warfare between the Free Silver Democrats and the followers of Grover Cleveland grew ever fiercer, each faction maneuvering for position in the coming battle. From Bryanism in the West and South, from Gormanism in Maryland, from Vest and Jones, Bland and Voorhees, from New York's Tammanyized Democracy, despite its normal sound money sympathies, he knew that he and his sound money allies could expect only vituperation and insult, despite the fact that the end of his political career was close at hand. Even had they not differed with him on this vital subject, they and the myriad other enemies, bred of many conflicts, were eager to send him forth at the end of his public service repudiated, like the ancient Hebrew scapegoat upon whose fleecy back the highpriest laid the sins of the people.

Meanwhile the voice of the scandalmonger was again heard in the land, fashioning ever new lies. Indignant at the utter baseness of their attacks, Don M. Dickinson wrote to the President:

666 Jefferson Avenue.

My dear Mr. President:

I want to thank you not only for your note of the 19th inst., but also for your good letter of the 18th ulto., of which I expected when in Washington, to have had an opportunity to speak to you but did not.

No one has a clearer realization of the situation than I, no one has seen what you have passed through with a keener or more sensitive appreciation of the general demoralization and prevailing madness, and of your situation in the midst of it. History will set down your four years as the most difficult period—war work excepted—in the life of this government, for its Chief Executive, and history will surely set down against the epoch, that the Chief, standing alone, was great in his place, equal to every occasion, a patriot always, and in and of himself the bulwark that turned back the flood of destruction.

Surely you hold up the only beacon. Outside and around, God and Truth and Right and Honor seem a dream. Self-sacrifice, bravery, loyalty, friendship, seem to have left you alone on the field. *Friendship!* it sneaks or whispers its professions in hiding. *Friendship!* in public and in private, it listens to insult with lowered eyes, or covertly smiles or winks at the enemy at the vilest ribaldry at the expense of a friend. One is not to challenge any vile spawn from the mouth of "rank" (rank save the mark) for fear of getting into the papers and being lied about. Who stays the liars and the mouthers of billingsgate from saying and printing broadcast the foulest screeds under the sanction of "high" official station? A man who is so bound that he cannot move, so held, that he cannot speak, is attacked by none of the human race except the digger Indian. But he who stands by and sees a digger Indian do it is meaner than the digger. Democrats, yes, but they are among the rank and file. I am glad I am among them. If I had been in office in these times I would have fought myself back to the ranks in some highly improper way, no doubt.

The people, not as Democrats or Republicans, but the American people, a part of the great mind of the Infinite, *do* understand and *do* appreciate, and will accord, not mere justice, but reward of merit; of this I have no more doubt than I have the sun shines. In the meantime I can only emulate Smollett when he said:

"Thy spirit, independence, let me share,
Lord of the lion heart and purpose high.
Thy steps I follow with my bosom bare,
Nor heed the storm that howls along the sky."

Faithfully yours,
DON M. DICKINSON.

Commodore Benedict wrote in the same strain, and to him Mr. Cleveland replied: " . . . Such expressions are my only comfort, except my wife and babies, in these troublous, perplexing days. The next week will be especially harassing and anxious, and what will follow may add to my burdens. Do you know, my dear Commodore, that I have never been so sure as now that there is a high and unseen Power that guides and sustains the weak efforts of man? I feel it all the time and somehow I have come to expect that I shall find the path of duty and right, if I honestly and patriotically go on my way. I should be afraid to allow a bad, low motive to find lodgment in my mind, for I know I should then stumble and go astray."

But though often discouraged, he kept up the fight for popular enlightenment. On May 20th, he wrote to a conference of New York Democratic newspaper editors:

"There is a temptation now vexing the people in different sections of the country which assumes the disguise of Democratic party principle, inasmuch as it presents a scheme which is claimed to be a remedy for agricultural depression and such other hardships as afflict our fellow citizens. Thus, because we are the friends of the people and profess devotion to their interests, the help of the members of our party is invoked in support of a plan to revolutionize the monetary condition of the country and embark upon an experiment which is discredited by all reason and experience, which invites trouble and disaster in every avenue of labor and enterprise, and which must prove destructive to our national prestige and character.

"When a campaign is actively on foot to force the free, unlimited and independent coinage of silver by the government at a ratio which will add to our circulation unrestrained millions of so-called dollars, intrinsically worth but half the amount they purport to represent, with no provision or resource to make good this deficiency in value, and when it is claimed that such a proposition has any relation to the principles of Democracy, it is time for all who may in the least degree influence Democratic thought to realize their responsibility.

"Our party is the party of the people, not because it is wafted hither and thither by every sudden wave of popular excitement and misconception, but because while it tests every proposition by the doctrines which underlie its organization, it insists that all interests should be defended in the administration of the government without especial favor or discrimination.

"Our party is the party of the people because in its care for the welfare of all our countrymen it resists dangerous schemes born of discontent, advocated by appeals to sectional or class prejudices, and reinforced by the insidious aid of private selfishness and cupidity.

"Above all our party is the party of the people when it recognizes the fact that sound and absolutely safe money is the life blood of our country's strength and prosperity, and when it teaches that none of our fellow citizens, rich or poor, great or humble, can escape the consequences of a degeneration of our currency."

In such letters, sent to leading Democrats throughout the nation, President Cleveland sounded the call, before the measure of his second term was more than half accomplished. And it was this educational feature which later made the campaign of 1896 unique in our history. His alarm increased as the months passed, and his language strengthened with his sense of danger. In July he wrote to Dickinson: "The devils that were cast out of the swine centuries ago have, I am afraid, obtained possession of some so-called Democratic leaders. Good times and justification of Democratic policy, with gifts in their hands, are driven out from the Democratic camp. If there was a penitentiary devoted to the incarceration of those who commit crimes against the Democratic party, how easily it could be filled just at this time."

While such views more and more infuriated the silver men, they created among sound money men of whatever party the feeling that Grover Cleveland was the safest man in public life. "The amount of third term feeling that exists in New York is amazing," wrote William Elroy Curtis. "President Cleveland seems to be the only man in the Democratic party, and although there is general dissatisfaction with the financial and foreign policies of the administration, the same people who condemn them predict that he will be the next candidate for president.

"I sat the other day in a business house which is very prominent in the South American trade, and where all the five partners are Democrats, some of whom have been very active in politics. They condemned the administration for revoking the reciprocity treaties, for preventing the annexation of the Hawaiian Islands, for permitting Great Britain to blackmail Nicaragua, for not interfering in the Cuban revolution, for the Venezuela

boundary dispute, for enforcing the payment of the
Mora claim, for permitting Chile to get the better of us
in the recent claims commission, and for almost everything else that has been done or omitted in our foreign
relations, and declared the Cleveland administration had
done more to injure our foreign trade than years of careful cultivation could correct. Then when we began to
talk of the future every one of them declared his belief
that the President would be nominated for a third term
and would be the strongest candidate the Democrats
could offer to the country.

"Nor is this an exceptional instance. You hear the
same talk everywhere—at the hotels, at the clubs and
restaurants, in the banks and brokers' offices and wherever
men who talk politics gather together."

The more the third term idea gained in strength, the
more violent were the denunciations heaped upon the
President by political opponents. "I have never felt so
keenly as now the unjust accusations of political antagonists," he wrote to Dickinson, on February 18, 1896,
"and the hatred and vindictiveness of ingrates and traitors
who wear the stolen livery of Democracy. . . . You
know my supreme faith in the American people. While
I believe them to be just now deluded, mistaken and
wickedly duped, they will certainly return to sound principles and patriotic aspirations; and what I may suffer
in the period of aberration is not important. I have
studied laboriously to discover or imagine what, if anything, is in the minds of those who assume the rôle of
Democratic leaders. Hatred of the administration seems
to be the only sentiment that pervades their counsels.

"It is absolutely certain that this issue [free silver]
will not wear during the campaign nor lead to success.

It will be the irony of fate, if in the hour of defeat, thus invited, the air is filled with democratic clamor accusing me of destroying party prospects. And yet this is precisely what I expect.

"I have a consciousness within me, however, and an experience behind me that will permit me to bear even this injustice with resignation; and I will patiently wait for the final verdict of my countrymen, which will certainly in due time be returned.

"I cannot be mistaken in believing that if the Democratic party is to survive, its banner upon which shall be inscribed its true principles and safe policies, must be held aloft by sturdy hands which even though few, will in the gloom of defeat, save it from the disgraceful clutch of time-serving camp followers and knavish traitors."

A few weeks later, he wrote again to Dickinson:

Executive Mansion, Washington,
March 19, 1896.

My dear Mr. Dickinson

I was made very happy yesterday by the receipt of the painting you sent me of the duck hunter. It is a very *relieving* picture to look at and every time my eye falls on it in these dreadfully dark and trying days, I say to myself, "I wish I was in that old fellow's place."

Two things I am longing for—the adjournment of Congress and the 4th day of March, 1897.

I honestly believe the present Congress is a menace to the good of the country if not to its actual safety. If the Democratic party was in proper condition and inclined to half behave itself the wildness and recklessness of this Republican Congress would turn many thousands of recruits to our party; but every day develops more and more plainly the seeming desperation and wickedness of those in the Senate and House for whose conduct our party will I suppose be held responsible.

I am positive there is but one chance for future Democratic successes—a perfectly and unequivocal sound money platform at Chicago. If this means the loss of votes, present defeat, or even a party division, the seed will be saved from which I believe Democratic successes will grow in the future.

But I must not be morbid on this subject—all the same it is outrageous that Democracy should be betrayed "in its hour of might."

Hoping that your short rest has done you good, I am

Yours very sincerely

GROVER CLEVELAND.

HON. DON M. DICKINSON,
    Detroit, Mich.

Although determined that under no circumstances would he consider the idea of a third term, his letters of this period show a more eager interest in the coming presidential campaign than he had shown regarding the three contests in which he himself had figured as a candidate. Visions of disaster to his party, if seduced to error by the growing free silver wing, haunted him, and he eagerly watched the progress of state elections, those gauges which indicate the direction of the winds of politics. To Dickinson he wrote on May 1st:

Executive Mansion, Washington,
May 1, 1896.

My dear Mr. Dickinson

I steal a moment from working hours to write this, because I feel that I cannot longer refrain from expressing my thanks as a citizens and a democrat, to you and those who worked with you, for the splendid achievement . . . in Michigan.

Whatever else may be done before July 7th to save the country and the party, the result of the Michigan Democratic State Convention will be, *must* be, looked upon as the most important incident of all that will crowd the intervening time. I know you do not want the least invidious mention, when so many have done so well, but I must tell you how much prouder than ever I am of your friendship, and how glad I am to know more of the splendid material in Stevenson's construction. No two men in the country have better cause for self-congratulation.

New York hangs fire and delays speaking, though she can say but one thing, and though she now owes that speech to the party and the cause. I am much humiliated and ashamed that she should be thus kept in the background by the same dickering, petty, ignoble, criminal figuring that will confront us "in our hour of might" at Chicago. The treacherous cry of harmony and the false pretense of compromise will still I fear be in the path of those who may fight valiantly and well as you have done.

Thanking and trusting you, and with sincere remembrances to Mr. Stevenson, I am

        Yours very sincerely

            GROVER CLEVELAND.

HON. DON M. DICKINSON.

President Cleveland was working for no mere temporary party victory. He already distinguished "the true Democracy" from the body of death which was slowly donning its livery. "We can survive as a party without immediate success at the polls," he wrote to Dickinson, "but I do not think we can survive if we have fastened upon us as an authoritative declaration of party policy, the free coinage of silver."

As the date of the Democratic National Convention drew near, however, it became increasingly difficult for him to believe that the Democrats would refuse the silver bait. The party was unmistakably being prepared for the transformation which would make of it the Free Silver party, and Mr. Cleveland was compelled to face, however reluctantly, the question, "What then?" He knew that he could not serve a free silver party, even as a private in the ranks. On the other hand, the Republican party offered no allurements, even had he been able to forget the McKinley tariff which had stamped it forever, in his mind, as the party of the interests. Moreover, McKinley, though now the leading candidate for the Republican nomination, had as yet recanted none of his silver views, and the chance seemed not too remote that the Republicans would sidestep the issue.

Under these circumstances he could but cling to the hope that the Democratic National Convention might after all be controlled by sound money men. "I am praying now," he wrote to L. Clarke Davis, on May 14th, "that the prevalent infection may pass away, leaving life and hope of complete recovery. In the meantime, the brood of liars and fools must have their carnival." Should the Democratic Convention declare for free silver, the only chance for the gold standard lay in the adoption by the Republicans of an uncompromisingly sound money platform, for he still believed that there were gold money men enough to elect a President if only they could have a party through which to express their views.

During the early months of the year, President Cleveland and Colonel Lamont had arranged to have the body of the late Secretary of State removed to a place of honor in Arlington Cemetery, and in May, Mrs. Gresham and her son, Otto Gresham, accompanied the remains to the new resting place. During his few days' visit to Washington Mr. Otto Gresham had frequent talks with the President on the currency question. "During these conversations," writes Mr. Gresham, "the President confidently declared that 'if the Democrats should adopt a free silver platform, that is silver at 16 to 1, and the Republicans straddle, silver would win, because no sound money Democrat would vote for a silver Republican for President, and the silver Republicans will vote for 16 to 1.'"

Mr. Gresham left Washington convinced of the soundness of this prophecy, and convinced also that the President, too, would bolt the Democratic ticket if the coming convention should father the free silver heresy. On his way back to Chicago, he stopped at Indianapolis to give the Indiana Democratic leaders the benefit of Mr. Cleveland's views, and sought out as well his father's old friends in the Republican camp.

According to his own account of his interviews, his most fruitful conversation was with Charles W. Fairbanks, who showed him the keynote speech which he had prepared for the coming Republican National Convention, of which Mr. McKinley had asked him to be temporary chairman. The speech was at best a straddle, Mr. Gresham writes: "He quoted from McKinley's speeches in favor of the Bland-Allison act, and in support of silver propaganda looking to some measure to take the place of the Bland-Allison act, as it was expiring by limitation. After he had finished reading it, he asked

me what I thought of it. I told him it would not do
at all."

For a time they argued the situation, Fairbanks, a
sound money man at heart, but planning a keynote speech
controlled by considerations of political expediency, and
Otto Gresham, a sound money enthusiast, filled with faith
in Cleveland's prediction that a straddle on the part of
the Republicans would mean a free silver President.
"Mr. Cleveland," finally declared Gresham, "is going
to bolt to your side, provided you give him something to
bolt to. The silver Republicans will leave you and go
to the silver Democrats if you straddle; the only chance
for you to win is to get on a sound money platform."
After a few moments' hesitation, Mr. Fairbanks replied:
"I see it. You are right. I will tear this speech up, and
write another one."

This second speech, duly delivered at the opening of
the St. Louis Convention, gave notice that the Republican
party, so long complacent toward the free silver heresy,
was now ready to stand four-square for the gold standard.
"We protest," it declared, "against lowering our standard
of commercial honor. We stand against the Democratic
attempt to degrade our currency to the low level of
Mexico, China, India and Japan. The present high
standard of our currency, our honor and our flag will
be protected and preserved by the Republican party."

This change, in the opinion of Mr. Gresham, would
not have been made had Mr. Fairbanks not "learned Mr.
Cleveland's opinion. . . . He had unbounded faith in
Mr. Cleveland's judgment and patriotism. . . . I am
just as sure as I am of anything that I did not personally
participate in, that Fairbanks sent McKinley Grover
Cleveland's views as I brought them." "I have no
doubt," he later declared, "that it was Grover Cleve-

land's views, financial and political, that switched William McKinley from . . . soft money to hard money in 1896."

While not too nearly akin to McKinley's own ideas, as interpreted by his past actions, these views were identical with those of Mark Hanna, McKinley's political manager. Hanna, a "gold bug" from the beginning, felt certain that McKinley could be nominated, but wished to be equally sure that if nominated he would stand upon an out-and-out gold platform. He therefore allowed the Platform Committee to debate the silver question for two days, and waited to be approached by the gold men, whom he had purposely left in doubt as to his position. At last they came, with an ultimatum. He must within one hour side with the gold wing or they would fight McKinley on the floor of the convention. Within the limits of the hour, the gold plank which Hanna had brought ready prepared with him to the convention was in the hands of the triumphant gold men, and William McKinley was secure of a place in history as the leader of the sound money crusade of 1896.

Upon the adoption of the platform, as sound in its financial plank as either Cleveland or Hanna could wish, the silver Republicans fulfilled to the letter Mr. Cleveland's prediction. Headed by Senators Teller, of Colorado, DuBois, of Iowa, Pettigrew, of South Dakota, and Cannon, of Utah, they marched, thirty-four strong, out of the Republican house of gold to find honored places in William Jennings Bryan's Democratic house of silver.

Such is the strange story of the influence exerted by a Democratic President upon a Republican campaign program, as told by one who saw matters from the inside. It is confessedly only a section of the picture, for, as Mr. Gresham's memorandum fully recognizes, many other leaders had their parts in the work of writing sound money principles into the Republican platform of 1896. Thomas C. Platt, for example, has modestly confessed: "In 1896 I scored what I regard as the greatest achievement of my political career. This was the insertion of the gold plank in the St. Louis platform." But Thomas C. Platt has confessed other things, and still others have been confessed for him, and therefore the world will not accept his voice as the voice of Clio, the muse of history, even though it accepts the fact that he played an important rôle in this drama, in company with a host of others: Herrick, Payne, Morrison and Lodge, Reed, Allison, Morton, Depew, and many more. Mr. Kohlsaat and Senator Foraker has each blushingly confessed himself the *deus ex machina,* and their part none can question. But the truth, while including them all, shows also the dominant figure of Grover Cleveland, the man who played in both companies in the interest of neither, but that the people's honor should be above reproach.

But though thus able to influence the Republican National Convention, Mr. Cleveland knew how small was his chance of changing the sentiments of the National Convention of his own party. Four weeks before the assembling of the latter he wrote to Dickinson:

Executive Mansion, Washington.
June 10, 1896.

My dear Mr. Dickinson

I so fully approve of your suggestions concerning delegations of sound and solid men to attend the convention as non-delegates with a view of exerting a wholesome influence on delegate sentiment, that I immediately began to agitate the subject in quarters where I thought it would effect the best results. My ideas seemed to meet with approval and I had some assurances of co-operation, though I am bound to say to you that they were even then accompanied with that sort of reserved enthusiasm which seems to have for the most part characterized all movements in favor of sound financial policy. Since the receipt of your letter, however, events have occurred so discouraging to the cause of sound finance, that I am afraid the efforts promised will not be made. The fact is, people whom I see here who believe with us, appear to be thoroughly impressed with the idea that nothing can be done to stem the tide of silverism at Chicago.

I believe I am by nature an undismayed and persistent fighter and I do not believe in giving an inch until we are obliged to; and yet it is hard to call on friends to maintain a struggle which seems so hopeless.

It does not seem to me that there should be any relaxation in the effort to prevent our party from entering upon a course which means its retirement for many years to come. If we cannot succeed in checking the desperate rush, perhaps a demonstration can be made which will indicate that a large section of the party is not infected. I don't know how this can best be done, but I very much desire that we shall not all have to hang our heads when our party is accused of free silverism.

Of course I have never seen anything like this craze before, but my faith in the American people is so great that I cannot believe they will cast themselves over the precipice.

But there is our old party with all its glorious traditions and all its achievements in the way of safe and conservative policies, and its exhibitions of indestructibility. Is it to founder on the rocks? Will not sanity return before we reach the final plunge? While I am not completely discouraged, I confess the way looks dark.

The most astounding feature of all this matter is the lethargy of our friends and the impossibility of stirring them to action. Michigan seems to be the only state whose work was needed and was forthcoming.

Events sometimes crowd closely upon each other and much may be developed within even four weeks.

Yours sincerely

GROVER CLEVELAND.

HON. DON M. DICKINSON.

When the Democratic National Convention assembled at Chicago on July 7th, it was at once apparent that the free silver men would control. Senator Daniel was chosen temporary chairman of the convention, to the discomfort of David B. Hill, who was now prominent as leader of the gold Democrats. Another ardent silver leader, Senator White of California, was made permanent chairman; and pending the report of a platform, the convention listened entranced to eloquent proponents of a currency reform guaranteed to save the nation.

The adoption of a platform demanding the free and unlimited coinage of both silver and gold at the ratio of 16 to 1 without waiting for the aid or consent of any other nation; the rejection by a vote of 564 to 357 of a resolution commendatory of the Cleveland administration, which David B. Hill introduced with the gleeful consciousness that it would be overwhelmingly defeated, and the nomination of William Jennings Bryan on the fifth ballot made Mr. Cleveland's dethronement complete. "Never before in American history," wrote a correspondent who witnessed his eclipse, "has a President sunk so low as Cleveland has fallen. Never has a President been so held in contempt by the people. No one is interested enough to care what he does or says. . . .

Cleveland has been driven out of his party, and it was Hill who closed the door and double locked it with his resolution as Cleveland departed."

It was here that Bryan made his "Crown of Thorns and Cross of Gold" speech. Up to that time, Bland was the leading Democratic candidate for President, and had a majority of the delegates, but from the moment of the "Cross and Crown" speech, state after state planted its banner beside the Nebraska standard, until two thirds of the convention were so represented.

It was felt by many of the onlookers that the sound money men would bolt, but this conviction was not justified. Tammany Hall was apparently ready to depart, but the counsels of Mr. Whitney, Governor Russell of Massachusetts, and other sound money leaders prevailed, and Tammany sat in silent protest as the platform was adopted and Bryan was nominated. When the nomination was announced, Senator Vest remarked in a stage whisper: "Now we are even with old Cleveland."

In accepting the nomination, Mr. Bryan amplified the protest, already made in the platform, against federal interference in local affairs. Taking Article IV, Section 4, of the Federal Constitution as his warrant, he pledged himself against such interference as that to which President Cleveland had resorted when he sent troops to Chicago in 1894.

Nothing could have more graphically illustrated the determination of the Bryanized Democracy to repudiate the former chief, for it was the Honorable John W. Daniel, of Virginia, president of the convention which nominated Bryan, who had proposed the resolution unanimously passed by the United States Senate on July 12, 1894, that: "The Senate indorses the prompt and vigorous measures adopted by the President of the United

States and the members of his administration to repulse
and repress, by military force, the interference of lawless
men with the due process of the laws of the United States,
and with the transportation of the mails of the United
States, and with commerce among the States."

In commenting upon the subject, the eminent Democratic leader, Judson Harmon, wrote: It is "a far more
serious matter than the money question or any of the other
questions before the people, grave as they all are. If a
candidate for President may properly pledge himself in
advance, as Mr. Bryan has done, to do nothing to protect
the property, maintain the authority, and enforce the laws
of the United States, unless and until the officers of another government request or consent, then we really have
no Federal Government, for a government which is not entirely free to use force to protect and maintain itself in the
discharge of its proper functions is no government at all."

The results of the convention gave President Cleveland a new phrase. Instead of the "free silver heresy,"
his fight was henceforth against "Bryanism." An abstract
idea which he abhorred had become incarnate. His indignation at this conquest of an organization, this appropriation of an honored name, was boundless. While Hill
was content to follow the new banner, declaring, "I am
still a Democrat, very still," Cleveland, acting upon his
own maxim, "a just cause is never lost," prepared to bolt,
advising his friends, however, to hold their peace until
a definite plan of action could be agreed upon.

"I really do not see what I can properly do or say,"
he wrote to Colonel Lamont, a few days later. "Those
who controlled the convention displayed their hatred of
me and wholly repudiated me. Those who at the convention differed from them, seem to have thought it wise
to ignore me in all consultation fearing probably that

any connection with me would imperil success. I do not say they were not right. I only say that events have pushed me so much aside that I do not see how I can be useful in harmonizing or smoothing matters.

"I have an idea, quite fixed and definite, that for the present at least we should none of us say anything. I have heard from Herbert to-day. He says he has declared he will not support the ticket. I am sorry he has done so. We have a right to be quiet—indeed I feel that I have been invited to that course. I am not fretting except about the future of the country and party, and the danger that the latter is to be compromised as an organization.

"I suppose it has occurred to you that since the Chicago Convention there cannot be a fool stupid enough or malicious enough to attribute to the present administration any calamity that may befall the organization of the Democratic party. While I would be willing to incur that accusation to save or benefit the party in a good cause, what is the use of inviting such an accusation by saying something which at this time can have no influence for good? I feel well out of it by the condemnation I have received at the hands of those who have managed affairs, and by the nomination of men whose personal hatred of me seemed to be a prerequisite for convention honors. Others who fought on the other side were not anxious to see me gain anything from the outcome, whatever it might be.

"I am receiving a good many letters from all sorts of people, which confirm me in the belief that, whatever the rest think they ought to do, I ought to keep silence—at least until conditions change.

"In the meantime I am having some good fishing and promptly attending to all official work sent me."

But though fully conscious of his position in the party

at large, he believed that every member of his Cabinet was with him. It was, therefore, a shock to receive from Hoke Smith, Secretary of the Interior, the information that he considered it his duty to support Mr. Bryan publicly in his paper. This appeared to Cleveland almost incredible. The Atlanta *Journal* had been regarded by sound money men as one of their chief instruments for presenting the gold cause to the South, and an elaborate sound money supplement was ready for the press when it was suddenly decided to swing the paper over to the support of Bryan. The cause of the swing, as Secretary Smith confessed in a letter to Mr. Cleveland, was local. "I consider the protection of person and property involved in the local Democratic success which can only continue through Democratic organization. I would strike my own people a severe blow if I repudiated a nominee of a regular convention, thereby setting a precedent for disorganization. While I shall not accept the platform, I must support the nominee of the Chicago Convention."

After some delay the President sent the following answer:

Gray Gables
Buzzards Bay, Mass.
August 4, 1896.

My Dear Mr. Smith.

I suppose I should have replied to your letter of July 20th before; but to tell you the truth I have delayed and hesitated because I could not satisfy myself as to what I should write.

I have determined to say to you frankly that I was astonished and much disappointed by your course and that I am by no means relieved by the reasons you present in justification of it.

When you addressed the citizens of your state so nobly and patriotically, you were discussing the silver question alone; and when you assured them that you intended to support the nominee of the National Convention you could certainly have intended no more than to pledge yourself that in case you were overruled by the convention *in the question under discussion* you would accept your defeat and support the platform and candidates which represented that defeat. This—considering your strong expressions on the silver question, your earnest advocacy of sound money and your belief in its transcendent importance—was going very far.

You surely could not have intended to promise support to a platform directly opposed not only to sound money but to every other safe and conservative doctrine or policy, and framed in every line and word in condemnation of all the acts and policies of an administration of which you have from the first been a loyal, useful and honorable member. You could not have intended a promise to uphold candidates, not only pledged to the support and advancement of this destructive and undemocratic platform, but whose selection largely depended upon the depth and virulence of their hatred to our administration. I say "our" administration because I have constantly in mind the work we have done, the patriotism that has inspired our every act, the good we have accomplished and the evil we have averted in the face of the opposition of the vicious forces that have temporarily succeeded in their revolt against everything good and glorious in Democratic faith and achievement.

It is due to our countrymen and to the safety of the nation that such an administration should not be discredited or stricken down. It belongs to them and should be protected and defended, because it is their agency

devoted to their welfare and safety. None can defend
it better than those who constitute it, and know the sin-
gleness of purpose and absolute patriotism that have
inspired it. You say, "While I shall not accept the platform, I must support the nominees of the Chicago Convention." I cannot see how this is to be done. It seems
to me like straining at a gnat and swallowing a camel.

The vital importance of the issues involved in the
national campaign and my failure to appreciate the
inseparable relation between it and a state contest, prevent
me from realizing the force of your reference to the
"local situation." I suppose much was said about the
"local situation" in 1860.

I am perfectly satisfied that you have been influenced
in the position you have taken by the same desire to do
exactly right that has guided you in all your acts as a
member of the Cabinet. You know how free my association with my official family has been, from any attempt to influence personal action, and how fully that
association has been characterized by perfect confidence
and a spirit of unreserved consultation and frankness.

In this spirit I now write. I have no personal grievance that any one need feel called on to even notice. My
only personal desire is to make as good a President as
possible during the residue of my term, and then to find
retirement and peace; but I cannot believe that I will do
my duty to my countrymen or party—either as President
or citizen, by giving the least aid and comfort to the
nominees of the Chicago Convention or the ideas they
represent.

Yours very sincerely,
GROVER CLEVELAND.

HON. HOKE SMITH,
   Washington, D. C.

Before this letter reached him, Mr. Smith wrote again:

Department of the Interior, Washington,
August 5, 1896.

Mr. President:

I had the honor, on July 20th, of advising you that I felt it to be my duty to support the nominee of the National Democratic Convention, notwithstanding the declaration by that Convention adverse to the views I entertain on the financial question.

I felt then, as I do now, that, in view of the contrary position assumed by some of the members of the Cabinet, the proprieties of the occasion would be best subserved by stating these conditions of embarrassment, and leaving to your judgment any suggestion that would insure the unanimity of counsel which you might desire.

To that communication I have received no reply.

I am constrained to infer that the embarrassments suggested by my letter of the 20th ult. are recognized by you as existing.

I therefore tender my resignation as Secretary of the Interior.

Very respectfully,
HOKE SMITH.

This letter crossed in transit Mr. Cleveland's reply to Secretary Smith's first letter; and accordingly the Secretary wrote again:

August 6, 1896.

My dear Mr. President:

I was very much pleased to receive your letter of this morning, which passed mine on the road. I must admit that I was a little hurt by your continued silence, for I can scarcely tell you how much I would feel the loss of your confidence.

I can hardly expect you to see the situation as I do, and I shall not undertake further to present it. I hope to still contribute in part toward helping the people to appreciate the great, patriotic work of your administration, nor do I believe my opportunity to do so will be lessened on account of the course which I pursue. My New England and German blood do not fit me to show feeling, but none the less my admiration for the President has grown during the last three years into an attachment scarcely less than that I have for my immediate family.

I hope I am sufficiently devoted to the nation, but in 1860 I should have gone with my state, and now I must stand by it.

Very respectfully,
HOKE SMITH.

For the Cleveland wing of the party, as for the President himself, neither Bryanism nor McKinleyism had any appeal. Of the two they preferred the latter, although McKinley's enthusiasm for sound money had come so late as to smack of opportunism. With no hope but the election by indirection of the Republican candidate, they organized the National Democratic party, that sound money and Clevelandism might not be without witnesses in the coming campaign.

On September 2nd, this third party, belated but determined, met in National Convention at Indianapolis. "This convention," declared their platform, "has assembled to uphold the principles upon which depend the honor and welfare of the American people, in order that Democrats . . . may unite their patriotic efforts to avert disaster from their country and ruin from their party."

Denouncing the heresies of "protection and its ally, free coinage of silver," it reaffirmed the doctrines which the Cleveland *régime* had striven to promote, and praised "the fidelity, patriotism, and courage with which President Cleveland has fulfilled his great public trust, the high character of his administration, its wisdom and energy in the maintenance of civil order and the enforcement of the laws, its equal regard for the rights of every class and every section, its firm and dignified conduct of foreign affairs, and its sturdy persistence in upholding the credit and honor of the nation."

Such praise at such a time was sweet even to so unegotistical a nature as the President's, and its sincerity was attested by the following telegram, which came the day the platform was adopted:

Indianapolis, Ind., *Sept. 3, 1896.*
To HON. GROVER CLEVELAND:
You will be nominated to-morrow unless you make a definite refusal. Strongly urge that you communicate privately to be used publicly if necessary with some friend on the ground. Otherwise every indication you will be nominated by acclamation.
D. G. GRIFFIN.

Mr. Cleveland at once telegraphed in reply:

Buzzard's Bay, Mass., *Sept. 3, 1896.*
To DANIEL G. GRIFFIN,
Chairman New York Delegation,
Indianapolis, Ind.
My judgment and personal inclinations are so unalterably opposed to your suggestion that I cannot for a moment entertain it.
GROVER CLEVELAND.

But his heart was with the Gold Democrats, although his name was withheld; and when news came that on the first ballot John M. Palmer had been nominated, the President thus confided his approval to Colonel Lamont:

"I am delighted with the result of the Indianapolis Convention. Its platform is the best possible statement of the true doctrines of Democracy and makes all those who believe in and love the grand old organization [feel] that they still have a home. I am gratified to know that you are willing to declare your sentiments and the quicker and stronger you and any other member of the Cabinet speak the better I shall like it. My notion is that the tone should be, or at least one note of it, that the Indianapolis platform and candidates are democratic and the Chicago platform and candidates are not.

"I am perplexed concerning the course I should pursue. My inclination, of course, is to join the chorus of denunciation, but I am doubtful as to the wisdom of such action, in the light of a chance that [it] might do more harm than good. My position cannot be misunderstood by any man, woman, or child in the country. I am President of all the people, good, bad, and indifferent, and, as long as my opinions are known, ought perhaps to keep myself out of their squabbles. I must attempt to co-operate with Congress during another session in the interest of needed legislation, and perhaps ought not to unnecessarily further alienate that body and increase its hatred of me, and if I take an active and affirmatively aggressive position it may aid the cause we have *not* at heart, in increasing the effectiveness of the cry of presidential interference. In addition to all this, no one of weight or judgment in political matters has advised me to speak out—though I shall be surprised if Palmer does not urge it soon.

"If you say anything, I do not care how plainly you present the inference that I am in accord with your views."

Mr. Cleveland's praise was for those who "loved the principles of their party too well to follow its stolen banners in an attack upon those national safeguards which party as well as patriotism should at all times defend." But he was too shrewd to cherish the hope that Palmer could be chosen. Thus he found himself, a Democratic President of the United States, hoping to see a Republican victory which would place McKinley at the head of the nation.

Although determined to take no active part in the coming campaign, he felt that he could, without violating this purpose, accept one invitation which reached him in the early autumn. The College of New Jersey was to celebrate on October 22d her Sesquicentennial, and to mark the passage of one hundred and fifty years of public service by taking the name of Princeton University. With the escort and dignity appropriate to his high office and to the importance of the occasion, he appeared at Princeton on the day appointed, and in the presence of a company of scholars from many lands, and of leading Americans from many sections, delivered one of the most carefully prepared addresses of his life. The glory of an educated citizenship; the duty of a college or university toward the state; the dangers latent in ignorance concerning the great natural laws upon which organized society rest—these were his themes. He spoke in terms suitable to a purely academic function; but many of his carefully phrased sentences turned the minds of his auditors, and of the millions who later read the address, toward the question of the hour: "the free silver heresy," never once mentioned, but always implied.

"When popular discontent and passion," he said, "are stimulated by the arts of designing partisans to a pitch perilously near to class hatred or sectional anger, I would have our universities and colleges sound the alarm in the name of American brotherhood and fraternal dependence. When the attempt is made to delude the people into the belief that their suffrage can change the operation of natural laws, I would have our universities and colleges proclaim that those laws are inexorable and far removed from political control. . . . When a design is apparent to lure the people from their honest thoughts and to blind their eyes to the sad plight of national dishonor and bad faith, I would have Princeton University, panoplied in her patriotic traditions and glorious memories, and joined by all the other universities and colleges of our land, cry out against the infliction of this treacherous and fatal wound."

While the newspaper men sent his speech broadcast, the President and Mrs. Cleveland gave themselves up to the enjoyment of the students' enthusiasm. Remembering that whatever the result of the coming election, he must seek a new home on the fourth of the coming March, he observed Princeton with the eye of a prospector, and the prospector became in spirit the intending settler as he stood with his wife that evening on the steps of Nassau Hall, where Washington had received the first French Ambassador.

The hour of the scholar, the statesman, the savant from many lands, had passed with the formal meetings. This was the hour of the undergraduate. The students had arranged a parade, dotted with illuminated transparencies, touched with the humor which is the ever-present asset of student life the world over. As the President and his beautiful wife gazed upon the passing show, they got a glimpse of a transparency bearing the inscription: "Grover, send your boys to Princeton." At that moment the Cleveland "jewels" consisted of three daughters: Ruth, Esther, and Marion, born, one in New York, one in the White House, and the third at the President's summer home at Gray Gables on Buzzard's Bay. No son had appeared. But there was the transparency, which, as they looked, moved forward and halted immediately in front of them: "Grover, send your boys to Princeton." The President had entered Princeton an admirer of the college. He left it a Princeton man, although he had declined the honorary degree which was offered him.

From the academic shades of the university he passed again into the hot furnace of political strife. The campaign was nearing its close. Mr. McKinley upon his front porch at Canton, Ohio, and Mr. Bryan from an hundred platforms throughout the land, had discussed the issue, which was now about to be submitted to popular vote.

With election day came a landslide. Mr. McKinley received over half a million more votes than Mr. Bryan, with the comfortable assurance that he would enter the Presidency with a Republican majority in both House and Senate. The fight had been made for principles that are too high for party property, and the fight was won. With a courage that few men in his situation have displayed, and a patriotism that will be honored in all coming time, Mr. Cleveland had resisted a pressure strong enough to have overwhelmed any man less ready to sacrifice self in obedience to conviction.

Mr. Bryan summed up the cause of Democratic defeat in one sentence: "I have borne the sins of Grover Cleveland." But Mr. Bryan had not borne the sins of Grover Cleveland. He had borne the sins of a fundamental financial heresy, in the making of which Grover Cleveland had had no part nor lot. And Mr. Cleveland, as he watched the celebrations of the triumphant goldbugs, knew that they were the rejoicings of sound money men of all parties, and was satisfied that, like the strong man, he had slain more in his last great effort than he had slain in his life. His enemies were tireless in abuse, but the noise and vaporings of the few were not the sentiment of the millions who were patriots before being partisans.

"When the history of the present time comes to be seriously written," declared the Baltimore *Evening News* of November 4, 1896, "the name of the hero of this campaign will be that of a man who was not a candidate, not a manager, not an orator; the fight which has just been won was made possible by the noble service of one steadfast and heroic citizen, and the victory which was achieved yesterday must be set down as the crowning achievement of his great record. . . . It is impossible to overestimate the value of the service Grover Cleveland has done through his twelve years of unswerving fidelity to the cause of honest money. . . . This is Cleveland's day, the vindication of his course, and the abundant reward of his steadfast adherence . . . to that principle of honor which he has held above self, above party, above expediency."

CHAPTER VIII

THE FOUR LEAN MONTHS

"I have done my duty as I saw it. I feel that I need no defense."

—GROVER CLEVELAND.

IN the life of every President there comes at last the trying period which, from the point of view of national leadership, might well be called the four lean months. During this time, which the Constitution, in obedience to former conditions of travel, allows for a retiring President to stand aside, he is in effect a broken vessel. If he has served the two terms fixed by custom as the limit of an executive's official days, he stands as a "has been," a leader who can no longer lead. If he has served but one term and has been defeated for re-election, he is an Ichabod, whose glory has departed.

But of all our Presidents, Grover Cleveland alone knew both these periods of political poverty. In 1888 he was a defeated President. Now he was to have the still more trying experience of a President repudiated by his own party, which had itself been defeated, and which, not without reason, blamed him for its defeat. And truly but little power remained to him. Either he was no longer a Democrat, or the Democratic party had shrunk to strangely small dimensions, for he was determined to acknowledge no kinship with William Jennings Bryan or the infatuated crowd which hailed him with the cry, "Bryan is our savior."

Grimly he accepted his position of "splendid isola-

tion," rejoicing in the conviction that he had remained
right, even when his party had gone wrong. He knew
that what he termed "The True Democracy" was composed of his followers, not of the majority now wor-
shipping strange gods and who, as he expressed it, had
with "the blight of treason blasted the councils of the
brave." Nor were Mr. Bryan and his friends less bitter.
They, in their turn, denounced the ex-President as one
who had used his party for his own selfish gain, and sold
it out to the enemy.

From time to time came rumors of impending magazine articles planned to interpret to the world outstanding incidents in his presidential career, but he viewed
them lightly. To Mr. Gilder, who wrote him an anxious
letter upon the subject, he replied:

> Executive Mansion, Washington.
> *November 20, 1896.*
>
> My dear Mr. Gilder:
>
> You are quite right. There are now three projects
> on foot to serve me up and help people to breast or dark
> meat, with or without stuffing. The one I have heard
> the most of was, when I last got a sight of it, running
> towards Professor —— the man who made *The Nation*
> at Princeton. I've forgotten his name. [Woodrow
> Wilson.]
>
> I don't know in the shuffle what will become of me
> and my poor old battered name, but I think perhaps I
> ought to look after it a little. I shall probably avail my-
> self of your kindness.
>
> > Yours sincerely,
> > GROVER CLEVELAND.

Mr. Gilder having offered his own brilliant pen in
defense of the "poor, old, battered name," the President

gratefully accepted the proffered service, despite his life-
long aversion to biographical work with himself as the
theme:

Executive Mansion, Washington.
Dec. 27, 1896.

My dear Mr. Gilder:

I was very much touched to receive on Christmas day,
your beautiful and valuable gift, made more impressive
by the sentiment suggested on the card accompanying it.
Of all men in the world you know best that I do honestly
try to "keep the compass true," and I am convinced that
you appreciate, better than others, how misleading the
fogs sometimes are. I frequently think what a glorious
boon omniscience would be to one charged with the
Chief Magistracy of our nation.

I can only thank you from the bottom of my heart,
for this last, of many, proofs of your friendship, and
assure you of the comfort and encouragement it has been
to me. I should be afflicted if my barometer ever indicated anything but "clear weather" in our relations.

I have been afraid sometimes since I left you here
a week ago, that you might not feel like bothering us
too much in the preparation of the article you had in
proof. I want to say to you that you must draw on us
to any extent you desire, to make the article suit you. Of
course your magazine instinct fits you to judge as to the
items that will interest readers, but you must understand
that everything, personal or otherwise, that would be at
all suitable for such publication is at your disposal.

For example, I have been sometimes surprised and
irritated by the accusation or intimation that I lacked in
appreciation of friendship and did not recognize sufficiently what others did for me. Of course this is as far

from the truth as it can be, and can only have its rise in a refusal on my part to compensate friends by misappropriation from the trust funds of public duty. To this I plead guilty on many charges; but no one is more delighted than I when friendship and public duty travel in the same way. Would it add a bit to the interest if the reader was given a little more of a peep at the home life and the sustaining influence of wife and children— working in the remark I have many times made, in dark and trying times of perplexing public affairs, in answer to inquiries after the welfare of my family: "They are as well as they can be. It is this end of the house that troubles me. If things should go wrong at the other end I would feel like quitting the place for good"? Having made these suggestions, I am so impressed that they are useless and foolish that I feel like telling you to utterly disregard them, except as they indicate my willingness to do anything you wish in the premises.

A few days ago Mr. Gardiner Hubbard and Mr. McClure (of *McClure's Magazine*) called on me and said Carl Schurz was to write an article for that magazine on the administration; and they wanted to know if Mr. Cox could take some pictures, etc. Of course I could not object, but the *Century* article was spoken of and Professor Wilson's too. They seemed to understand or to know about both, and thought Mr. Schurz could hold his own with anyone in the same field. I suppose his article will be far removed from the track of yours.

I was delighted in my late interview with Mr. Schurz to see that he had recovered from his Venezuelan scare and was quite satisfied apparently with the civil service reform situation. He is a good and useful man and I am always pleased to have him friendly, but as I told him once, he is "a hard master." I only hope he will gain the best information attainable and be just. I know he will try to be.

This is a horribly long letter. Give my love to Mrs. Gilder and believe me

Sincerely your friend

GROVER CLEVELAND.

R. W. GILDER, ESQ.

But conflicts awaited him which related to pending questions and which perforce took precedence over mere matters of his own place in history. From the beginning of his troubled life as President, with its not infrequent threats of war, some undoubtedly induced by his masterful method of conducting foreign affairs, Mr. Cleveland had worked to secure the adoption of an arbitration treaty between the United States and England. Mr. Carnegie, already famous for his services to the cause of arbitration, had pronounced him "as strong a supporter of that policy as ever I met." But the ceaseless disputes about fisheries, which had raged with ever-increasing bitterness since the Senate's rejection of his treaty of 1888, had fostered emotions unfavorable to the project. Now, however, beneath Secretary Olney's guiding hand, the irritating question, "What are the rights of American fishermen?" had given place to the greater question: "Are we willing to agree that all matters in difference between the United States and Great Britain shall be settled by friendly arbitration?"

On January 11, 1897, a treaty to that effect, negotiated by Secretary Olney and Sir Julian Pauncefote, was sent by Mr. Cleveland to the Senate. It bound the two nations, for a period of five years, "to submit to arbitration, in accordance with the provisions and subject to the limitations of this treaty, all questions in difference between them which they may fail to adjust by diplomatic negotiations," and provided for the appointment of arbritrators. It was Mr. Cleveland's hope that this treaty might stand beside the pending Venezuelan treaty as his last great act of service, not only to England and America, but to the general cause of peace. "Its ultimate ensuing benefits," he said, "are not likely to be limited to the two countries immediately concerned. . . . The example set and the lesson furnished by the successful operation of this treaty are sure to be felt and taken to heart sooner or later by other nations, and will thus mark the beginning of a new epoch in civilization."

The publication of the message, with an outline of the treaty, was the signal for demonstrations of enthusiasm in both countries. The New York *Tribune,* after a canvass of the members of Congress, announced that: "From each came expressions of cordial satisfaction. There was not a discordant note." The London *Standard* declared that it was proof positive that the lessons of the panic that followed the Venezuelan Message had not been thrown away, and the London *Times* ventured to predict that the Senate would not "defeat a policy that has obtained a decided and unusual degree of approval among the American people." And indeed the whole country recognized the treaty not only as the crowning glory of Mr. Cleveland's administration, but as a fitting climax to the century of civilization that was drawing to its close. Chambers of Commerce, boards of trade, church congresses, and the leading newspapers throughout the length and breadth of the land were urgently insistent upon the ratification of this treaty of lasting peace between the two greatest nations of the world.

On February 2d, Senator Sherman, Chairman of the Committee on Foreign Relations, reported the treaty favorably, five out of six Republican members of the committee having voted in favor of such a report, while three out of the four Democratic members had opposed it. For six weeks thereafter it remained under debate in executive session. Some Senators objected that such a treaty, if ratified before the Clayton-Bulwer Treaty of 1850 was definitely abrogated, would amount to a surrender of the American dream of building and controlling a canal across the Isthmus of Panama. Others devised amendments which brought on renewed discussion, while still others talked for the sake of passing the time. Toward the end of the session, the treaty was referred back to the committee, and in consequence the end of the Cleveland administration saw it still in the possession of that body, no vote having been taken in the Senate itself.

On March 17th, when Sherman, now Secretary of State, met the Senate Committee on Foreign Relations, he was told that the Arbitration Treaty would be reported favorably on the following day, and this was done; but more discussion was the only immediate result. At last, on May 5th, it came up for decision and was lost, only forty-three votes being cast in favor of what remained of it after months of senatorial amending had left it a mere skeleton.

To Mr. Cleveland and Mr. Olney, now private citizens, this outcome was a bitter disappointment. "The treaty," sarcastically declared the latter, "in getting itself made by the sole act of the Executive, without leave of the Senate first had and obtained, had committed the unpardonable sin. It must be either altogether defeated or so altered as to bear an unmistakable Senate stamp—and thus be the means both of humiliating the Executive and of showing to the world the greatness of the Senate.

Hence, the treaty has been assailed from all quarters and by Senators of all parties, and although the present Executive advocated its ratification no less warmly than his predecessor. The method of assault has been as insidious as it has been deadly. . . . Before the treaty came to a final vote, the Senate brand had been put upon every part of it, and the original instrument had been mutilated and distorted beyond all possibility of recognition. The object of the Senate in dealing with the treaty—the assertion of its own predominance—was thus successfully accomplished and would have been even if the treaty as amended had been ratified." Its defeat was, Olney declared, "a calamity, not merely of national but of world-wide proportions."

The other subject which disturbed the closing months of Mr. Cleveland's public life, was that of the revolution in Cuba. In February, 1895, the Cubans had rebelled against their Spanish masters, and on September 25th of that year Secretary Olney had reported to the President: "The situation of affairs in Cuba seems to me one calling for the careful consideration of the Executive. The Spanish side is naturally the side of which I have heard, and do hear, the most. It is, in substance, that the insurgents belong to the lowest order of the population of the Island, do not represent its property or its intelligence or its true interests, are the ignorant and vicious and desperate classes marshaled under the leadership of a few adventurers, and would be incapable of founding or maintaining a decent government if their revolution against Spain were to be successful. . . . There are, however, grounds for questioning the correctness of this view. . . . The Cuban insurgents are not to be regarded as the scum of the earth . . . In sympathy and feeling nine tenths of the Cuban population are with them. . . . The property

class to a man is disgusted with Spanish misrule, with a
system which has burdened the Island with $300,000,000
of debt, whose impositions in the way of annual taxes
just stop short of prohibiting all industrial enterprise,
and which yet does not fulfill the primary functions of
government by insuring safety to life and security to
property."

As an illustration of Spanish methods, he cited "the
short and effective way the government has of dealing
with non-combatant suspects. A file of soldiers visits
certain designated houses at night—the proscribed persons are carried off—but, partly for the torture of the
thing, and partly because the noise of the firearms is to
be avoided, they are not shot but chopped to pieces
with the small axes that the Spaniards call *machetes.*"
He summed up his conclusions with the declaration that
the Cuban revolution was "just in itself, commanding the
sympathy, if not the open support, of the great bulk of
the population affected, and capable of issuing in an
established, constitutional government," and expressed
the conviction that within a few months either Cuba
would be smothered in its own blood, or be "in the
market, for sale to the highest bidder," as Spain would
never be able to suppress the rebellion. He warned the
President that American "politicians of all stripes, including Congressmen," were "setting their sails, or preparing to set them, so as to catch the popular breeze,"
which blew in the direction of a recognition of Cuban
belligerency.

Since then the soundness of Mr. Olney's observations
had been amply demonstrated. Spain's weakness and
increasing cruelty, the unconquerable persistence of the
insurrectionists, and the drift of American public sympathy, all had revealed themselves with unmistakable

clearness. Other dangers, too, had emerged. The rights of American citizens in Cuba had become manifestly unsafe, their lives manifestly in danger.

As these facts had appeared, Congress had shown an increasing tendency to seize control, or as Ambassador Bayard expressed it, had seemed "strangely inclined to reverse the order of the Constitution, and . . . send messages and information to the Executive—not to receive them from him." This undoubted tendency Congress had already expressed in a concurrent resolution declaring that Cuban belligerent rights should be promptly recognized, a resolution which Secretary Olney ironically characterized as "an interesting expression of opinion." It had, however, apparently made not the slightest impression either upon him or upon Mr. Cleveland, who insisted that the conduct of America's foreign affairs belonged by law to the Executive, and that while Congress had the right to declare war, it was the President's duty to maintain peace until war was declared.

The end of October brought developments which made the task of preserving peace vastly more difficult. On the 21st of that month, Valeriano Weyler, the Spanish Captain-General of Cuba, issued his order of reconcentration, and with it the Spanish policy of suppression became a policy of extermination. The simple peasants from the outlying districts, most of whom had shown sympathy for the rebellion, were driven into the fortified towns and there subjected to treatment which called pestilence to the aid of the sword for their destruction. Four hundred thousand *reconcentrados* were soon kenneled in these urban pens of disease and starvation, while the world looked on in horror. The situation thus created required firm and wise leadership, as a declaration of war was inevitable unless some new solution could speedily be made effective. Such a solution Mr. Cleveland believed to lie in the purchase of the island, though he held the mailed fist ready, should this or other peaceful methods fail to secure protection for American life and property.

In his last annual message of December 7, 1896, he made this fact clear, declaring that from thirty to fifty million dollars of American capital was involved in the fate of Cuba, and that the revolution had virtually ruined American trade in the island, and added: "It cannot be reasonably assumed that the hitherto expectant attitude of the United States will be indefinitely maintained. While we are anxious to accord all due respect to the sovereignty of Spain, we cannot view the pending conflict in all its features and properly apprehend our inevitably close relations to it and its possible results without considering that by the course of events we may be drawn into such an unusual and unprecedented condition as will fix a limit to our patient waiting for Spain to end the contest, either alone and in her way or with our friendly co-operation.

"When the inability of Spain to deal successfully with the insurrection has become manifest, and it is demonstrated that her sovereignty is extinct in Cuba for all purposes of its rightful existence, and when a hopeless struggle for its re-establishment has degenerated into a strife which means nothing more than the useless sacrifice of human life and the utter destruction of the very subject matter of the conflict, a situation will be presented in which our obligations to the sovereignty of Spain will be superseded by higher obligations, which we can hardly hesitate to recognize and discharge.

"Deferring the choice of ways and methods until the time for action arrives, we should make them depend upon the precise conditions then existing, and they should not be determined upon without giving careful heed to every consideration involving our honor and interests, or the international duty we owe to Spain. Until we face the contingencies suggested, or the situation is by other incidents imperatively changed, we should continue in the line of conduct heretofore pursued, thus in all circumstances exhibiting our obedience to the requirements of public law and our regard for the duty enjoined upon us by the position we occupy in the family of nations.

"A contemplation of emergencies that may arise should plainly lead us to avoid their creation, either through a careless disregard of present duty or even an undue stimulation and ill-timed expression of feeling. But I have deemed it not amiss to remind the Congress that a time may arrive when a correct policy and care for our interests, as well as a regard for the interests of other nations and their citizens, joined by considerations of humanity and a desire to see a rich and fertile country, intimately related to us, saved from complete devastation, will constrain our government to such action as will subserve the interests thus involved, and at the same time promise to Cuba and its inhabitants an opportunity to enjoy the blessings of peace." And he added this phrase, characteristically Clevelandesque: "The United States is not a country to which peace is necessary." This hint of possible intervention fanned the flame of public opinion, and encouraged Congress to hope that it might force the President's hand.

"I was with the President at Woodley, near Washington, one Sunday afternoon," says Mr. A. B. Farquhar, "when some members of Congress came in and said, 'Mr. President, we wish to see you on an important matter.' I got up, but he motioned me to keep my seat. They said,

'We have about decided to declare war against Spain over the Cuban question. Conditions are intolerable.'

"Mr. Cleveland drew himself up and said, 'There will be no war with Spain over Cuba while I am President.'

"One of the members flushed up and said angrily, 'Mr. President, you seem to forget that the Constitution of the United States gives Congress the right to declare war.'

"He answered, 'Yes, but it also makes me Commander-in-Chief, and I will not mobilize the army. I happen to know that we can buy the Island of Cuba from Spain for $100,000,000, and a war will cost vastly more than that and will entail another long list of pensioners. It would be an outrage to declare war.' "

Mr. Cleveland's belief that Spain might be induced to sell Cuba for $100,000,000 doubtless rested in part upon the information obtained in a letter kept among his private papers, and written from London by H. Plasson to Senator Call, of Florida. It is marked "the strictest secrecy," and declares that in 1892 a group of London bankers had raised £20,000,000, with which to purchase the independence of the island, provided Cuba would assume the responsibility of the debt, and that a negotiator had been sent to Madrid with this purpose in view. Mr. Plasson was cabled to join this agent, but two days before he reached the capital the Spanish Cabinet had fallen. At the close of the letter Mr. Plasson suggested to Senator Call: "If you think I can be of any use to you . . . I will undertake to group again the bankers referred to."

With the idea of purchase in mind, Mr. Cleveland summoned the well-known international lawyer, Frederic R. Coudert, in a note which shows that he had continued his custom of late working hours:

Feb. 28, 1897. (Sunday)

My dear Mr. Coudert:

Can you not call on me at some hour this evening to suit your convenience? Any time from 8 P. M. to 2 A. M. will do for me.

Yours sincerely,

GROVER CLEVELAND.

HON. F. R. COUDERT,

Arlington Hotel.

When Mr. Coudert arrived, the President confided to him his fear that war with Spain was imminent unless an adjustment could be reached at once, and expressed the belief that such a war would be the result of the activities of Americans in Cuba. He mentioned the American Consul General, General Fitzhugh Lee, as their ringleader. He proposed that Mr. Coudert undertake a mission to the Spanish authorities in Cuba, and expressed the belief that, through his command of the Spanish tongue and his unusual knowledge of Spain and Cuba, war might yet be avoided.

Mr. Coudert objected that within a few days there would be a new President of the United States, and a new Cabinet, who would naturally wish to form their own policies and choose their own personnel in the face of the Cuban situation. To this the President replied that in his opinion Mr. McKinley, as a high-minded and patriotic American, would never enter an unnecessary war, and that if Mr. Coudert would accept the appointment, he himself would take up the matter with the incoming administration. Pressed at last to an immediate decision, Mr. Coudert answered that his health was so impaired that he would not dare to undertake so arduous and difficult a mission. And so, when the fourth of

March came, the Cuban situation remained unsolved, and with forebodings of impending conflict Mr. Cleveland was compelled to hand over this great responsibility to the new administration, to be by it handled in the interests of peace, and ultimately disposed of by the grim methods of war.

The last official hours of President Cleveland were spent in the same careful service to the public which he had always given. Patiently he waded through the accumulation of official business, making the greatest elective office in the world ready for the leader of the opposing party. He had known abuse, party treachery, malicious personal slander, and scarcely veiled contempt from many loyal Americans who should have recognized his greatness. All that, however, was now history, and as such did not concern him overmuch.

Three days before his retirement his friend, A. B. Farquhar, wrote a defense of the President and sent it to the White House with the request that it be endorsed for publication, and on March 4th, despite the excitement incident to his last hours in office, Mr. Cleveland answered:

My dear Friend:

In a few hours I will cease to be President. The people seem to have deserted me, and I would advise you to withhold this publication. Any defense of me will only hurt you, and since I have done my duty as I saw it, I feel that I need no defense.

Yours sincerely,

GROVER CLEVELAND.

The pæan of thanksgiving raised by the free silver and the Populist press expressed a far different opinion.

Their denunciations are reminiscent of those with which the extreme Democratic press greeted Washington's retirement in 1797. Human ingenuity for the coining of billingsgate was taxed to the utmost to invent phrases more insulting than those with which Benjamin Bache and his fellow scribes had daubed their pages as parting insults to the man who had made America. "Grover Cleveland will go out," declared the Atlanta *Constitution* on March 4, 1897, "under a greater burden of popular contempt than has ever been excited by a public man since the foundation of the government." "The Democratic party which he has deceived, betrayed and humiliated," said the Kansas City *Times* of the same date, "long ago stamped him as a political leper and cast him out as one unclean. The reproaches and contumely of the entire American people accompany him in his retirement." A Populist orator of Minnesota assured the Legislature of that State that Grover Cleveland would leave the White House "with the ignominious distinction that he is the first President who ever accumulated millions during his term of office." To this slander Lamont replied with the following statement: "The retiring President has property amounting all told to $300,000 or $350,000 acquired from salary during two terms, fees received during the period of New York law practice, and about $100,000 of profits from the purchase of real estate just outside Washington."

Before completing his arrangements for his final departure, Mr. Cleveland called William and told him to take the portrait by Eastman Johnson and put it in the attic. He saw no good reason why the White House should treasure his picture, and he had not vanity enough to wish to see it left there.

At the hour appointed for the inauguration ceremonies, he joined the President-elect and drove with him to the Capitol, and as he gravely greeted the crowds which lined his pathway, or rather the pathway of the President soon to be, he rejoiced in the thought that, while his party had been defeated, his policies had won a signal victory. Such also must have been his thoughts as he stood a little behind his successor, with head bowed, listening to the solemn oath of office administered by Chief Justice Fuller.

It is doubtful whether a President and an ex-President of opposite political parties ever separated with such cordial relations as did McKinley and Cleveland. McKinley thanked the retiring President for all that had been done to make things smooth for the new administration, and said: "Now, Mr. Cleveland, isn't there something you would like me to do for you?" "No, Mr. President," replied Mr. Cleveland, "there is nothing that I want personally; but I beg you to remember that the time may come again when it will be necessary to have another union of the forces which supported honest money against this accursed heresy; and for this reason I ask you to use all your influence against such extreme action as would prevent such a union."

McKinley answered that he fully appreciated the danger and the necessity, and that he had already begun to act in that direction in the make-up of his Cabinet. Both were much moved and both spoke with deep feeling. Mr. Cleveland expressed the hope that the new President, when it came his turn to go out, would not have so many reasons to be glad. To this Mr. McKinley replied courteously that his [Mr. Cleveland's] place in history was assured.

The ceremony of handing over a nation being complete, Grover Cleveland, not President but simple citizen, joined Admiral Evans, Captain Lamberton, and Leonard Wood for a fortnight's outing. "I remember him as he came aboard the ship, immediately after the great inaugural parade," writes General Wood. "He was tired and worn from weeks of hard work and the strain of the long hard day, and as we were pulling off from the dock . . . he sat down with a sigh of relief, glad that it was all over. 'I have had a long talk with President McKinley,' he said. 'He is an honest, sincere, and serious man. I feel that he is going to do his best to give the country a good administration. He impressed me as a man who will have the best interests of the people at heart.' Then he stopped and added, with a sigh: 'I envy him to-day only one thing, and that was the presence of his mother at his inauguration.'"

For the next two weeks, by day in shooting boxes, by night in the cozy cabin of the ship, he enjoyed his liberty as only the true sportsman can enjoy it. "If he found himself in a poor position for shooting," said General Wood, "he would always insist on staying there, never permitting any of us to be displaced . . . nor would he allow anything to be done for him which would seem to give him an undue advantage." He scorned special privileges, and any suggestion of carrying his gun was certain to be rejected with the words: "On this expedition, every fellow does his own carrying."

At the end of the trip, when the last of his companions, Leonard Wood, left him on the platform of his home-bound train, Mr. Cleveland suddenly realized that he was alone, and again a free man. Waving his hand in farewell, he called gayly: "If you don't mind, just ask the conductor to roll me off at Princeton."

CHAPTER IX

RETIRES TO PRINCETON

"I feel like a locomotive hitched to a boy's express wagon."
—GROVER CLEVELAND.

WHEN the conductor "rolled him off at Princeton" on March 18, 1897, his sixtieth birthday as it chanced, Mr. Cleveland believed himself the most unpopular man in America, and there was some justification for the belief. The Bryanites hated him for having caused the defeat of their leader, while the triumphant Republicans were not yet ready to give him any of the credit for their success. Thus reviled by the one and disregarded by the other, he was a man without a party.

He arrived in Princeton in a pouring rain and was driven to his new home, "Westland," a substantial colonial mansion of stone covered with stucco and set in spacious grounds dotted with fine old trees. As he had made the purchase without seeing the property, he was eager to inspect it, but the rain prevented. But though he chafed under this enforced restraint, he weathered the storm as he had weathered so many before it, and frankly luxuriated in the unaccustomed freedom from pressing responsibilities. "I am enjoying the first holiday of my life," he remarked to an inquisitive reporter. "I have worked hard. Now I am entitled to rest. My mission in life has been accomplished."

Dropping at once into the spirit of the place, he watched with interest the arrangement of his books, and adjusted the angle of his desk with a critical eye to the

256

question of light. A careful survey of his accumulated volumes convinced him that there were many which would never interest him. There were books in unknown tongues, sent by foreign admirers, ignorant of the fact that Grover Cleveland's reading was all done in his native language. There were presentation copies of works on science, works on art, works on music, medicine, and mines, for which he saw no reason to provide house room. He accordingly telephoned to the University Library that if one of the librarians would come up he might choose such of these books as the University wished. One of the young assistants, Varnum Lansing Collins, later Secretary of the University, was accordingly dispatched. He found the ex-President friendly, cheerful, and of a disposing mind. "Come in," he said, "and take what you want." Then, selecting a large volume, gorgeously bound in red leather and inscribed in gold, he remarked, "This is the Bible in the language of Borneo. I seldom read it. Could the Library make use of that?"

The transfers made, the remaining volumes arranged according to his fancy, and the furniture adjusted to his taste, he began summoning the elect. To Dean West he wrote on March 23rd, "Unless I see you within a very brief period, I shall pull up stakes and clear out." To Commodore Benedict, "I want to play cribbage with you. We are settled enough to make you comfortable and I suppose I might lend you a nightshirt *again,* though it would probably be better for you to bring one." To Evans and Gilder, L. Clarke Davis and Dan Lamont, Joe Jefferson and the rest, he sent invitations expressed in terms of the kind of intimacy which he had with each. Into his letters there had crept again the spirit of banter which they had lacked of late. After the Commodore's visit he wrote: "I discovered after you left . . . a perfect wealth of fine cigars which you brought. I don't think you can afford that on $2 winnings."

Mr. Cleveland intended to make his "at homes" distinctly exclusive affairs, open only to the elect, among whom he included none of those priests of the limelight— newspaper reporters. To one of the latter who eagerly pleaded for an interview, on the ground that "a vast number of people are interested in knowing what you do," he replied, "Well, we'll see how they get on without knowing." He had no interest in headlines with his name as the central theme. What he wanted was the privilege of living his life as other men live theirs, the privilege of privacy so long and at times so insolently denied him, and above all the privilege of selecting his own companions, and of meeting them upon a basis of personal relations only. Long years of officialdom had made these things loom large among the rights of man.

In dress he chose to be informal. A brown slouch hat, loose clothes, not too fresh from the shop, and wide, comfortable shoes added greatly to his new-born sense of freedom. He studiously avoided everything calculated to make him resemble the traditional political magnet, supremely content to be what Andrew Jackson once declared Sam Houston: "A man made by God and not by a tailor."

His manner of receiving such visitors as he chose to see was bluff, hearty, sincere, and surprisingly informal; but his natural dignity and self-restraint served to protect him from undue familiarity, and he never lost the consciousness of what was due to the office which he had occupied.

Over all, however, and not to be shaken off, was the disturbing feeling that he had lost the love and confidence of the American people. It crept, unbidden, into his conversations, and stood out in clear relief in his intimate letters. Upon one occasion when Jesse Lynch Williams was calling at "Westland," his fine setter dog, excluded at the door, searched for and found another entrance. When he trotted triumphant into the drawing-room and laid his cold muzzle on the ex-President's hand, his owner rose to expel him. "No, let him stay," remarked Mr. Cleveland. "He at least likes me."

When asked why he did not use his leisure in the preparation of an autobiography, Mr. Cleveland answered: "There is no reason for my writing my autobiography. My official acts and public career are public property. There is nothing to say about them. What I did is done and history must judge of its value, not I. My private life has been so commonplace that there is nothing to write about." This idea he emphasized more strongly one evening when Dean West interrupted a shot at billiards to urge "at least a brief, dictated personal memorandum." "I tell you, I won't do it," replied Mr. Cleveland, "and I'll tell you why. The moment I began, the newspapers would cry: 'There goes the old fool again.'"

With freedom from conflict, there came more fully to light the gentler qualities of his nature, among which was his tender sympathy with children. One St. Valentine's Day his little daughters came home from school with excited stories of the giving out of valentines to the classes. "Isn't it a shame," remarked one, "that Jean was the only child who did not get a valentine?" Mrs. Cleveland glanced at her husband and to her surprise saw the tears coursing down his cheeks. He could not stand the thought of the disappointment of the little girl who had been inadvertently overlooked, and at once a messenger was dispatched to carry her a valentine from Grover

Cleveland. Nor could he bear to attend the Christmas tree celebrations held each year in the Princeton church which he attended, because the voices of the children singing Christmas carols always brought the tears to his eyes.

He passed his days in reading, planning additions and changes in his new house, and always, when opportunity offered, in fishing. The diaries which he kept during his later years are fuller of fishing entries than of all others combined, and his personal letters show an almost equal interest in duck hunting. "I am more deeply interested in the plans for preserving the fish and game of this community," he remarked to a friend, "than I ever was in being President of the United States." When such sports were out of season, cribbage supplied the want. The stakes were "shiners," new dimes which changed hands without material alteration in the relative financial positions of the contestants. The Benedict collection of Cleveland letters is liberally supplied with these trophies, which the Commodore never thought worth while to remove. The challenges sent by Mr. Cleveland were of varied form, but always measurably insulting to the Commodore's pride of conflict:

Commodore:

I've got ten more shiners. If you will come up to-night and can win them, you can put them in the contribution box to-morrow. G. C.

My dear Commodore:

I was glad to hear that you had received and squandered the ten dollars I sent you and that you had returned to sobriety and decency. . . . As far as cribbage is concerned, I am prepared for the fray and think I have some new dodges. G. C.

Upon one occasion, in the practice of these new dodges, Mr. Cleveland won the Commodore's yacht, the *Oneida,* and, although this departure from the established policy of shiners was entirely fictitious, from that day Mr. Cleveland became "the Admiral" when the "Poverty Club" was in action. In one letter to "the Commodore," "the Admiral" declared: "You may be sure, my dear Commodore, that I shall not acquire the habit of abandoning old companionships, and means of transportation, in my journeys homeward from Gray Gables. I like them both too well." And suddenly remembering that he was "Admiral," he added: "Besides, the owner of a yacht that pays for other travel is, as you often say, like the man who keeps a cow and buys milk."

The students' sports furnished a never-failing source of interest and at important games seats were always reserved for the ex-President and Mrs. Cleveland. It was not unusual at one of these games to hear a commotion in the grand stand, accompanied by good-natured boos and cat-calls, and if a stranger inquired the cause of the trouble his student neighbor would reply laconically: "Some guy got into Grover's seat."

The manner of his life had thus completely changed, but his attitude toward Bryanism never altered, though his enthusiasm for McKinley cooled rapidly. A few weeks after his arrival in Princeton, he wrote to Mr. Olney: "I have been a little amused at the cackling over eggs that were substantially in the nest before we left the scene, like the release of Americans in Cuba, etc., but have been on the whole much gratified by the apparent conviction among the people, that the new administration after all could find but little to amend. You know what I hope will be the result of the Senate's tomfoolery in the arbitration treaty business. I am satisfied I can indulge in the hope I have expressed to you without the least unpatriotic feeling, and I do want this Senate to get the hot end of the poker as long as present influences control it."

A week later he added: "Of course you and I are too patriotic to gloat over the condition and you no doubt feel as much humiliated as I do by the silly exhibition our government is making in its conduct of foreign affairs. I am willing, however, to confess to enough of the 'old Adam' to feel a little bit of satisfaction in a situation that crowds this bitter dose down the throats of the dirty liars who attempted so hard to decry and depreciate your dignified, decent, and proper management of our foreign relations. The present administration must soon find that the Executive Department cannot drift through public duty on the wave of public applause and adulation and that the day comes when popular tickling and humbug will not do."

"The Dingley bill," he wrote later, "has not done anything for me yet, and therefore I am still 'agin it.'" Indeed, he gradually grew almost as much 'agin the Government' as 'agin' the leaders of the Democratic organization, which now composed the opposition. In replying to an invitation from Mr. Fairchild to speak at a dinner of the Reform Club, he wrote:

> Westland, Princeton, N.J.
> *April 2, 1897.*

My dear Mr. Fairchild:

Yours of March 30th is received. I am perfectly willing to say something at the dinner on the 24th if I can do any good in that way. . . . But to tell you the truth I am going to find it difficult, I am afraid, to be prudent and say just what I would like to say. I am very much disgusted with the silver Democratic leaders and am not inclined to credit them with sincerity or convictions. I am near the point of believing them to be conspirators and traitors and, in their relations with the honest masses, as confidence sharks and swindlers.

I don't suppose that the diners will all be Democrats and so a man can't cuss both parties as at present controlled, and yet it is not perfectly easy to see how a Democrat can condemn his party organization and steer clear of being struck in the face with the suggestion that the way out is to act with the Republican party. But we will have to get along with it somehow.

Yours sincerely,
GROVER CLEVELAND.

HON. CHAS. S. FAIRCHILD,
 New York City.

When the hour arrived, however, he did "cuss both parties," unhesitatingly proclaiming his friends "the true Democracy," and denouncing his enemies, whether Republicans or Democrats, as unprofitable servants. He described the Bryan organization as "born of sordid greed and maintained by selfish interest and partisan ambition," spending its energies in "inflaming those inclined to be patient with tales of an ancient crime against their rights, to be avenged by encouraging the restless and turbulent with hints of greater license, and by offering to the poor as a smooth road to wealth, and to those in debt as a plan for easy payment, and to those who from any cause are unfortunate and discouraged as a remedy for all their ills . . . cheap money." "It was a rude awakening . . . when the bold promoters of this reckless crusade captured the organization of a powerful political party, and, seizing its banners, shouted defiance to the astonished conscience and conservatism of the country. Hosts of honest men, in blind loyalty, gathered behind the party flag they had been accustomed to follow, failing to discover that their party legends had been effaced." "Let us . . . break through the influence of the mischievous leadership," he declared. "Let true Democrats meet the passion and bitterness of their former associates who have assumed the leadership of anti-Democratic wanderings, with firm expostulations, reminding them that Democratic convictions and Democratic conscience cannot be forced to follow false lights, however held aloft."

His appeal was for a return to "true Democracy, a party of noble origin and traditions, identified with the counsels of the nation from its earliest days, and whose glorious achievements are written on every page of our country's history. Always the people's friend, seeking to lighten their burdens and protect their rights, true Democracy has constantly taught conservatism, American fraternity, and obedience to law. . . . It enjoins the utmost personal liberty consistent with peace and order. It defends the humble toiler against oppressive exactions in his home, and invites him to the fullest enjoyment of the fruits of industry, economy, and thrift. . . . True Democracy declares that . . . there is a limit beyond which the legitimate results and accumulations of effort and enterprise should be denounced as intrinsically criminal. . . . Above all things, true Democracy insists that the money of the people should be sound and stable, neither shriveling in purchasing power in the hands of the poor, nor by its uncertain value driving enterprise and productive energy into hiding."

Nor did he spare those who in obedience to their fetish, party loyalty, had turned from the light to follow after darkness: "They are willfully wicked and stupid who believe that disaster waits upon the ascendancy of those forces, and yet turn away from the plain evidence of their dangerous strength." Defiantly, passionately, he repudiated "adherence to a party organization merely for the purpose of compassing governmental control," and declared that the only partisanship which could command his allegiance was "the support of certain principles and theories of government, and a co-operation and association in political effort and activity with others who believe in the same theories and principles." "It is an impeachment of the intelligence of the members of any political association to say that party management and discipline should at all times command implicit obedience, even when such obedience leads to the abandonment or radical perversion of party principles."

He scored the Republicans as men who, placed in power by splendid Democratic patriotism, had "returned in hot haste to their wallowing in the mire of extreme protection, offending millions of voters by their exhibition of a party's bad faith, and disgusting millions more by their unconcealed determination to repay partisan support from the proceeds of increased burdens of taxation placed upon those already overladen."

Upon his return to Princeton, Mr. Cleveland received an intimation that the honorary degree which he had declined as President was awaiting him as a private citizen, and having accepted the offer, he turned his mind to the pressing problem of his academic costume. On June 11th, he wrote to Mr. Gilder, in high glee:

"My gown and cap came to-day, and my wife says I look very fine in them. I suppose your wife gave you a like assurance. I shall look for you Wednesday morning and I mean to ask Professor West to-morrow if you won't be obliged to wear your toggery too. The fox that lost his tail tried to make all the other foxes believe that short tails were the fashion."

In similar vein, he wrote to Olney after the event: "You needn't put on any airs because you are settled on Cape Cod. I'll open up there myself in a few days—and I've got a degree that I'm going to bring with me. There may be others—I presume there are—but there are no rivals of my gown, hood, and cap: and the Latin investiture of the degree was to my certain knowledge faultless. I wonder if Brad and Jim Jones ought not to have some sort of a degree, so that you and I might feel a little more at ease with them."

His acknowledgment to President Patton who had performed the Latin investiture was in different vein; for as yet he did not understand how much his less formal thoughts would have been appreciated by that supremely humorous master of the Latin:

"I cannot forbear the expression of my profound appreciation of the honor just conferred upon me, and the assurance of my gratitude for the hearty welcome which has greeted my admission to the brotherhood of Princeton University. As I recall the commanding place which Princeton holds among the universities of our land, her glorious history, her venerable traditions, her bright trophies won on the field of higher education, and her sacred relation to the patriotic achievements which made us a nation, I am proud of the honor which has come to me through her grace and favor, and as I realize the sincere and friendly comradeship attached to this new honor, I cannot keep out of mind the feeling that an additional tie has this day been created binding me with

closer affection and deeper delight to the home where I
hope to spend the remainder of my days."

True to his promise, he took his degree to Buzzards
Bay soon after Commencement, and at once became intent upon squeteague, tautog, and the fighting blue fish,
which he insisted upon catching with a rod and reel,
contrary to the custom of those who "do business in great
waters." Automatically, Brad and Jim Jones, un-
doctored but unashamed, took the place vacated by Dean
West and President Patton in his daily scheme of social
intercourse, and his figuring concerned itself with boats
instead of libraries. The language of his letters, too,
became at times most unacademic, as valve trouble
dimmed the consciousness of what was due to his new
cap and gown.

"I am having the devil's own time with my launch,"
he wrote to the Commodore. "I have not had but one
satisfactory time with her since I came and that was the
day after I arrived when Brad ran her. I get so cursed
mad every time I go out that I almost swear I'll never
go in her again."

Politics seemed a long way off in those gloriously
damp and salty days, and his letters, even to the men who
had fought by his side against a varied foe, touched rarely
upon public questions, save for occasional pointed thrusts
called out by passing incidents. On August 1st he wrote
to Colonel Lamont: "As far as I can see the tendency at
present is to enjoy being humbugged by the administration now in power and to forget or decry all that was done
by the last one. Of all weak, milksop things, it seems
to me the Democratic press so far as it comes under my
observation is a prize winner." And to Harmon two days
later: "The administration seems at present to be so little

in the minds of the people and its achievements appear
to be so nearly forgotten that I feel like apologizing to
all the good and true men who cast in their lot with
it. . . . It seems to me that in Ohio better than anywhere
else the Bogus Democracy has turned itself up for a sound
spanking. The thing that strikes me with amazement
is the gullibility of Democratic newspapers and men that
want to be sound and yet do not see the mischief and
humbug of the Maryland platform. When anything
straight, honest or truly democratic emanates from Mr.
Gorman, neither you nor I will be there to see." "I am
such a political outcast these days," he wrote to Don M.
Dickinson on October 20th, "that the rôle of looker-on
seems quite a natural one; and yet I feel that matters are
brewing that may bring decent men into activity again."

On October 28th, Mr. Cleveland's first son was born
at Westland, and at once the Princeton students, remembering their transparency, "Grover, send your sons to
Princeton," formally adopted him by posting on their
bulletin board this notice: "Grover Cleveland, Jr., arrived
today at twelve o'clock. Will enter Princeton with the
class of 1919, and will play center rush on the champion-
ship football teams of '16, '17, '18 and '19." A deluge
of congratulations came from all parts of the land, and
from many lands, while the press cried "politics," as
they had done at every great achievement of his life.
The Pittsburgh *Leader* presented a picture of the ex-
President, dramatically pointing his oratorical finger at
a tiny white bundle in an old-fashioned cradle, and
soliloquizing: "If this doesn't mean a third term, nothing
does."

Mr. Cleveland's own comments seem meant to conceal
the emotion which he felt at the possession of a son. To
Olney he wrote: "I wish I could write something satis-

factory to the ladies of your household, touching our new boy. This I cannot do on my own responsibility, for I agree with you that when they can count but two weeks as the period of earthly experience, all babies are very much alike, both as regards their looks and conduct. As sort of second-hand information, however, I venture to say that the female members of our household declare that this particular child looks like his father, that he has blue eyes, a finely shaped head, and bids fair to be a very handsome and a very distinguished man. I have no doubt this is all true, because a neighbor lady who was to-day admitted to a private inspection of the specimen, told me that he was 'the loveliest thing' she ever saw. We have named him Richard Folsom—my father's first name and my wife's father's last name. Some good friends thought we ought to call him Grover Jr., but so many people have been bothered by the name Grover, and it has been so knocked about that I thought it ought to have a rest."

So far as he himself was concerned, however, there had already been rest enough, and he began to feel the need of active employment. To one friend who asked how he felt with no Senate to fight and no weight of official responsibility to bear, he replied: "I feel like a locomotive hitched to a boy's express wagon." Three years later, the position of Stafford Little Lecturer on Public Affairs was founded in his honor, and he became an organic part of the University. His duties consisted only in the preparation of one or two public lectures a year, but the task weighed heavily upon him. The honor pleased him; but the work appalled him. For months before each address his intimate letters were filled with lamentations and forebodings of evil; but he had a rich experience from which to draw, and the lectures at once became intellectual events in the life of Princeton.

The final step in his academic career was his election as trustee of the University, and the new duties thus added to the old he took with equal seriousness. "As a trustee of Princeton," writes Dr. Charles Wood, "where I sat at the meetings of the Board directly opposite him, he was a constant surprise to us all. He was an indefatigable attendant of all meetings, interested in the University details and speaking with the greatest simplicity and modesty, as if feeling that his opinion could not be of any great value, though no man in the Board was more convincing."

Every detail of University life, from football to social coördination, from entrance examinations to the standard of the degree of doctor of philosophy, received from his trusteeship as painstaking care as he had formerly given to currency, tariff and foreign affairs. When the trustees discussed the necessity of a social reorganization of the institution, Mr. Cleveland drafted an elaborate plan for correcting the evils of undergraduate club life. And when the graduate school committee proposed expansion, he wrote to his friend, Andrew Carnegie, a letter designed to secure for the project the financial support which he had refused to accept for himself. These things, together with his family and his friends, his rods, guns and hunting dogs, pleasantly filled his life.

CHAPTER X

WATCHING THE GAME FROM THE SIDE LINES

"Your every voter, as surely as your Chief Magistrate, under the same high sanction, though in a different sphere, exercises a public trust."
—GROVER CLEVELAND.

ALTHOUGH out of politics, Mr. Cleveland had not lost his interest in the affairs of the country and from his home in Princeton he watched the passing show, sometimes with approval—often with dismay. By the 1st of December, 1897, it was apparent that a crisis was at hand in Cuba. Spain had continued her cruelties, and the following January, in response to appeals from General Fitzhugh Lee, American vessels of war were ordered to occupy vantage points, to be ready should action become necessary.

The North Atlantic squadron took up its vigil at the Dry Tortugas within six hours of the Cuban shores. Captain Sampson, with a squadron of battleships and cruisers, sailed for Key West, and on the 25th the Spanish Government was notified that the second-class battleship, *Maine,* had been ordered on a friendly visit to Havana. Thus the stage was set for the tragedy of February 15, 1898, when the *Maine* was wrecked by an explosion, with the loss of two officers and 264 enlisted men.

Even this disaster, which was interpreted by many as a deliberate act of war on the part of Spain, did not alter Mr. Cleveland's opinion that "it would be an outrage to declare war." "If the President's backbone holds out," he wrote to Mr. Olney the next day, "our Cuban policy will, I believe, be fully justified." He was far from being a pacifist, but he was a firm believer in the doctrine that nations should mind their own business, and he did not consider the Cuban situation our affair. He deeply resented the use made of the *Maine* disaster by the press, and freely expressed this resentment. On February 28th he telegraphed to William Randolph Hearst:

Feb. 28, 1898.

To W. R. HEARST,
N. Y. *Journal,* New York.

I decline to allow my sorrow for those who died on the *Maine* to be perverted to an advertising scheme for the New York *Journal.*

GROVER CLEVELAND.

Week by week he sought to keep his faith in the ultimate success of the policy of 'hands off.' "Notwithstanding warlike indications," he wrote to Olney on March 27th, "I cannot rid myself of the belief that war will be averted. There will be infinitely more credit and political capital in avoiding war when so imminent than to carry it on even well. And then there is Spain's condition and the reflection that may come to her that 'the game is not worth the candle.'" And to Commodore Benedict he declared: "I wish the President would stand fast and persist in following the lead of his own good sense and conscience, but I am afraid he intends to defer and yield to Congress. I cannot yet make myself believe there will be war. If there is and it is based upon present conditions, the time will not be long before there will be an earnest and not altogether successful search by our people for a justification."

A few days later the ambassadors of six European countries ventured to intimate the same opinion in a note to President McKinley, expressing the hope that he would avoid war for humanity's sake. Mr. McKinley's reply, that if war came it would be a war for humanity's sake, sounded to the ears of these diplomats like cant and hypocrisy. And when, on April 25th, Congress, by unanimous consent of both houses, with the approval of President McKinley and the vast majority of the American people, declared war and pledged the nation to the altruistic policy of giving Cuba back to her own people, the Continent's sarcastic comment was that this was a gesture planned to prevent European interference with a scheme to annex Cuba. England, on the other hand, took the part of the United States. When news of the declaration of war reached London, crowds of Englishmen went to the American Embassy and cheered, and the Stars and Stripes were displayed in every part of the city. There had been talk of foreign intervention to stop the war, but at this attitude of England it quickly died down.

Mr. Cleveland's view, however, was not changed, although he felt, as he wrote to Commodore Benedict, that: "We, the people, have but one thing to do when the storm is upon us and that is to stand by the action of our government."

"With all allowances I can make . . . ," he wrote to Olney, "I cannot avoid a feeling of shame and humiliation. It seems to me to be the same old story of good intentions and motives sacrificed to false considerations of complaisance and party harmony. McKinley is not a victim of ignorance, but of amiable weakness not unmixed with political ambition. He knew, or ought to have known, the cussedness of the Senate and he was abundantly warned against Lee, and yet he has surrendered to the former and given his confidence to the latter. The Senate would not hesitate to leave him in the lurch, and Lee will strut and swagger, I suppose, as a Major General and the idol of the populace. Roosevelt, too, will have his share of strut and sensation, and Miles will be commissioned General of the army. In the meantime, we who have undertaken war in the interest of humanity and civilization, will find ourselves in alliance and co-operation with Cuban insurgents—the most inhuman and barbarous cutthroats in the world. I suppose the outrages to which we shall then be privy, and the starvation and suffering abetted by our interference will be mildly called the 'incidents of the war.'

"My only relief from the sick feeling which these thoughts induce consists in the reflection that it affects no one but myself, and in the hope, almost amounting to expectation, that we shall find Spain so weak and inefficient that the war will be short and that the result may not be much worse than a depreciation of national standing before the world abroad, and at home, demoralization of our people's character, much demagogy and humbug, great additions to our public burdens, and the exposure of scandalous operations."

On June 21st, in the height of the war spirit, Mr. Cleveland delivered the Commencement address at Lawrenceville, choosing as his subject "Good Citizenship," and in ringing sentences denouncing, not the war, but the spirit of imperialism which he feared would follow war:

"Never before in our history have we been beset with temptations so dangerous as those which now whisper in our ears alluring words of conquest and expansion, and point out to us fields bright with the glory of war. . . .

Our government was formed for the express purpose of creating in a new world a new nation, the foundation of which should be man's self-government, whose safety and prosperity should be secure in its absolute freedom from Old World complications and its renunciation of all schemes of foreign conquest. . . .

"If you believe these things, do not permit any accusation . . . to trouble you. If . . . the suggestion is made that the time has come for our nation to abandon its old landmarks and to follow the lights of monarchical hazards, and that we should attempt to employ the simple machinery of our popular and domestic government to serve the schemes of imperialism, your challenge of the proposition is entirely in order. If you are satisfied that foreign conquest and unnatural extension or annexation are dangerous perversions of our national mission . . . you will not necessarily be wrong. . . .

"It is difficult to deal with the question of war at this time and avoid misconception and misrepresentation. But we are considering American citizenship, and endeavoring to find its best characteristics, and how they can be most effectively cultivated and securely preserved. From this standpoint, war is a hateful thing, which we should shun and avoid as antagonistic to the objects of our national existence, as threatening demoralization of our national character and as obstructive to our national destiny. . . . If you believe this, you should stand bravely for your belief, even though a shower of stupid calls should fill the air."

As the problems of a short war merged into those of a victorious peace, he became more and more fearful that the United States had entered upon an era of conquest which would surely enroll her among the imperialistic nations. Among his papers is a faded manuscript, in his own hand, evidently written as his anti-imperialistic creed:

"We believe that the spirit of our free institutions, the true intent and meaning of the Constitution, and the interest and welfare of our people forbid either the absolute and permanent control of the Philippine Islands as colonies or dependencies, or their admission to the family of states; and we insist that a consistent adherence to the American idea of freedom and liberty, an honest and sincere belief that the consent of the governed is essential to just government, and a scrupulous and American regard for the obligations of good faith, demand that an occupation and control of these Islands shall only be for the purpose of leading their inhabitants to the establishment of their own government; that these inhabitants shall be at once reassured and pacified by an immediate declaration of such purpose, and that when with our friendly aid such purpose is accomplished, our control and occupation by force in the Isles shall cease—save only so far as they may be desired or be necessary for the maintenance of peace and order under the new government."

In this opinion he had the full sympathy of Mr. Bryan who, though he raised the 3rd Regiment of the Nebraska Volunteer Infantry for the war and became its Colonel, was as suspicious as was the ex-President of the aims of the McKinley administration, and as eager to lead a crusade against imperialism. Truly peace problems no less than politics make strange bedfellows, but Mr. Cleveland had no desire to make room for Mr.

Bryan, feeling, not without reason, that he was large enough to occupy the bed alone.

In letter after letter he poured out his distressed consciousness of his own unpopularity, his disapproval of the conduct of affairs under Republican administration, and his anxiety over the "prevailing American madness":

Westland, Princeton, N. J.
Jan. 12, 1899.

My dear Mr. Shepard:

. . . With a full realization of the fact that my relations with Mr. Bayard and my love for him should constrain me to join with enthusiasm in any movement to honor his memory, I have determined to decline participation in the meeting suggested. I cannot detail all my reasons for this conclusion; and I hope my justification does not require it.

I will say, however, that I have been controllingly influenced by a clear negative conviction on the following proposition contained in your letter to me: "Whether amid all the present din and noise, a worthy presentation of Mr. Bayard's career and services can be fittingly heard, is possibly open to doubt."

Unpleasant suggestions of "pearls" and "swine" *will* obtrude themselves.

My pride and self-conceit have had a terrible fall. I thought I understood the American people.

Yours very sincerely,
GROVER CLEVELAND.

EDWARD M. SHEPARD, ESQ.
New York.

"I am not the sort of man people want to hear these days," he wrote to Harmon. "My beliefs and opinions are unsuited to the times. No word that I could speak would do the least good and the announcement that I was to address my fellow countrymen on any subject whatever would be the signal for coarse abuse and ridicule. I am content in my retirement and am far from complaining of my elimination from public thought or notice; but I cannot see that I ought to uselessly give an opportunity to those who delight in misrepresenting and maligning me.

"You know me too well to imagine that such a consideration would have a feather's weight with me if over against it there was the slightest possibility of my being of service to the country in these perilous days. Indeed I would gladly do such service. The time may come when I can see such an opportunity, but I cannot now; and it may be that this opportunity will more surely come to me, if I am silent now."

To Dr. Ward he declared: "Those who delight in my elimination from popular thought and consideration have no need to struggle with a resisting victim. I go most willingly. The delights of life are way back of incidents or days related to political devotion or hate; and of these I cannot be robbed."

"Did you ever 'in all your born days,' " he inquired of Olney, "see such goings on as have been exhibited at Washington during the past year? I am in a constant state of wonderment, when I am not in a state of nausea. Sometimes I feel like saying 'it's none of my business,' but that's pretty hard for me to do, though it would be comfortable if I could settle down to that condition.

"The Democratic party, if it was in only tolerable condition, could win an easy victory next year; but I am afraid it will never be in winning condition until we have had a regular knockout fight among ourselves, and succeed in putting the organization in Democratic hands and reviving Democratic principles in our platform. I don't think the kind of 'harmony' we hear so much of will bridge over our difficulties, and I don't believe our people, notwithstanding the disgust the administration is breeding, are ready to accept Bryan and the Chicago platform; and if they are, what comfort is there in that for decent, sound Democrats?

"One thing I regard as absolutely certain: If the plans of those now in charge of our party management are not interrupted, the dishes served up to us will be Bryan and the Chicago platform. To suppose anything else will occur in the contingency suggested, is to ignore every indication in the political sky." Then, with an effort to turn his mind to happier themes, he added: "Other questions, however, of utmost importance confront us. Bryan is alive and his followers active, numerous, and determined; but is Jim Jones alive, and are the bass in Long Pond numerous, and will they in due time prove active and determined?"

Mr. Olney replied in the same vein:

Boston, *22 March, 1899.*

My dear Mr. Cleveland:

I have your last favor—to receive which is a pleasure of itself, while, as always, I find the contents full of interest. It was high time, I have long been thinking, that communication between us was restored, and as one or the other of us had to begin, I am greatly obliged to you for not waiting for the other feller.

I think my surprise—not to say consternation—at the

performances in Washington equals your own. While believing the policy of the government in its foreign relations might well be liberalized and broadened, and certainly should not be hampered by rules not made for present conditions, I have never been able to understand why McKinley wanted to rush upon problems so momentous and why he should conceive it to be either the interest or the duty of the United States to undertake the thankless and enormously expensive task of civilizing and Christianizing some seven or eight millions of Malays. I have been told on good authority—and I have seen some evidence—that the Methodists of the land labored with him in the line of the policy to which he seems to be inclined—although he evidently means to be in a position to disclaim having any policy of his own and to load the whole responsibility upon Congress. But while that is his attitude in his speeches, is he not in fact committing the country to a course from which retreat, even were Congress so disposed, will be well-nigh impossible?

By the way, I had quite a talk with Senator Hoar the other evening. He asserted with much warmth—what I suppose to be true—that but for Bryan and his influence with Democratic Senators, the treaty would not have been ratified. That being so, will it not be quite impossible for him to pose successfully as an anti-imperialist? . . .

But though I put this in type rather than in my own elegant handwriting, to save your eyes and time and patience, I fear I am taking advantage of your welcome note to inflict upon you a reply of most inordinate length. The really important thing, after all, is what you suggest —namely, how to get to Cape Cod and Jim Jones and the bass at the earliest possible moment. I shall get there as soon as my family will permit—probably early in June—and that Jones and the bass will be on hand with their customary cordial greetings I have no reason to doubt.

Have you noticed what a handsome start our Ambassador in London has made? If they take him seriously on the other side, what a nice sort of nation they will deem us to be.

I hear that the Zorn portraits of Mrs. Cleveland and yourself are most successful—also that they are coming on here soon for exhibition—and hope both rumors will prove to be well founded.

My best regards to Mrs. Cleveland and the children, with the same for yourself and, looking forward with eagerness to a personal meeting before many weeks, I am

Sincerely yours,

RICHARD OLNEY.

P. S.

Miles is here—called on me yesterday—to my disappointment in plain clothes and not in his gold uniform. What he wanted to find out or what he did find out, I don't know. I think I found that the presidential bee in his bonnet has swelled to the size of a full-grown peacock.

"The poor old Democratic party!" Mr. Cleveland lamented in reply. "What a spectacle it presents as a tender to Bryanism and nonsense. If there should be a glimmer of returned Democratic sense between now and the next National Convention, it might, as its best (or worst) result, ascend (or descend) from Bryan to Gorman—nothing better in my opinion."

As the currency question upon which Mr. Cleveland had broken with his party was no longer an issue, thanks to the fact that the newly discovered gold fields of the Klondike, the Nome district, Cooks Inlet, etc., had fully met the demands of business, the Democrats began to hope that the ex-President would return to the party fold and work with Bryan to stem the tide of imperialism. But Mr. Cleveland had no intention of fighting in ranks headed by Bryan. He did not wish to command, but if he followed it must be some other leader than the Prophet of Free Silver. Of this his letters left no doubt.

"Don't you in these days," he wrote to Dickinson, on November 11th, "sometimes pinch yourself to see if you are awake, when you contemplate so-called Democratic management? I actually find myself wondering whether or not those who are leading us do not deliberately intend to assassinate the organization, and bury it completely out of sight and for all time."

Princeton, N. J.
February 7, 1900.

My dear Mr. Shepard:
Your letter is just at hand. I have not sufficiently recovered from a tedious disability to permit my attendance at the dinner appointed for next Saturday evening.

Perhaps I ought not to add anything to this; and yet I feel that I would not be candid if I suppressed the further statement, that even though the obstacle I have mentioned were not in the way, I should still be constrained to avoid appearing as a somber figure at the feast. This is written under the influence of so strong a desire to see true Democracy rehabilitated that it outweighs every other wish. It is written, too, I beg you to believe, uninfluenced by the least feeling of personal irritation or resentment.

Considered in the light of judgment and expediency, I am satisfied you are wrong in suggesting my presence at your meeting of conciliation. Thousands of those who have struggled to maintain the true Democratic faith, may be forgiven by the apostles of a newly-invented Democracy; but it seems that I am as yet beyond the pale of honorable condonation.

Prominent among your guests of honor, there will be those who lose no occasion, on the floor of Congress or elsewhere, to repudiate me as a Democrat, and to swell the volume of "jeers" and "laughter" that greet the mention of my name in that connection. Perhaps they are justified; but if I have sinned against Democracy, I am ignorant of my sin; and in any event, my love of country and party will not permit me to sue for forgiveness while being dragged behind the chariot of Bryanism. I know your motives are pure and your purposes exalted. Have I not written something, that should challenge your thought, in support of my opinion that I would be an ill-selected guest at your dinner?

If a movement shall be there inaugurated tending toward a revival of true Democracy, I shall be glad that I have taken no risk of interrupting it. If it should lead to loading more securely upon our party the fatal burdens of the Chicago platform and Bryanism, I shall be glad to have had no part nor lot in the matter.

Yours very sincerely,
GROVER CLEVELAND.

HON. EDWARD M. SHEPARD,
    Brooklyn, N.Y.

His letters were equally denunciatory of McKinley and the Republicans who seemed to him, he said, likely "to get their feet into the trough and upset it." Even the signing of the Currency Bill on March 14, 1900, which legalized the gold standard, fixed the reserve at $150,-000,000, and authorized the Secretary of the Treasury to protect it by effective bond issues, did not restore his confidence in McKinley. It seemed only to deepen his resentment that it had been left to the Republicans thus to serve the country while his own party was "in the hands of charlatans and put to the ignoble use of aiding personal ambition."

"The political situation is too much for me—that is, I cannot put it before me in any shape for satisfactory contemplation," he wrote to Olney on June 25th. "I see Massachusetts' sweet-scented 'scholar in politics' played true to his despicable nature at Philadelphia. As for our own party, the old Adam occasionally dominates me, to the extent of prompting me to second the suggestion of a queer old woman who said a few days ago, anent the *Herald's* suggestion that I run for President, 'Let them that got into the scrape, get out of it.'"

And so, he sought to absorb his faculties in academic activities, and to hold aloof from politics. But politics, in one form or another, inevitably crept in, though sometimes unawares. Richard Watson Gilder has left this account of such an occasion:

"Stayed at Westland, Saty., 25th to Tues., 28th, '99.

"Sunday night I brought Prof. W. W. [Woodrow Wilson] down to the house, wanting him to talk with the President on the subject W. is thinking and writing about—namely, high politics and the relation of statesmanship to practical partisanship, etc. The Professor wants to arrive at a working theory—to set forth considerations which will make it easier for men of conscience to remain in touch with the machinery of party. G. C. said that it was sometimes perplexing to draw the line, to know how far one could go in yielding to the views of others. . . . After W. W. went, G. C. entered into details."

On June 29th, William Elroy Curtis drew the following picture for the readers of the Chicago *Record:*

"Ex-President Cleveland is living a quiet, dignified life at Princeton in a congenial atmosphere and apparent contentment. He has plenty of time for study and reflection; he can command the society of many learned and agreeable men whose political views are more or less sympathetic, if not similar, to his own; he can accept consultation cases from New York firms and corporations that pay big fees and thus make an income sufficient for his wants; he can receive a sufficient amount of deference, adulation, and honor to satisfy his pride and keep his name before the public, and can have all the fun he needs watching the pranks of the students—all this without going out of Princeton; and what more can an ex-President ask for? The chaplains pray for him; the university professors quote from his public papers in their lectures to the students and hold him up before them as an eminent example; he is himself a member of the faculty, occupies the chair of 'lecturer on public affairs,' and the students admit him to the general circle of fun and good fellowship, which is the most gratifying, no doubt, to a man of his sentiment and sense of humor of all his experiences here.

"Whenever anything happens to excite a demonstration the ex-President is always remembered. The other evening when the youngest class in college, having completed their annual examinations, were celebrating their promotion from freshmen to sophomores in a rather boisterous way, their procession marched from the residence of President Patton to Mr. Cleveland's modest home. He heard them coming—the entire town could trace their movements by the unearthly noise they made—and was standing on the veranda when they reached his house. They gave him the college yell, as they always do, and he responded with a pleasant little speech, congratulating them upon the onward step they had taken, wishing them a successful course in the university and successful careers in after life, and thanking them for calling upon him.

"When the Princeton baseball nine defeated Yale the entire body of students in their enthusiasm marched to his house and let him congratulate them and the university upon the victory. 'I wish I could give the Princeton yell, boys,' he said, 'but, as I can't, you must give it for me. Now, together, with a will!' And thus he maintains an intimate and sympathetic relation with 1,200 or 1,500 boys that keeps him young and is good for both sides. . . .

"On all formal occasions Mr. Cleveland appears with the rest of the faculty in a mortar-board cap, a silk gown, a hood lined with orange, which is the university color, and a band of purple, which denotes a doctor of laws."

When the Democratic National Convention assembled at Kansas City on July 4th, it manifested little desire to tempt the old leader from the enfolding academic shades. Instead it nominated Bryan by acclamation and, although making anti-imperialism the chief issue, reaffirmed and indorsed the principles of the Chicago platform of 1896, specifically demanding "the free and unlimited coinage of silver and gold at the present legal ratio of 16 to 1, and without waiting for the aid or consent of any other nation."

So overwhelming was Mr. Cleveland's disappointment at this outcome, that for several months he ceased to discuss public questions, even with his intimate friends. During those dark days, the darkest of all his life, his fish and his family were his consolation. Day after day, he hid himself in some quiet cove of Buzzards Bay, starting at dawn, with "Brad" and some chosen companion, Joe Jefferson, Dean West, Professor McClanahan, the Commodore, or some other member of the Poverty Club, not too closely associated with political memories. When the last ounce of joy had been extracted from his favorite nooks where bottom fish abound, he would troll for blue fish until, wearied at last, he landed at his little wooden wharf, climbed the grassy knoll to the privacy of his home, a quarter of a mile from the nearest neighbor, and sought the never-failing cheerfulness of wife and children, who alone had power to make endurable his St. Helena.

Amid the sadness of that summer of 1900, each mail brought from his friends requests for political advice, and from his foes indignant demands that he aid the party which had thrice honored him with its highest honor, while the newspapers gossiped over the question, "Why does he not speak?" Though declining to enlighten his enemies, the general public, or the press, he continued to state his views to his intimate and trusted friends. To Harmon he wrote:

Gray Gables, Buzzards Bay, Mass.
July 17, 1900.

Personal

My dear Mr. Harmon:

I was very glad to hear from you—though it is difficult to write as full and frank a reply as I would like.

Letters similar to yours come daily to me from all classes and conditions of men, who still love the old faith, and who cannot plainly see the path of duty. So with the arrival of every mail I have a season of cursing the criminals who have burglarized and befouled the Democratic Home.

I have refrained from replying to those letters, because I have not been forgiven by Mr. Bryan for lack of support in 1896; and *pending his pardon,* have no standing in the new Democracy, and cannot therefore speak from that standpoint; and if I should speak according to the principles and teachings of the old Democracy, the notions of the rank and file of the party are so mistaken and confused, that the charge against me of ingratitude, and other accusations and abuse, would do as much or more harm than good.

Of course the "old Adam" rebels against the demagogue and insolent crusader, whose title to Democracy is far from unquestioned, but who notwithstanding assumes to say what Democracy is, and to grant certificates of membership. It is humiliating to feel that Democrats who were fighting its battles before Bryan was born should be obliged to sue to him for credentials; and as a condition of obtaining them forego all the political beliefs of former days. But personal feelings should be sacrificed if by doing so the country can be saved from disaster.

As between imperialism and a continued struggle against sound money, you and many other good and patriotic Democrats, see more danger in the first. The latter and much more trouble we would surely get with Bryan. How certain can you be that he would save you from imperialism? What did he do towards that end when the treaty of peace was before the Senate; and how do you know what such an acrobat would do on that question if his personal ambition was in the balance?

My feeling is that the safety of the country is in the rehabilitation of the old Democratic party. It would be a difficult task to do this, at the end of four years of a Bryan administration and its absurdities, for which the Democratic party would be held responsible. With the defeat of Bryanism and the sham Democratic organization gathered about him, and his and its disappearance in the darkness of aroused Democracy's scorn and contempt, the old guard untainted with either Bryanism or McKinleyism could gather together the forces—checking, through fear of the indomitable force of *true* Democracy, Republican excesses and promising to the country the conservation and safety of Democratic principles.

Bear in mind that McKinleyism has not so far committed itself concerning the treatment and disposition of our new possessions, that it could not be frightened into decency by the organization of an opposition resting upon sane principle, solid character, and substantial appeal to the sense and judgment of our people.

I am afraid that the Republicans cannot be dislodged until Bryanism and all in its train is abandoned if not expressly repudiated; this cannot be done until new men are at the helm of the party; and when such new men are called for, it seems to me those most useful and acceptable will be those who now decline Bryanism because it is not Democracy, and Republicanism because it is in every way and at all times un-Democratic.

When the collapse of Bryanism comes, the rank and file, who have been deceived and misled, will in my opinion look for just such leaders. I shall remain an intensely anxious looker-on. The activities will fall on such men as you.

I have written you my thoughts as I have to no other person. I may be all wrong, but if I am I don't intend to influence others to do wrong too. I am quite happy in political exile—or should be if I did not love my country so well. I will only add that I am not in favor of an independent Democratic ticket; and further that what I have written is for you alone.

Give our love to Mrs. Harmon and believe me

Yours very sincerely,

GROVER CLEVELAND.

HON. JUDSON HARMON,
Cincinnati, Ohio.

Early in the fall, the Baltimore *Sun* called his attention to the fact that Mr. Olney had expressed the view "that the best interests of the country again require . . . the triumph of the Democratic party, despite the defects which he recognizes in its platform, and its leadership," and asked for Mr. Cleveland's opinion on the subject, "strictly confidential, or as matter for publication, as you may desire." The same mail brought an indignant letter from John P. Irish: "Mr. Olney and Mr. Wilson may lie down with Mr. Hearst and Morgan, Altgeld, Towne, and Eugene Debs, if they wish. I decline, though I lie alone. . . . I prefer that you shall go into history as the last Democratic President of the Republic, rather than that Bryan shall go there as the first Populist President. . . . The party in whose conventicles your name is mentioned only to be hissed is not the Democratic party." At once Mr. Cleveland answered the *Sun's* question, but his reply was not for publication:

Buzzards Bay,
Sept. 11, 1900.

MESSRS. A. S. ABELL CO.

Gentlemen:

I hope that I have not grown heedless of any duty I owe my countrymen; but I am not inclined to declare publicly my thoughts and opinions on the political situation. This I supposed was quite clearly expressed in my note recently published in the New York *Herald*.

For a number of years I have been abused and ridiculed by professed Democrats, because I have not hesitated to declare that Bryanism is not Democracy. I have had the consolation of seeing those who professed my belief run to cover, and of noting a more headlong Democratic rush after anti-Democratic vagaries. My opinions have not changed, why then should I speak when bedlam is at its height? Perhaps I am wrong in my opinions; at any rate I should say unwelcome things; and all to no purpose except to add to the volume of abuse, which *undefended,* I have so long borne.

I received this morning a clipping from a German newspaper containing my note to the *Herald* with this comment: "That was wise. That part of the American people who most need instruction at this time would not listen to Grover Cleveland, but the only thanks they would give him for his well-meant advice would be to open upon him a new bombardment of poison and dirt; the other part do not need to be taught by anyone how to vote rightly next November." That's about it.

You are not, however, to suppose for a moment that I could be induced to do anything in aid of McKinleyism or any phase of Republicanism. I suppose it is a case of being "damned if I do and damned if I don't," but I have made up my mind that I am entitled to decline enlistment in the war between Bryanism and McKinleyism.

This communication is strictly confidential. It is written because I cannot ignore your letter.

Yours truly,

GROVER CLEVELAND.

Five days later he poured out his heart to Bissell.

Buzzards Bay,
Sept. 16, 1900.

My dear Bissell:

I was very glad to get your letter of the 8th. Somehow, in these days, I think I am more than ever glad to hear from old friends.

The President wrote me asking if I would accept the appointment as one of the arbitrators under the Hague Convention. In reply I wrote that my disinclination to assume any duty of a public nature was so great, that I should ask him to permit me to decline the proffered honor. He replied urging me to accept the place, and informed me that Ex-President Harrison had accepted, &c. Oscar Straus, who was then in Washington, also wrote seconding the President's request; and Secretary Gage wrote to Hamlin in the same way, and his letter was sent to me by Hamlin. Notwithstanding all this, I felt constrained to adhere to my determination; and a number of days before the receipt of your letter, I had definitely disposed of the matter, by writing to the President that upon a re-examination of the subject I failed to persuade myself that I ought to accept the appointment.

I think the conclusions arrived at by the Hague Conference were lame and disappointing ones. I did not care to be one of four men, the majority of whom would probably be quite under the lead of Mr. Harrison; and in my peculiar relation to the organization of my party, I thought it better not to hold a place under the appointment of the present administration.

The pending campaign has brought upon me much unhappiness. First there came numerous letters from apparently honest Democrats in every part of the country, asking my advice as to how they should vote. These have been largely succeeded by persuasions and demands from self-styled rock-ribbed Democrats, that I should publicly declare myself in favor of the ticket of the "party which has so greatly honored me"; and in many cases the insistence is made that a word from me would insure the success of the ticket. With these came appeals from anti-imperialists, asking all sorts of things.

Through all this I have maintained silence, except to say that I have nothing to say. To four letters, I think, from people I could not ignore, I have written my views. I cannot write or speak favorably of Bryanism. I do not regard it as Democracy. But many good party men do. I cannot conceive that anything I might say would better conditions or change results. It would, however, add to the volume of abuse which for a long time has been hurled at my "defenseless head," and by a bare possibility destroy an opportunity for usefulness in the future.

I have some idea that the party may before long be purged of Bryanism, and that the rank and file, surprised at their wanderings, and enraged at their false leaders, will be anxious to return to the old faith; and in their desire to reorganize under the old banners will welcome the counsel of those who have never yielded to disastrous heresy. This may never be; or it may be that, however complete the return, those who now refuse to aid in the struggle made in the name of Democracy, whether for right or wrong, will still incur Democratic hatred and discontent. Still it is worth all, to be conscious that at all times one has been consistent and patriotically Democratic.

I have seen Olney but once this summer. I put the matter before him as I have to you. He expressed his inclination to vote for Bryan, and suggested that those who did so might better secure the confidence of the party in the future. He may be right on this proposition, as *there may have been something more in his mind than there was in mine.* It seems to me strange that a man who in my judgment is largely responsible, through his *Atlantic* article, for the doctrine of expansion and consequent imperialism, should now be so impressed with the fatal tendency of imperialism, as to be willing to take Bryanism as an antidote. But the times are as full of strange and untoward things as they can be; and no one can foretell the issue.

I cannot believe Bryanism will win. I am sure Democracy if it was in the field would win; and in any event we shall the most of us, I think, be surprised at the number who will follow the spurious banner to the polls. . . .

Yours very sincerely,
GROVER CLEVELAND.

The idea of forming a third party he disapproved as probably unnecessary and certainly untimely. "I am a strong Democrat," he wrote to A. B. Farquhar, on September 20th, "and my great affliction is that the present so-called Democratic organization does not represent Democratic principles as I understand them. I am not, therefore, perhaps, a very good adviser in the premises. I believe, however, if the organization of a third party becomes hereafter a strong movement, and is thought necessary by strong men, the present effort will not be a factor, but will be entirely ignored and passed over. . . . If such an emergency should arise, I am afraid identification with an insignificant and inopportune movement *now*, might impair usefulness that would be greatly needed *then*. The projectors of the present effort have been so very unfortunate, and the time left for action is so short, that I do not see how any national good can result from it."

Toward the end of September, Mr. John S. Green, a gold Democrat of Kentucky, sent him a copy of the letter to Chicago business men, written on April 13, 1895, denouncing Bryan. With it came the questions: "Are you still opposed to the Chicago platform, and do you advise your old friends to support Bryan and his present platform?" To which Mr. Cleveland replied:

Buzzards Bay, Mass.
October 7, 1900.

JOHN S. GREEN, ESQ.
Dear Sir:

I have received your letter enclosing a copy of my letter written more than five years ago to the business men of Chicago. I had not seen it in a long time; but it seems to me I could not state the case better at this time if I should try.

I have not changed my opinion as then expressed in the least.

Yours truly,
GROVER CLEVELAND.

This correspondence, having been given to the press by Mr. Green, was at once explained by the Bryanites as referring to currency alone. Currency, they argued, is no longer the vital issue; imperialism has taken its place, and upon the question of imperialism Mr. Cleveland and Mr. Bryan are one. Therefore Mr. Cleveland favors Mr. Bryan over Mr. McKinley. This conclusion, though perhaps logical, was without a shred of justification, as the following confidential letter makes abundantly clear:

Princeton, *Oct. 12, 1900.*

My dear Mr. Dickinson:

. . . I am still pestered to death nearly with appeals "to come out for Bryan" and for advice "how to vote." It is surprising how many letters I receive purporting to come from people who opposed Bryan in 1896 and are supporting him now. A comparative few of my correspondents ask me to oppose Bryan publicly. Since, however, I cannot do what the large majority desires, and since I am very far from wishing to aid McKinleyism affirmatively, I have thought I might satisfy my conscience and avoid the accusation of open and pronounced ingratitude by keeping silence. This is a thing very hard for me to do at a time when I am so clear in my convictions; and occasionally I am very restive. You see there are millions of our fellow citizens who believe that the organization now supporting Bryan is the same that on three occasions nominated and supported me; and it is hard for them to reconcile my silence, and would be more difficult to reconcile my open and avowed opposition, with a proper appreciation on my part, of the honors and favors freely accorded me by Democracy in the past.

On the other hand, the day I hope is not far distant when sanity will succeed insanity and the Democratic masses will cry out for deliverance from Bryanism and a resurrection of true Democratic faith. If that day dawns, there must be those untainted with heresy to hold aloft the standard. I do not assume for a moment that I shall or can be one of these; but perchance I may encourage and rejoice. You can hardly believe [how] deeply I am concerned lest I should miss doing that which is best for my country and—what in the present emergency seems to me almost the same—best for my party.

I know you will pardon this long uninvited letter. I would be glad if you could give me any advice or comfort.

Yours very sincerely,
GROVER CLEVELAND.

HON. D. M. DICKINSON,
    Detroit, Mich.

If more evidence be needed, it is found in another letter to Dickinson, written a few days later, which declared: "I don't see how an honest man, holding the views I then expressed, can favor Bryanism now." Also when Eckles, his former Comptroller of the Currency, and close personal friend, wrote from Chicago: "The followers of Bryan . . . are attempting to deceive honest and respectable Democrats to the support of Bryan by saying you are so much against McKinleyism that . . . you are accepting Bryanism," he declined to publish a statement, and when the Democratic Headquarters in New York, on October 21st, sent him an S. O. S., he answered: "My silence is the best contribution I can make."

A few days before the election certain of his enemies played their last card. On October 29th, a reporter named Black brought to the office of the Philadelphia *Times* what he declared to be an interview recently granted him at Princeton by ex-President Cleveland. He asked no compensation for the article, which circumstance should have aroused suspicion, and in the absence of the editor, Mr. A. K. McClure, the interview was passed and printed. It startled both parties with its astonishing declarations:

"Grover Cleveland . . . in an interview which I had with him, predicted a landslide to William Jennings Bryan. . . . Mr. Cleveland said: 'My young man, you will see a landslide for Bryan the morning after election; of that I am confident.' To this I replied that the indications, according to Republican leaders, are favorable to McKinley, but he quickly retorted: 'Of course they are; that is policy. What I tell you is my private opinion.'"

There was much more in the same vein, intended to create the impression that Grover Cleveland was back in the Democratic fold, eagerly waiting a Democratic victory which would place Bryan in the White House.

When he saw the interview in the morning papers of October 30th, Mr. Cleveland issued a prompt denial: "The whole thing from beginning to end is an absolute lie without the least foundation or shadow of truth. I have never uttered a word to any human being that affords the least pretext for such a mendacious statement."

Upon which Black as promptly made the following deposition:

Philadelphia, *Oct. 30, 1900.*

I, Robert J. Black, had an interview with Grover Cleveland, on the 23rd day of October, 1900, in his home in Princeton, N. J., and during a lengthy talk with him in his parlor he told me that he favored Bryan, and said: "My boy, you will see a landslide for Bryan on the day after election," that he also said "Bryan was a great orator."

R. J. BLACK, Vinton, Iowa.

Witness: JOHN A. BRADLEY.

Sworn and subscribed before me this
30th day of October, 1900.

JOHN A. THORNTON, Magistrate of Court No. 23.

During the remainder of the campaign, this pretended interview continued to be used by unscrupulous politicians, but there is no evidence that it was with the connivance of responsible national leaders of the Democratic party.

When the election of 1900 was over, the most competent critics felt that Bryan had led his last charge, and that as a candidate he was "without hope, unless the [next] convention should be made up of political lunatics," as a Washington correspondent of the New York *Times* phrased it.

Theodore Roosevelt, the newly elected Vice-President, expressed his personal appreciation of Mr. Cleveland's part in this result in the following letter:

Private.

State of New York,
Executive Chamber,
Albany,

Nov. 22nd, 1900.

HON. GROVER CLEVELAND,
Princeton, N. J.

My dear President Cleveland:

During the last campaign I grew more and more to realize the very great service you had rendered to the whole country by what you did about free silver. As I said to a Republican audience in South Dakota, I think your letter on free silver prior to your second nomination was as bold a bit of honest writing as I have ever seen in American public life. And more than anything else it put you in the position of doing for the American public in this matter of free silver what at that time no other man could have done. I was delighted to find that Governor Shaw of Iowa had just the same feeling about it that I had and made an even fuller acknowledgment of the debt due to you in one of his speeches at which I was present. I think now we have definitely won out on the free silver business and therefore I think you are entitled to thanks and congratulations.

With regards, and best wishes both for Mrs. Cleveland and yourself, I am

Very sincerely yours,

THEODORE ROOSEVELT.

Mr. Cleveland, too, believed that McKinley's re-election meant an end of the menace of free silver; but, through the columns of the Atlanta *Constitution,* he assured his friends of the South that William McKinley and Theodore Roosevelt were not President and Vice-President by virtue of his vote. If, on the other hand, he voted for Bryan, he violated the conscience and the desire of Grover Cleveland, and it is, therefore, safe to assume that he cast no vote in 1900.

On April 27, 1901, he wrote to Dickinson: "It is a little comforting to see the end of Bryanism in politics, but on the Democratic side I am constantly asking, 'What next?'" Although living in Princeton, in almost daily touch with the only Democrat destined within a quarter of a century to stand as the victorious leader of Democracy, the idea that Wilsonism was next never crossed his mind.

CHAPTER XI

THE TURN OF THE TIDE

"Unswerving loyalty to duty, constant devotion to truth, and a clear conscience will overcome every discouragement and surely lead the way to usefulness and high achievement."
—GROVER CLEVELAND.

EARLY in September, 1901, a small company of childhood friends of Vice President Roosevelt received on their dahabeah on the Nile the startling news that President McKinley had been shot by a half-crazed fanatic at Buffalo. "He will not recover," remarked one of the party. "We all know the Roosevelt luck." A few days later, upon the assurance of the physicians that the President was making good progress, Colonel Roosevelt left Washington for a wilderness journey of rest and recreation in little frequented parts of the Adirondacks. On September 13th he reached Lake Colton, near the summit of Mount Marcy, accessible only by means of a human messenger. Toward noon one such arrived, a mountain guide sent to bring the news that the President was sinking rapidly.

Within a few hours Colonel Roosevelt had returned to the house where he had left his family, and by midnight, attended by none save the driver, he was descending the mountain in a buckboard, heedless of rain, darkness, and almost impassable roads. Before dawn he had covered the thirty miles to the nearest railway station, to find a special train awaiting him, and a despatch which announced that once more a Vice President had suc-

ceeded to the office of Chief Executive. When he reached
Buffalo, the Cabinet was assembled, and within a few
moments he had taken the solemn oath which made him,
at the age of forty-two, the youngest of American
Presidents.

From his retreat at Princeton, Mr. Cleveland
watched the career of the new Chief Executive, at first
with sympathy, but soon with growing trepidation.
Although anxious to do Mr. Roosevelt justice, he found
it difficult to appreciate his sterling qualities, being constantly offended by methods which he considered wholly
out of keeping with the dignity that should surround the
office of President. Nor did he come under the wonderful magic of the Colonel's personality. His own slower
mind mistook Roosevelt's rapidity for superficiality, and
he interpreted the latter's instinctively dramatic appeals
to the people as the works of the demagogue. Temper-
amentally, the two were as far apart as the poles. Roosevelt was mercurial, Cleveland was phlegmatic. Roosevelt
was quick to form friendships or to conceive enmities.
Cleveland did nothing in haste. Roosevelt was ready of
speech, whether written or spoken, while a speech to
Mr. Cleveland was like a mountain in the pathway, to
be laboriously surmounted. But both were courageous
and resourceful in danger, loyal and true to the traditions
of America in the face of temptation, not self-seeking in
public work, and of sterling honesty.

President Roosevelt's admiration for Mr. Cleveland
was almost boyish. "I always regarded him as a fresh-
man regards a senior," he once declared, and when
leaving instructions to his biographer, Joseph Bucklin
Bishop, he said: "I wish you would put in all the letters
of mine to him. I was very fond of the old fellow."

About a year after Mr. Roosevelt's accession to power,

began the great coal strike of 1902, which offered him a chance to employ Mr. Cleveland's personal influence for an important public service. On May 12th, 145,000 coal miners ceased work, in obedience to the call of the United Mine Workers of America, under the leadership of John Mitchell. Throughout the summer the owners sought in vain to replace the strikers and resume the work of mining. As August advanced it became apparent that a coal famine must follow unless effective action was taken, for, though the mine owners had an abundance of coal within easy reach of the public, they were deliberately holding it out of the market in the hope that public opinion would drive the strikers to submission. They "had banded together, and positively refused to take any steps looking toward an accommodation," as President Roosevelt expressed it. The sympathy of the public was with the strikers, and the opinion was freely expressed that the federal government should seize the mines and produce the coal.

As Mr. Cleveland watched conditions, he became increasingly uneasy, being uncertain what use President Roosevelt might make of such a situation. "If the coal strike and some other matters do not change soon," he wrote to Commodore Benedict on August 24th, "I believe there will be serious trouble before we are six months older. I don't like to see so many things depending on one man's nod." Far from assuming unauthorized power, however, President Roosevelt was as determined as Mr. Cleveland could have been to adhere to the strictest constitutional limitations. "I had in theory," he later wrote, "no power to act directly unless the Governor of Pennsylvania or the Legislature . . . should request me, as Commander-in-Chief of the United States, to intervene and keep order."

On September 26th, New York closed her schools to save her scant supply of coal, the price of which was already almost prohibitory. By October, retail dealers were demanding $30 a ton, and the President was being bombarded with prayers for federal intervention.

In the absence of an appeal from the governors of the coal states, however, Mr. Roosevelt decided to try the rôle of peacemaker. He accordingly sent to the presidents of the anthracite coal companies the following telegram:

I should greatly like to see you on Friday next, October 3rd, at 11 o'clock A. M., here in Washington, in regard to the failure of the coal supply, which has become a matter of vital concern to the whole nation. I have sent a similar despatch to Mr. John Mitchell, President of the United Mine Workers of America.

THEODORE ROOSEVELT.

The meeting was an excited one, and much strong language was used. Mr. Roosevelt himself said of it: "There was only one person there who bore himself like a gentleman and it wasn't I." Later, in his Autobiography, he stated that it was John Mitchell who "kept his temper admirably and showed to much advantage." Mitchell readily agreed to arbitration, stipulating only that the President should have power to name the Commission, but the operators refused to arbitrate, insisting instead that the President aid them in breaking the strike. The session lasted throughout the afternoon, and, at the end, the operators boasted that they had "turned down both the miners and the President."

The next morning, on his way from Gray Gables to Princeton, Mr. Cleveland read in the New York *Herald* an account of the conference, under the heading: "President's Coal Conference a Complete Failure; Operators Reject Mitchell's Arbitration Offer."

Arrived at Princeton, he sent the President the following letter:

Princeton, *Oct. 4, 1902.*

MY DEAR MR. PRESIDENT:

I read in the paper this morning on my way home from Buzzards Bay, the newspaper account of what took place yesterday between you and the parties directly concerned in the coal strike.

I am so surprised and "stirred up" by the position taken by the contestants that I cannot refrain from making a suggestion which perhaps I would not presume to make if I gave the subject more thought. I am especially disturbed and vexed by the tone and substance of the operators' deliverances.

It cannot be that either side, after your admonition to them, cares to stand in their present plight, if any sort of an avenue, even for temporary escape, is suggested to them.

Has it ever been proposed to them that the indignation and dangerous condemnation now being launched against both their houses might be allayed by the production of coal in an amount, or for a length of time, sufficient to serve the necessities of consumers, leaving the parties to the quarrel, after such necessities are met, to take up the fight again where they left off "without prejudice" if they desire?

This would eliminate the troublesome consumer and public; and perhaps both operators and miners would see enough advantage in that to induce them to listen to such a proposition as I have suggested.

I know there would be nothing philosophical or consistent in all this; but my observation leads me to think that when quarreling parties are both in the wrong, and are assailed with blame so nearly universal, they will do strange things to save their faces.

If you pardon my presumption in thus writing you, I promise never to do it again. At any rate it may serve as an indication of the anxiety felt by millions of our citizens on the subject.

I have been quite impressed by a pamphlet I have lately read, by a Mr. Champlin of Boston, entitled, I believe, "The Coal Mines and the People." I suppose you have seen it.

Very respectfully,
Your obedient servant,
GROVER CLEVELAND.

To the President.

A more detailed statement of the thoughts aroused by the situation is contained in the following undated manuscript found among his papers, and showing many revisions:

"The stubborn and serious disagreements that have broken out from time to time in our industrial localities between employers of labor and those in their service who work with their hands, have given rise to much discussion concerning their origin and the blame for their existence. . . . They must be regarded as the outcome of a persistent effort on the part of labor to secure at any cost, a larger share of the fruits of American opportunity, and opposition to these efforts by employers, as based upon demands unreasonable in substance and unjustifiable in method of enforcement. In the meantime the situation they invite and their frequent accompaniment of strike, lockout, boycott, paralysis of production and interruption of important undertakings, inflict loss and injury upon numerous citizens absolutely innocent of the least complicity in these contentions and utter strangers to all they directly involve. . . .

"Wherever our sympathies may be, we can hardly escape the conviction that labor has made demands, adopted policies and permitted if not encouraged conduct, which cannot be justified; nor can we safely deny that in too many instances, employers of labor have been heedless of the just and reasonable claims of their employees, regardless of their interest and disdainful of their presentation of grievances. . . .

"Manifestly it cannot be necessary to dwell upon the sad consequences visited upon the actual participants in these labor quarrels. Those who run may read these consequences, in the pinching deprivation that enters the homes of our working men; in their idleness and its malevolent influence on character and habits; and in the morbid discontent and irritation that comes from brooding over wrongs.—Nor is the depressing story less plainly read in the dispiriting loss and perplexity of employers; in their inability to meet contract engagements and trust expectations; in the hardening of their sympathy with the mass of working men, and in their blinding resentment against those whom they accuse of guilty responsibility for afflictive conditions. . . .

"With all our efforts to escape it, the consciousness is forced upon us that neither the liberality and equal advantages of our scheme of government nor the patriotism which is abroad among our people has been found sufficient to prevent the birth and existence of labor disturbances. . . . Human nature when left to its own devices can be so blinded by interest or prejudice, and so strongly led by stereotyped methods of thought, as to be unable, of its own motion, to pass a fair judgment upon the quality of its operations or to correctly define its springs of action.

"These suggestions lead us to recall the ease with which disagreements between individuals are frequently settled, when the parties are brought to a calm review of their differences by a trusted intermediary. . . . No reason can be given why such a course cannot be followed with the same good results when the dispute, instead of merely involving individuals, is between organized working men and their employers. . . .

"The method . . . certainly savors of interference, but only with the consent of the disputants; and in view of the broad interests involved, and the multitude of our people affected by labor disputes, surely as much interference as this ought to be allowed. . . . It is the only remedy within our reach. It embodies every effort but force; and force is not suggested as a real cure by anyone who has studied the situation. . . .

"Any intermediary attempting to bring the parties in difference together for amicable deliberation should be absolutely disinterested and impartial, and should possess the unqualified respect and confidence of all the parties concerned. . . . Beyond doubt some concessions might also be made in advance of conference, which would better prepare the contestants in labor quarrels for friendly discussion. It is quite generally believed by those who would be glad to see the rights and interests of our working men fully recognized, that labor organizations are much too radical in some of their demands and too far-reaching in the objects of their efforts. If these were so far reduced that the claims and demands of labor could be presented to unprejudiced reason as only such as are relevant to its needs, and necessary to the exigencies of its just protection, the way to a peaceful adjustment of their complaints would be made very much easier; and if these organizations could be freed from the suspicion of taking advantage of pending necessities and emergencies in industrial conditions to enforce questionable demands, it would give great encouragement to our conservative citizens who approve the legitimate purposes of labor unions. . . .

"Labor unionism is with us to stay; and whatever the result may be, it has become a permanent element of our industrial system. Its further development must be expected. It behooves us therefore to ask whether this development will be in the direction of more reasonable demands, less menacing methods, and a larger, more conscientious conception of the wide and vital interests affected by the movements of labor, or in the direction of a more sullen insistence upon excessive demands, greater heedlessness of the comfort and prosperity of our people at large, and vindictive and revengeful conduct, instead of protective precautions? . . .

"It has been suggested that it would be well for employers to organize for the purpose of acting together in dealing with labor disputes. Such organization would be useful if prompted by a desire to facilitate pacification and if not allowed to originate and stimulate obstructive resentments, or to keep on constant exhibition an ugly collection of real or supposed wrongs. . . . With organization on both sides of a labor dispute the field for review and deliberation would be so enlarged, and such an aggregate of varied and individual situations would be presented that any conclusion arrived at in adjusting the dispute would be more widely binding and more easily enforceable than any that could be otherwise reached. . . ."

The operators having refused his attempts at mutual agreement, President Roosevelt formed a drastic plan, conceived upon the theory, as he later explained, "that occasionally great national crises arise which call for immediate and vigorous executive action, and that in such cases it is the duty of the President to act upon the theory that he is the steward of the people, bound to assume that he has the legal right to do whatever the needs of the people demand, unless the Constitution or laws explicitly forbid him to do it." Through Senator Quay, he arranged that the Governor of Pennsylvania, at a preconcerted signal, should request federal aid for the coal fields, and that Major-General Schofield should then promptly set troops in motion and seize the mines.

Wishing, however, to avoid this extreme measure if possible, he decided to threaten the operators first with an investigation by a commission so commanding in its personnel as to insure popular support for any verdict it should render. "Ex-President Cleveland's letter . . ." he explained, "gave me the chance to secure him as head of the Arbitration Commission. I at once wrote him, stating that I would very probably have to appoint an Arbitration Commission or Investigating Commission to look into the matter and decide on the rights of the case . . . and that I would ask him to accept the chief place on the Commission. He answered that he would do so."

After sending his reply, Mr. Cleveland proceeded to divest himself of the holdings which he had in the stock of certain coal-carrying railroads, as he was unwilling to be a judge in matters in which he had a personal interest. By this transaction he lost $2,500, and unnecessarily, as it developed.

Had the fictitious millions which the enemy press had brought with him from Washington been real millions, such a sacrifice would have meant nothing. But Mr. Cleveland felt that it was by no means negligible, as he regarded his savings as scarcely sufficient for the dignified maintenance of his family. That his more intimate friends had a similar view is shown by numerous letters offering financial aid, in manners more or less guarded. More than one had suggested nominal business posts with salaries attached, and Andrew Carnegie only a few months before had offered to solve the difficulty by direct financial aid, an offer which Mr. Cleveland declined in the following letter:

Jan. 13, 1902.

MY DEAR MR. CARNEGIE:

I was so touched and overcome by your last letter that it has taken me some time to fit myself to reply to it. You and I both began to really live late in life—that is to say we were late in knowing the blessedness and joy of wife and children, and the homes they made for us. When I remind you of this I have an idea you will understand me better than other friends would, if I say to you that it has been with much anxiety that I have looked the "course of nature" in the face, and contemplated the time when the mother of my children would have to bear the burden of their care and maintenance alone.

I have never written or said as much as this before; but somehow as I have read and reread your letter, it has seemed to me that something of the kind must have been in your mind, and that I ought to be thus frank with you.

So far as the present is concerned, I am getting on I think as well as I deserve. If the law lately introduced in Congress, providing an annuity for ex-Presidents should pass, I would be glad, and would without the slightest compunction avail myself of it. Indeed I think I should nearly feel that I had earned what such a law would give to me.

But how can I ever bring myself to accept the private benefaction you suggest? And how can I take it from you, who in no sense owe me anything, but have always been a disinterested and warm friend? I am asking things of you in these days. I have just asked you to allow me to decline a great honor you sought to confer upon me; and now I ask you to allow me to pull and worry along in my own way—with permission to go to you, when the Fates are so hard with me that I must have a strong friendly hand; and whether I have this permission or not, let me assure you that your kindness and what you have offered to do, will always remain among my most cherished possessions.

> Yours most gratefully
>
> GROVER CLEVELAND.

Armed with Mr. Cleveland's consent to accept a place on his Commission, Mr. Roosevelt now played his trump card. Selecting as his agent the ablest member of his Cabinet, Mr. Elihu Root, Secretary of War, he dispatched him to New York to interview J. Pierpont Morgan, the man best able to influence the actions of the operators. At ten o'clock on the evening of October 11th, a watchful reporter from the New York *Herald* saw a boat put off from the pier and five minutes later a glass showed the Secretary climbing up the side ladder to greet Mr. Morgan, who stood on the deck. But the glass could not give the conversation in which Mr. Root made known the President's plan of an arbitration committee, and announced that upon it among other distinguished names would appear that of a man "whose word would have the ear of the nation, Grover Cleveland."

This warning had the desired effect. The meeting was followed by a hurried gathering of operators, who, the next day, notified the President that they were ready to submit all matters involved to a commission, consisting of one judge of the United States Court, one engineer of the army or navy, one mining expert, one eminent sociologist, and one man experienced in mining and selling coal. As arbitration had been Mr. Mitchell's desire from the beginning, he readily consented, insisting only that one of the commissioners should come from the ranks of labor.

Mr. Cleveland being neither a judge, an engineer, a sociologist nor a mining expert, President Roosevelt sent him the following telegram and letter, and headed the list of commissioners with the name of Judge Gray:

White House, Washington, D. C.
October 15, 1902.

HON. GROVER CLEVELAND
Princeton, N. J.
Strictly personal

Deeply grateful for your letter. Propositions that have been made since have totally changed situation so that I will not have to make the demand upon you which three days ago it seemed I would have to for the interest of the Nation. I thank you most deeply and shall write you at length.

THEODORE ROOSEVELT.

White House,
    Washington.

                                        October 16, 1902.

Personal.

MY DEAR MR. CLEVELAND:

I appreciated so deeply your being willing to accept that it was very hard for me to forego the chance of putting you on the commission. But in order to get the vitally necessary agreement between the operators and miners I found I had to consult their wishes as to the types of men. Of course I knew that it was the greatest relief to you not to be obliged to serve, but I did wish to have you on, in the first place, because of the weight your name would have lent the commission, and in the next place, because of the effect upon our people, and especially upon our young men, of such an example of genuine self-denying patriotism—for, my dear sir, your service would have meant all of this. I do not know whether you understand how heartily I thank you and appreciate what you have done.

                    Faithfully yours,
                            THEODORE ROOSEVELT.

Hon. Grover Cleveland,
    Princeton, N. J.

President Roosevelt's views in regard to the influence of the ex-President's name were in no wise exaggerated. Even when the denunciations of his enemies had been loudest, Mr. Cleveland had had the staunch support of a great body of men who understood and appreciated his struggles to uphold the law of the land, and his public activities of the last few years had but added to the number of these admirers and increased the regard in which he was held by the country at large—political antagonists included. From many were beginning to arise the whisper that Grover Cleveland was again coming back, and that he would lead the Democratic ranks to victory in 1904. "There appears to be a strong and steadily growing sentiment in the Middle Western States in favor of your nomination," wrote Joseph Garretson, of Cincinnati. "The *Times-Star* has made a great effort to investigate this sentiment, and the general tenor of all our correspondents is along the line that you are the only logical candidate in the field."

But Mr. Cleveland brushed all such suggestions impatiently aside. To this letter and the plea for a few words in reply, he sent the following note:

Princeton, February 6, 1903.

JOSEPH GARRETSON, ESQ.
Editor, &c
DEAR SIR:

I have received your letter of the 4th instant asking me on behalf of the *Times-Star* for an expression regarding my intentions as related to the next Democratic nomination for the Presidency.

I cannot possibly bring my mind to the belief that a condition of sentiment exists that makes any expression from me on the subject of the least importance.

Yours very truly,
GROVER CLEVELAND.

This cryptic utterance was interpreted by the press as indicating a spirit of submission should the people call again. "His letter . . . to an Ohio newspaper," commented the New York *Times*, " . . . is taken as an assurance that at the proper time the reformer Buffalonian will enter the field." The papers in other sections, too, took up the theme, and, lacking facts, printed fiction, some stating positively that he would run again, others as positively that he would not. To such as came to his notice Mr. Cleveland dealt out such stinging reproofs as the following:

"Words have been put in my mouth which entirely misrepresent my position in politics. I never said I had retired from active politics to act as the party's adviser. To be thus pictured as an old Brahmin seated in the background and aspiring to manage things my own way is alike distasteful to me and absolutely false as to my true position."

His true position was never in doubt among his friends, to whom he repeatedly declared that no conceivable condition could tempt him back into public life. "There is nothing that presents anything like the same allurement to me," he wrote to Commodore Benedict, "as a retreat somewhere that would give me freedom from nagging annoyances and exhausting importunities." And later: "It seems to me . . . that I have expressed myself with sufficient clearness to enable all who believe in my sincerity, to understand how settled is my determination to spend the remainder of my life in the ranks of private citizenship. I can understand why the dirty little scoundrel who is allowed to scatter filth through the columns of the Louisville *Courier-Journal,* and a few vile imitators, pretend to understand me; and I am not inclined to give them the satisfaction of plainer speech. I doubt if the time will ever come when a more explicit declaration will be necessary for the satisfaction of my friends and the decent people of the country. When in my judgment that time has arrived, such a declaration, in my own way, will be forthcoming."

Had he known, as others knew, that the tide of public

sentiment had turned toward him, he would doubtless have been more patient with those who persisted in the belief that he would be a candidate for the fourth time in 1904, for even Tammany Hall showed a realization of the fact that this political Samson's hair was growing. At the Jefferson banquet on April 13, 1903, eight hundred braves, who had evinced little interest when letters from Hill and Bryan were read, leaped to their feet with cheers for "the next President," when the toastmaster read a simple note of regrets from Grover Cleveland. The cheers of Tammany Hall, however, affected him no more than had its curses. He believed that the people's faces were turned from him, and the belief was gall and wormwood.

But a revelation was in store for him, and at no distant date. With great reluctance he had yielded to the demands of his friends and had promised to attend the opening of the Louisiana Purchase Exposition at St. Louis, on April 30th. Before leaving he wrote to ask Mr. Dickinson's advice as to whether the time had arrived to announce his determination not to run again. To which Mr. Dickinson replied: "I cannot say what you would like me to say. . . . I feel that it ought not to be said just now, much as you are assailed by the Ass of Nebraska and others less worthy than he. . . . Recently in the South, I heard his name spoken, and spoke it when not otherwise called out, and it was invariably received with a cuss. . . . Men of good standing . . . who were regular in 1896 and 1900, *as I know,* are saying that they have been Democratic all their lives but 'Bryanism was not Democracy and I helped kill it,' and so on. The President's popularity [too] is waning remarkably." The letter urged him not to drive his friends into the arms of the Republicans: "If you speak now," it declared, "just about that will happen."

Acting upon this advice, Mr. Cleveland continued to deny to the public any declaration of his intention, and on the appointed day started to St. Louis. All along the line, in the various states through which the train passed, the entire population seemed to have gathered to see and cheer the ex-President, but their enthusiasm only puzzled him; he did not know that the day of the shadow had passed. That knowledge was soon to come. Standing beside President Roosevelt on the platform at St. Louis, he received in one great thunder of applause the whole-hearted plaudits of his fellow countrymen, and the sound was a healing balm to his wounded spirit. The scene is described in the following editorial sent him a few days later from Electra, Texas.

"Mr. Cleveland so far overshadowed President Roosevelt in popular applause, when both stood on the same platform, as to make the latter feel aggrieved. With every department of the administration on the platform, and a former Republican National Committee chairman acting as the spokesman of the occasion; with Governor Odell, of New York, at his feet, and Senator Hanna at his back; and with a circle of distinguished Republicans all around him, Mr. Roosevelt, the President, ought easily to have drawn out the most vociferous and con-tinued applause when he stood before the multitude at St. Louis last Thursday. Yet when he sat down and Grover Cleveland, the private citizen, arose, the crowd, on the platform, and out in front, so instantly and so vigorously applauded, and so wildly manifested delight, that the President's greetings a few minutes before seemed like a whisper compared with a long-continued peal of thunder. It was an unexpected, instantaneous, generous, unmistakable ovation. It indicated clearly the state of the public mind toward the ex-President. It was a revelation to the politicians. It was an eye-opener to the anti-Cleveland Democrats. It was a warning to the Roosevelt Republicans. It was plainly the voice of public sentiment, and it thrust Grover Cleveland to the front as the strongest man in American politics to-day."

This editorial bears the marks of contemporary politics, and is, therefore, unfair to the memory of the great statesman whom it sought to belittle in order to gain additional glory for another great statesman whom it rightly desired to honor. Mr. Roosevelt himself, several years later, described the scene with as frank an enthusiasm as that shown by the editor in question: "I was at St. Louis as President when Mr. Cleveland, then a plain private citizen, arose to make an address in the great hall of the Exposition; and no one who was there will ever forget the extraordinary reception given him by the scores of thousands present. It was an extraordinary testimony to the esteem and regard in which he was held, an extraordinary testimony to the fact that the American people had not forgotten him, and, looking back, had recognized in him a man who with straightforward directness had sought to do all in his power to serve their interests."

To Mr. Cleveland, more than to any other soul in that vast assemblage, this overwhelming reception at the hands of an audience gathered from every part of the world was a revelation. Suddenly, without a shaft of light to warn him of its coming, the full noonday sun had broken through the black clouds that for years had covered his sky from horizon to horizon. At last he knew that the tide had turned; that the people whom he loved, and whom he had served with so unselfish and so untiring a devotion were again his friends. The joy that came to him with the knowledge lasted throughout the remainder of his life. "From that moment," declared his wife, "he was a different man."

CHAPTER XII

THE ELECTION OF 1904

"Men and times change, but principles—never."
—GROVER CLEVELAND.

MR. CLEVELAND left the St. Louis Exposition with a new joy in the realization of the people's confidence, but with no new ambitions. He still did not desire the nomination, but he delighted in the effect of third term talk upon Mr. Bryan. On May 8th he sent Mr. Gilder a cartoon by McCutcheon, showing four successive expressions upon his own face as he was interviewed by four successive reporters. In the background stand the figures of Bryan and Watterson, whose expressions change as Mr. Cleveland's change. "I find in the situation," reads the accompanying letter, "two satisfactory things—the hopping and jumping in certain cages of Democratic zoological specimens, and the belief that the Democratic party will get a hint that no Bryanism or Bryan conciliation will get enough votes to do the business."

On that same day "the faithful" read in Bryan's newspaper, the *Commoner,* a two-page editorial of denunciation of the ex-President as "an office-boy in a Wall Street institution . . . the logical candidate for the Presidency in case the Democratic party returns to its wallow in the mire. . . . He has been faithful to the financial interests that made him and have kept him, and if those interests are to dominate the Democratic party it would be unfair to deny to him the honor of being their representative. The third-term objection will have no influence upon those who are in sympathy with Mr. Cleveland's masters, for those who see no objection to making the White House the rendezvous for financial conspirators against the public, who will not be disturbed by the fear of continued authority in one man, the men who are willing to risk imperialism to secure the gold standard, would keep a President in power for life if they thought it would keep the control of the government in the hands of the financiers. The logic of events is forcing Mr. Cleveland more and more into the leadership of the reorganizing element. The New York *World* suggested him some months ago, and now the Brooklyn *Eagle* has withdrawn Mr. Parker and suggested Mr. Cleveland as the proper presidential candidate."

This editorial served as the caisson from which the petty officers of "Bogus Democracy" at once drew ammunition for further attacks. In the opinion of the Cleveland Democrats, however, they drew "duds," and on May 13th Lamont gleefully wrote to St. Clair McKelway: "The more the papers and the politicians discuss Cleveland, the smaller Bryan will grow, and they will get the habit of demanding the Cleveland type of President. Therefore, I have written him, urging him to say nothing at present."

During the summer, amid the delights of Gray Gables, it was comparatively easy to say nothing about politics, for other and more attractive thoughts engaged his attention. On July 4th he wrote to Mr. Gilder: "I am waiting for a new census report of the Cleveland race, which I expect will be in order within the next two or three days." And to Commodore Benedict, eleven days later:

Buzzards Bay
July 15, 1903.

DEAR COMMODORE:

I received your letter a few days ago and was glad to know that we might expect to see you soon. I cannot refrain from saying to you, however, that there are two conditions now existing which I would like to see changed before you come. One is the state of expectancy and anxiety which the *hover of the stork* over our house creates; and the other is the abominable fishing here just at this time. Both of these conditions will, I hope, give way for better before very long.

We have not been on the Bay to fish since the Doctor arrived. The fishing is not good enough to be tempting, and I guess we both feel like keeping fairly near home. The Doctor has been working in the hay all day and I have been trying to keep warm at home.

We may go out a little while to-morrow morning and try Rocky Point near home for squeteague. I will keep you posted as to the fish and the other event; and when conditions assume a more favorable aspect I will promptly give you the word.

With love to Mrs. Benedict, I am

Yours very sincerely

GROVER CLEVELAND.

Com. E. C. Benedict
80 Broadway, New York

Within three days the stork had descended, and the ex-President, father of a second boy, wrote to Mrs. John Grier Hibben, wife of the future President of Princeton:

Buzzards Bay
July 18, 1903.

MY DEAR MRS. HIBBEN:

I sent you a telegram this morning that a tramp boy had trespassed upon our premises. He was first seen and heard at 10 o'clock A. M. (I hear him now), and I sent the dispatch a few moments thereafter, to Redfield where, according to the itinerary you sent me, you were to be from the 5th to the 20th instant. I have heard since that there was difficulty in transmitting the dispatch from Camden to Redfield; and I shall not be surprised if this letter or the newspapers give you the first information touching to-day's important event.

The shameless naked little scoundrel weighed over 9 pounds. Richard was very much tickled as long as he thought it was something in the doll line, and was quite overcome with laughter when he found it was "a real baby." He and I have been planning for the amusement of the newcomer when he shall arrive at Richard's present age. He denies with considerable warmth any intention of taking him by the hair and throwing him down. In point of fact we have agreed upon no particular line of conduct, except an engagement on Richards' part to teach the young brother to swim if all goes well.

The dear Mother is as well apparently, as possible; and seems to me very self-conceitedly happy—as if she thought she had done a good job.

She sends her love—and so do I. And we both include the Professor.

Yours very sincerely

GROVER CLEVELAND.

To his neighbors at Buzzards Bay he announced the good news with even more elaboration:

"It may possibly be that some of you are aware of a very recent event in my household which has increased by one the present population of the town of Bourne, and has also added another to the future fishermen in Buzzards Bay. This newcomer was weighed on the scales I use for weighing the fish I catch; and he registered nine pounds and a half. That's not a wonderful weight for a child. For a fish it would be all right and among fishermen no explanation need be made. But it was not a fish that was weighed, and others besides fishermen have an interest in the truthfulness of all that pertains to the vital statistics of Bourne Township. Therefore I take this opportunity to say that the nine and a half pounds registered on my fishing scales honestly means nine pounds—no more and no less. The extra half pound is a matter of special and private arrangement between me and the scales. By this statement I satisfy all my conscientious scruples and disdain any attempt to gain credit for half a pound more increase in population than I am entitled to.

"It must not be for a moment supposed that my fish weighing scales are unique in the particular referred to, nor that I am by any means the only fisherman who resorts to such a mechanical contrivance to substantiate his stories. The fact is, anything I have done in that direction may be regarded as frivolous when compared with other transactions of a like character. In proof of this let me cite an instance of a medical fisherman who, having provided himself with one of these fish story supporting appliances, was called while on a fishing trip in a remote region with a party of companions, to attend the wife of one of the few inhabitants of the locality in the pains and perils of maternity. The child, it was insisted by the parents and all cognizant of its advent, must be weighed; and no scales but the Doctor's fish scales were at hand. After some demur on his part they were finally pressed into the service, with the astounding result that quite an ordinary looking newborn infant was found to weigh nineteen pounds and a half."

Shortly after his return to Princeton, his most intimate friend, Wilson S. Bissell, died, and to Commodore Benedict he wrote: "Bissell's death is another reminder . . . that the shafts are flying." But, though saddened by the loss, he was by no means inclined to chronic melancholy, and his native wit often enabled him to baffle inquisitive reporters and maintain the sphinx-like silence enjoined by his friends. At Chicago, about the middle of October, when compelled out of consideration to his host, Mr. Eckels, to make some reply to a group of eager questioners seeking a headline concerning the coming presidential campaign, he told the following story:

"A friend of mine went with me on one of my recent duck-shooting expeditions. Two ducks rose over our heads. One had a white breast and the other a brown one. They were plainly marked. As I raised my gun to fire, my friend said:

" 'Mr. Cleveland, I have named one of those ducks Nomination.'

"I fired and one duck fell." Here Mr. Cleveland paused.

"Which duck came down?" demanded his hearers breathlessly. But Mr. Cleveland only smiled.

At length, however, he sent to St. Clair McKelway the following letter with leave to print:

Princeton, *November 25, 1903.*

MY DEAR DR. MCKELWAY:

I have waited for a long time to say something which I think should be said to you before others.

You can never know how grateful I am for the manifestation of kindly feeling toward me, on the part of my countrymen, which your initiative has brought out. Your advocacy in the *Eagle* of my nomination for the Presidency came to me as a great surprise; and it has been seconded in such manner by Democratic sentiment, that conflicting thoughts of gratitude and duty have caused me to hesitate as to the time and manner of a declaration on my part concerning the subject—if such a declaration should seem necessary or proper.

In the midst of it all, and in full view of every consideration presented, I have not for a moment been able, nor am I now able, to open my mind to the thought that in any circumstances or upon any consideration, I should ever again become the nominee of my party for the Presidency. My determination not to do so is unalterable and conclusive.

This you at least ought to know from me; and I should be glad if the *Eagle* were made the medium of its conveyance to the public.

Very sincerely yours,

GROVER CLEVELAND.

St. Clair McKelway, LL.D.
Brooklyn, N. Y.

Six weeks later, on January 6, 1904, his daughter Ruth, died of diphtheria, and his grief dwarfed all else. Her death was most unexpected, as his diary shows:

January 2d, "Ruth is a little sick with tonsillitis."
January 3rd, "Ruth still sick, but better."

January 6th, "Doctor said this morning Ruth had diphtheria . . . a trained nurse came at 5:25. Prof. West was here. Dr. treated us all with antitoxin and reported that Ruth was getting on well. Houghton Murray came in the evening and we played cribbage until 12. At 2 o'clock in the night word came . . . that Ruth was not so well. Dr. Carnochan came at 2:30 and Dr. Wykoff at 3:30. We had been excluded from Ruth's room, but learned that dear Ruth died before Dr. Wykoff came, probably about 3 o'clock A. M., Jan. 7th."

January 8th [in a trembling, almost illegible hand], "We buried our daughter, Ruth, this morning."

Deep natures suffer long, and the memory of that little grave in the old Princeton Cemetery haunted him, despite his deep religious faith. On January 10th, he wrote, "I had a season of great trouble in keeping out of my mind the idea that Ruth was in the cold, cheerless grave instead of in the arms of her Saviour." And the next day, "It seems to me I mourn our darling Ruth's death more and more. So much of the time I can only think of her as dead, not joyfully living in Heaven." On the 15th the diary declares: "God has come to my help and I am able to adjust my thought to dear Ruth's death with as much comfort as selfish humanity will permit. One thing I can say: Not for one moment since she left us has a rebellious thought entered my mind." "It seems so long since we buried Ruth," he wrote to Commodore Benedict, on February 20th, "and yet it is only six weeks yesterday. We are becoming accustomed to her absence. For the rest of it we have not a shadow of a doubt that it is well with the child."

So deep was the impression made by the loss of this daughter, whose intelligence and personal charm had

made her the life of the household, that his friends
advised him to divert his mind by re-entering politics.
Nathan Straus wrote: "While I have all along been very
much averse, purely through a friendly feeling, to your
being again drawn into politics, I have changed my
opinion since you have met with the misfortune that has
visited you. Nothing but time can heal such a wound
as you have received; but a change of scene, an active
life, the compelling of thoughts in other directions would
naturally leave you less time to dwell upon your sorrow.
. . . A short time ago I met Mr. Carlisle and told him
how I felt about the matter, and he agreed with me and
expressed the same sentiments. Further than this,
wherever I speak of it, and to whomever I speak of it,
I get only one reply, that the only hope of the success
of the Democratic party lies in you. I fully agree . . .
that you are the only man the Democrats can elect against
Mr. Roosevelt."

Mr. Straus also quoted a conversation between Mr.
J. S. Cram, of Tammany Hall, and Mr. Stillman, in
which the latter said: "If you will nominate Mr. Cleveland, I will personally see that there is a fund raised
bigger than was raised at the time McKinley was elected,
and you know when he ran they had more money than
they could use."

Tammany's friendly attitude toward the idea was expressed by Murphy to Lamont, who in turn reported it
to the ex-President:

Wednesday Evening, *February 10, 1904.*
2 West Fifty-Third Street

MY DEAR MR. PRESIDENT:

Murphy whom I had never seen before called on me
yesterday afternoon. He came alone and said he wanted

to get in touch with me so that he could confer with me about national politics. I was greatly pleased with him because he is evidently a man of sense and wants to put his organization to the front for the best in the party.

He is honest in his talk about you and says if it can't be Cleveland, "then let's get the nearest to him that can be found." I advised him to fight down any instructions and to take his delegation to the convention with the announcement that New York was there to confer and to bring about the strongest nomination possible. He gives out to-night just about what I said to him. He says you would be elected without question, and to some things I said to him in response to that he answered, "Then do ask Mr. Cleveland to do no further declining now. Let's have the benefit of his name to round up a Cleveland party and all will agree on a Cleveland candidate." He is opposed to Parker—because he says there is nothing in Parker to campaign on; he is against Gorman and he says he would have no idea of McClellan for such a place. Bryan he says should be absolutely turned down and ignored. . . . He has no patience with anybody who wants to placate Bryan. As for Hearst, he says he cuts no figure whatever.

I have never seen a leader of Tammany Hall talk as well about things as this man does. You will be interested in my story of his visit when I see you.

I hope you got home safely and that your trip did you no harm. I wish you would come oftener. The seeing you did us all great good, especially Mrs. Lamont. My love to all.

Sincerely yours,
Daniel S. Lamont.

The newspaper statement, to which Lamont refers, reads as follows:

"Charles F. Murphy to-day practically disposed of the Parker presidential boom, so far as New York is concerned. He volunteered a denial of reports that he was really for Parker, and declared emphatically that he would fight to a finish any plan to instruct the delegates from New York State to the Democratic National Convention. He also made it plain that Parker will not figure in the national convention as New York's candidate at any stage of the proceedings if he (Murphy) has anything to say about it; and he thinks he will have a great deal to say about it.

"Murphy was moved to talk about the Parker boom by reports from Albany that, at a dinner there last night, which Judge Parker attended, Tammany senators and assemblymen shouted for Parker and voted for him on a mock ballot. . . . The Tammany leader did not say it in so many words, but he plainly implied that nobody would have a chance to vote for Parker next November. . . . He volunteered this statement: 'I hear that it is reported up the State that I have been speaking favorably of Mr. Cleveland by agreement with certain persons, and that I am using Cleveland just now to conceal my purpose of bringing about the nomination of Judge Parker. I wish to say that these reports are absolutely untrue. As I have said more than once, I think Mr. Cleveland is the strongest man that could be named, and I mean it. I am not committed to Cleveland or anybody else, however, and I certainly have not made any agreement with anybody to send the New York delegation to the national convention with instructions to support Judge Parker. I am opposed to instructions by the convention for any candidate, and I will go into the convention and fight any effort to instruct. I don't believe in instructions. . . .'

"This declaration is plainly a notice served by Murphy on David B. Hill and his friends that Judge Parker cannot be put forward as New York's candidate at the spring convention, and that any attempt to do so will result in a fight in the convention. The outcome of such a fight, Murphy's friends say, would not be doubtful. They assert that he will have a considerable majority in the convention, and that the Parker boomers will be suppressed in quick order. It was also asserted at Tammany Hall to-day that if any attempt is made to instruct for Parker, Murphy will not permit David B. Hill to go to St. Louis as a delegate-at-large.

"The Tammany senators and assemblymen who shouted for Parker last night, under the influence of good cheer at a particularly cheery place—'The Tub'— will hear something not to their advantage by calling at Tammany Hall when they come down from Albany on Friday. Murphy does not seem to be able to appreciate the humor of that vote for Parker, and there is such a thing as 'discipline' in Tammany Hall."

A few weeks later, the Honorable James Smith, Jr., Democratic boss of New Jersey, called at Westland to urge the ex-President to enter the race; but he was met by a firm refusal.

Mr. Cleveland's letters and conversations of this period are full of hopes and fears, speculations, and at times lamentations, as he watched the uncertain progress of the party of his devotion struggling toward the light. In reply to Lamont's letter, he wrote:

Princeton, *Feby. 18, 1904.*

MY DEAR COLONEL:

I was very glad to learn from your letter that you had met Mr. Murphy and that your favorable impression of him agreed with that made upon me by a moment's chat with him a long time ago. It is exceedingly fortunate that he is at the head of Tammany at this critical time for Democracy, and so far as I can now see it is also fortunate that McClellan is Mayor, and our old friend McAdoo at the head of New York's Police Department.

Under all the circumstances Murphy's idea of an uninstructed New York delegation to St. Louis is very wise, and I hope he will inexorably insist upon it. I wish I could look differently upon Parker's candidacy, but what you write of Murphy's opinion on that subject, exactly expresses my feeling.

As matters now stand I hope to see a growth in the sentiment towards Olney or Gray.

I note what you write about the hope expressed in your interview with Murphy that I "do no further declining now."

I am willing to be silent up to the point that continued silence might be construed as indicating a departure from my expressed determination not to be a candidate, or until such silence will subject me to the accusation of misleading my good friends.

I see the *Herald* this morning publishes a part of my political article which is to appear in the *Saturday Evening Post.*

I have had some misgivings about the wisdom or propriety of that utterance; but I am entirely reassured when I hear so much about Bryan-Hearst nonsense and when I recall my right to have my position understood as uncompromisingly opposed to Democratic suicide. I will have no part or lot in such a crime.

I enjoyed my visit with you very much indeed. It seemed like old times; and I want to thank you for the time you spent for my convenience and comfort.

With love from Mrs. Cleveland and me to both you and Mrs. Lamont, I am

Yours faithfully
GROVER CLEVELAND.

Hon. D. S. Lamont
  No. 2 West 53d St., New York.

And ten days later:

DEAR COLONEL:

My notion is that if there is to be an effort to get our party in any kind of promising shape there ought to be a movement in a hard-headed sensible way. Perhaps Parker has such a start that he would be the best one to concentrate on. You know my idea has been that Olney or Gray would suit present conditions best.

I want you to tell all who talk "Cleveland" nonsense that it is a waste of time that might be profitably spent in other ways.

I would not accept a nomination if it was tendered to me—which of course it cannot be—and I don't want to be considered as a defeated candidate for nomination.

I am content. I want to see the party succeed, but I hope there will be no idea of playing any kind of trick on me.

Yours faithfully,
GROVER CLEVELAND.

Hon. D. S. Lamont,
  2 West 53rd St., New York.

The insistence of his friends in no way affected his determination to remain on the side lines, but their pleading pleased him, and his eagerness for party success was intense. He watched with expert eye the uncertain drifting of the bark once so steady in his own guiding hand, and his comments regarding possible candidates of both parties were frequent and specific. "There is one thing about our young President which I think cannot be denied," he wrote to Lamont. "He has but little idea of the proprieties that belong to his high office or, for that matter, to its incumbent. . . . There never was a time I believe when the country would be a greater gainer than now, by the clearing out of an administration." And to Hornblower, eighteen days later:

Princeton, *March 29, 1904.*

MY DEAR MR. HORNBLOWER:

I thank you for the pains you have taken to put in my hands the book I need. I expect to receive it to-day.

In reply to the other matter contained in your letter I have to say, that I have had doubts as to Mr. Parker's being the very best candidate in sight, considering all things; but I am not very strong in these doubts. One thing is certain, I think. He is clean, decent, and conservative and ought on those grounds to inspire confidence in quarters where it is sadly needed, if our party is ever going to be a political power again.

It is in my view immensely important that the sane portion of our party should be as united on a decent candidate as circumstances will permit—to the end that the movement now threatened in the direction of insanity and indecency may be run over and killed "beyond recognition." In this view it should be taken into account that Parker's candidacy has such a start and has so many elements ready to support it in the convention, that he appears to present a better rallying point than anyone else.

Personally I would prefer Olney or Gray; but they do not seem to me to be under much headway.

I believe if I were in your place I would signify a disposition towards Parker.

Yours faithfully,

GROVER CLEVELAND.

Hon. Wm. B. Hornblower
New York.

His leaning toward Mr. Olney pleased the latter, but it did not imbue him with presidential longings. "I am fairly astounded at some of your intimations about politics," wrote Mr. Olney, on May 18th. "I esteem any opinion of yours in my favor as about as high a compliment as it is possible for a man to receive. But I am sure it would not be to my advantage to be President, while at the prospect of a candidacy, if actually presented to me, I should be perfectly panic-stricken. Can you think of anyone less fitted for such an ordeal? I am not really disturbed, however, because I refuse to take the matter in the least seriously. Everything done here in Massachusetts has been done without my consent either asked or given, and but for the peculiar conditions of the Hearst invasion I should have publicly and expressly forbidden the use of my name in the contest for delegates at the St. Louis Convention."

Judge Parker's attitude was far more receptive, and he was in a position to point to a record of consistent opposition to free silver, even when the party had stood upon the silver platform. When Mr. Cleveland, toward the end of May, sent word that he could be counted upon to help in case Mr. Parker were nominated, the latter replied:

Albany, June 1, 1904.

MY DEAR MR. CLEVELAND:

Mr. Teague of the *North American* called on me last evening, and conveyed to me your very generous message, at the same time showing me your interview as it appeared in the *North American.* In the papers I had seen only excerpts. I wish to thank you for your expression of confidence, and the manner of it. I would not have had you put my name before that of Olney and Gray if you could conscientiously have done so, and am glad that you pointed to the fact that "circumstances" put the lead where it is at present. Your generous offer to help if the nomination should come to me is most welcome, for in that event I shall need your advice, and shall be greatly gratified if I may consult you about a few of the more important matters.

May I be permitted to suggest that you draft such a platform as seems to you to meet the situation? Am sure it will prove of great help to the party if you can find the time to do it.

Again assuring you of my great appreciation, I am

Very sincerely yours,
ALTON B. PARKER.

The Honorable Grover Cleveland.

As the date of their National Convention approached, Mr. Cleveland watched with astonishment the operations of the Republicans who were wise enough to realize —as he did not—that in Theodore Roosevelt, the "accidental president," they had a leader of the first order. When the latter's nomination was announced, he sent

Mr. Olney a clipping headed, "Is Bryan for Olney?" at the same time threatening the latter with the Presidency.

Princeton, *June 24, 1904.*

MY DEAR MR. OLNEY:

You had better look out. I cut the attached bit of news from the *Sun* of this morning.

Did you ever see such a boyish, silly performance as the Republican National Convention which has just adjourned? Perhaps Lodge & Co. think they can safely calculate on the stupidity of enough of the people to elect "Teddy"; but if our party was in proper shape, I am sure the conglomeration of the apostles of all good would find themselves reckoning without their host.

Somehow I cannot at all times feel very confident of Democratic success; but I honestly think if the hint contained in the clipping I sent could lead to a practical result, there would be brighter hopes than in any other condition—I mean of course for the country and party and not especially for the comfort and peace of the gentleman referred to. . . .

Yours faithfully,

GROVER CLEVELAND.

Hon. Richard Olney,
   23 Court St., Boston, Mass.

When the delegates were preparing to start for the Democratic National Convention at St. Louis, Mr. Cleveland wrote to the Honorable James Smith, Jr., head of the New Jersey delegation:

Princeton, *June 26, 1904.*

MY DEAR MR. SMITH:

You will, I suppose, head the delegation from my state to the St. Louis Convention. I am well aware of the favorable opinion you originally entertained touching my availability as a candidate for the Presidency in the coming campaign; and I remember with great satisfaction the friendly spirit in which you accepted the reasons I advanced against that proposition, when we met here a long time ago. My public declaration made before our conversation and the apparent reception of my refusal to be considered a candidate as justifiably conclusive, by you and other friends, have led me to regard all discussion of the matter as ended.

I have heard and read some things lately that disturb me. Perhaps that is unnecessary, but I am very anxious that there should be no misunderstanding which can be chargeable to me or to anything I may do or omit to do.

In view of all the circumstances, I have ventured to write you this, and to ask you as representing the state of my residence, as my friend, to prevent the use of my name in connection with the presidential nomination at the Convention. I certainly could not accept it.

I cannot think that any occasion will arise calling upon you to do me this service; but as I am just leaving here for my summer vacation, I regard it as not amiss to provide against even a very slight or possible contingency.

Yours very truly,
GROVER CLEVELAND.

Hon. James Smith,
    Newark.

To this Mr. Smith replied on June 30th:

"I remember well the reasons advanced by you at our meeting some months ago for not wishing your name presented, and I then fully agreed with you. Since that time events have so shaped themselves that the people of this country, without regard to politics, seem determined to have you again assume the duties of President. Of course I shall carry out your instructions in this matter, and will see that the New Jersey delegation does not present your name to the Convention. Should it become necessary, I will go further and say on the floor of the Convention that I have a letter from you in which you state that you cannot accept the nomination, provided this course meets with your approval; but should the time come when the Convention shall arise and demand your nomination, with almost unanimous voice, I think it would be unfair to ask me, as the head of the delegation from your state, to refuse to assent to such a demand. . . .

"Senator Hill's leadership of the Parker forces, to my mind, makes Judge Parker's election, if nominated, very doubtful. I have no personal feeling against either Senator Hill or Judge Parker, but I think it my duty, as a Democrat, to do all in my power to prevent the latter's nomination, as I am convinced that such an event would be disastrous to Democratic success."

In his keynote speech at the opening of the St. Louis Convention, the temporary Chairman, John Sharp Williams, declared that, through the dogged persistence and indomitable will of Grover Cleveland, in forcing the repeal of the silver-purchase clause of the Sherman Act in 1893, the gold standard was now an established fact. At the mention of Mr. Cleveland's name, the party which had deserted him in 1896, and scorned and insulted him in 1900, burst into applause which lasted so long that the speaker had twice to take his seat before it subsided.

In spite of this fact, however, Mr. Bryan, with the skill of a master of forensic oratory, once more pushed his fight for a declaration in favor of the free and un-limited coinage of silver at the ratio of sixteen to one. Again he charmed the galleries with his eloquence, but he could not charm the delegates. The St. Louis Convention had no mind to go before the country chained to a dead issue.

When the platform was at length adopted, it was silent upon the silver issue, but when the news of his nomination reached Judge Parker, he sent the following telegram which forced the Convention to the position consistently maintained by Grover Cleveland since his first battle with Bryan, in 1893:

HONORABLE W. F. SHEEHAN,
  Hotel Jefferson, St. Louis, Mo.

I regard the gold standard as firmly and irrevocably established, and shall act accordingly if the action of the Convention to-day shall be ratified by the people. As the platform is silent on the subject, my views should be made known to the Convention, and if it is proved to be unsatisfactory to the majority, I request you to decline the nomination for me at once, so that another may be nominated before adjournment.

                                        A. B. PARKER.

Upon reading this message, the Convention, by a vote of 774 to 191, directed that the following reply be sent:

"The platform adopted by this Convention is silent on the question of the monetary standard. It was not regarded by us as a possible issue in the campaign, and only campaign issues were mentioned. Therefore, there is nothing in the views expressed in the telegram received which would preclude a man entertaining them from accepting the nomination on the said platform."

These telegrams, to Mr. Cleveland's mind, meant party redemption. "True Democracy" was again in the ascendant, after eight years of almost total eclipse; and for the moment he was again a Democrat in full and regular communion with the leadership of his party. For these long, bitter years, he had stood on the side lines. Now, at last, he was able once more to join the team. He sent a cordial telegram to Judge Parker, to which the Democratic nominee responded:

Rosemount
Esopus-on-the-Hudson

MY DEAR MR. CLEVELAND:

I am deeply grateful for your telegram of congratulations, and pleased beyond expression that my action meets with your approval.

May I have the liberty of consulting you occasionally about matters that seem of larger moment? I will not trouble you except on very important matters.

Very sincerely yours,
ALTON B. PARKER.

July 11, 1904.

Mr. Cleveland's reply was the letter of a Democrat who is able to endorse his party's actions heartily and without reservations:

Buzzards Bay, Mass.
July 14, 1904.

MY DEAR MR. PARKER:

I received your letter yesterday at this place, where I have been stranded for more than a week on my way to join my family in New Hampshire.

I am certain that no man living appreciates your situation and its perplexities better than I; and I am equally positive that no one is more anxious for your election. Of course this does not necessarily mean that I can be of any great service to you—I wish it did. I hope, however, that you will feel absolutely at liberty to command me in every way. I am not afraid you will ask me to do anything inadvisable, and if at any time I am too forward with advice or suggestions you must go your way without the least embarrassment. Your judgment is too good, I am convinced, to be interfered with by *any one*.

Our best campaign material just now is—YOU. I mean "You" as you are manifested to your countrymen in the despatch you sent to St. Louis. The spirit and sentiment aroused by this utterance of yours, should be kept alive and stimulated from time to time during the campaign. Occasions will present themselves, when you respond probably to the Committee on notification and when you write your letter of acceptance. I do hope that you will insist upon a free hand in meeting these occasions and that you will not hesitate to paraphrase or give your own language to our platform, to such an extent as to convince our people that you propose to keep the reins you have in hand and that your conception of Democratic obligations will constrain you to protect all legitimate rights, and to restrain all harmful trespass upon the privileges and opportunities promised to *all* our people under our plan of government—so far as such an exercise of power is within executive limits. For myself I do not think expediency demands of you the distortion of anything your judgment suggests, in deference to the South or the radicals of our party. Bryan is doing the cause much good in his present mood; and I for one hope it will continue. We need Indiana; and if the Taggart

Chairmanship will help us to get it, it might be well to remember that after all the Chairman of the Executive Com. of the N. Y. Headquarters is the important man.

I am bothered about the question of retaining your judgeship while a candidate for President; but I hope there will be a safe deliverance.

Yours faithfully,
GROVER CLEVELAND.

Hon. Alton B. Parker,
  Esopus, N. Y.

"I am very much pleased with the outcome of the Convention as brought about by Providence and a gentleman living in Esopus," he wrote to Olney, on July 19th. "Such Democrats as you and I ought to be pretty well satisfied. Bryan and Bryanism are eliminated as influential factors in Democratic councils, true Democracy has a leader, and its time-honored and time-approved principles again are set before the people of the land without apology or shamefacedness.

"If we can only keep peanut methods out of our campaign management, I believe there is a good chance to rid the country of Rooseveltism and its entire brood of dangers and humiliations. At any rate, it seems to me there can be no excuse for lack of effort or half-heartedness on the part of any true Democrat who has waited all these years for party regeneration."

No sooner was the presidential nomination disposed of, than the demand was made that Mr. Cleveland allow his name to be used as candidate for Governor of New Jersey. "So many people have waited on me, as well as newspaper men, to urge your name," wrote James Smith, Jr., on July 22d. "I simply told them that while it would be a great pleasure to me to have you accept it, and that while it would insure the state for Democratic electors, I hardly thought that after refusing to accept a nomination for the Presidency, you were . . . 'patriotic' enough to accept Governor," a prediction which Mr. Cleveland's reply promptly justified.

As the campaign progressed, he grew more and more eager for Judge Parker's election, writing articles to that effect for *Collier's Weekly,* for *McClure's Magazine,* and for the *Saturday Evening Post,* after seeing one of which Judge Parker thanked him in the following letter:

Rosemount
Esopus-on-the-Hudson
July 22, 1904.

MY DEAR MR. CLEVELAND:

I wish to thank you for your very kind letter of the fourteenth, for all the generous things you say, and for all the suggestions you make. I shall always be most grateful for any advice that comes from you, and it shall always have great weight with me.

I have read with very grateful appreciation your most generous article written for *Collier's Weekly.* It is by far, in my opinion, the most telling contribution to the cause.

Thanking you again, and with best wishes for you always, I am,

Very sincerely yours,
ALTON B. PARKER.

Mr. Cleveland's diary records the events of November 8th with laconic brevity: "Election day. Voted about 10 o'c . . . Began to receive returns abt. ½ past 7 I think. It took but a few reports to enable me to see that we the Democrats were dreadfully left. Went to bed a little after 10." When the count was finished, it

was seen that Roosevelt was overwhelmingly elected.
He carried every state except the solid South, and Missouri and Maryland followed him into the Republican
fold. His popular vote was over seven and a half millions, and his plurality more than two and a half millions.

So great was Mr. Cleveland's disappointment that
for weeks he was silent on political matters, replying
when questioned: "My present state of mind does not
permit me to do the subject justice." To Mr. Farquhar,
however, he wrote, on December 12th:

A. B. FARQUHAR, ESQ.,
    York, Penna.
MY DEAR SIR:—
    I was glad to receive your recent letter after so long
a silence. The result of the election was so astounding
that I have hardly sufficiently recovered my composure
to contemplate the reasons which led to it or the results
likely to follow it. I am such an intense and unalterable
believer in the saving common sense of the American
people, that I cannot yet believe that the tremendous
Republican majority given at the last election should be
taken to indicate the people's willingness to allow the
principles and practices of Republicanism to be unalterably fixed in the affairs of our body politic. I believe
that the next swing of the pendulum of public sentiment
will be quite to the Democratic side of the dial, and that,
if Democracy is prepared to do its duty, when that time
arrives, it will become again the beneficent agent of the
people's salvation.

A number of the incidents involved in the election
have so surprised me that sometimes, for a moment, the
idea has entered my mind that a change in the character
of our countrymen has taken place. This is, however,

only for a moment, and the second thought immediately reinstates me in the confidence which I have always had in our people's right thinking. How the rejuvenation of the Democratic party which seems to be absolutely essential, is to be brought about, I do not know; but I am certain that in due time a way will be made plain.

Yours very truly,
GROVER CLEVELAND.

The defeat of Judge Parker served incidentally to heighten the prestige of Grover Cleveland, who remained the only Democrat since Buchanan strong enough to carry a presidential election. The oft-rejected prayer of friends, that he prepare an autobiography, grew more and more insistent, and flattering offers came from publishers, who understood far better than he the interest which his own story from his own pen would excite. He rejected them all, declaring the task distasteful to him as smacking too much of what he called "self-conceit." He admitted, however, the value of biographies of great men: "There is no sadder symptom of a generation's bad moral health than its lack of faith in its great men, and its loss of reverence for its heroes; but let this belief be coupled with the reservation that those called great shall be truly great, and that the heroes challenging our reverence shall be truly heroic, measured by standards adjusted to the highest moral conditions of man's civilization."

In this class he placed Washington, whom he described as "one whose glorious deeds are transcendently above all others recorded in our national annals . . . the incarnation of all the virtues and all the ideals that made our nationality possible"; and Lincoln, "A supremely great and good man . . . more and more sacredly enshrined in my passionate Americanism with every year of my life." But Grover Cleveland he persistently refused to consider even as a candidate for greatness. While fully conscious of a power to endure labor, far beyond that of the average man, of a courage that permitted him to steer his course regardless of opposition, of a purpose bent upon things outside his own personal gain, and of many other qualities of the warp and woof of greatness, he claimed no pedestal, no place among the immortals, content with the thought that he was a citizen who had done his duty. He felt he was in the world for quite another purpose than being great, as Dr. Merle Smith once expressed it.

But though disinclined to hear with favor the pleas of historians eager to become his biographers, he bitterly resented what he deemed the misrepresentations of pseudo-historians. To Gilder he expressed the wrath which the efforts of some of the latter had kindled:

Princeton, *January 28, 1905.*

MY DEAR MR. GILDER:

I want to thank you for your trouble in attempting to set Mr. ——— right. (PROF. ——— God save the mark!) I never heard of him until Nelson mentioned him in connection with his stuff; and I don't care what else he is, it must be that he is a lover of falsehood, who had rather, in the cloak of history writing, put down something new and striking, than tell the truth. There is another coyote in Kansas who is cut off the same piece; and I suppose such yelping and snarling as theirs is history.

I honestly think, my dear Gilder, that there are things in my life and career that if set out, and *read* by the young men of our country, might be of benefit to a generation soon to have in their keeping the safety and the mission of our nation; but I am not certain of this, for I am by no means sure that it would be in tune with the vaudeville that attracts our people and wins their applause. Somehow, I don't want to appear wearing a fur coat in July.

Mr. McClure and all the forces about him have lately importuned me, in season and out of season, to write, say twelve autobiographical articles, offering what seems to me a large sum for them [$10,000]; but I have declined the proposition. I went so far (for I softened up a bit under the suggestion of duty and money) to inquire how something would do like talking to another person for publication; but that did not take at all. I don't really think I would have done even that, but the disapproval of merely a hint that the "I" might to an extent be eliminated, made it seem to me more than ever that the retention of everything that might attract the lovers of a "snappy life" was considered important by the would-be publishers.

There is a circle of friends like you, who I hope will believe in me. I am happy in the conviction that they will continue in the faith whether an autobiography is written or not. I want my wife and children to love me now, and hereafter to proudly honor my memory. They will have my autobiography written on their hearts where every day they may turn the pages and read it. In these days what else is there that is worth while to a man nearly sixty-eight years old?

Give my love to Mrs. Gilder and believe me

Yours faithfully

GROVER CLEVELAND.

R. W. Gilder, Esq.,
13 E. 8th St., New York.

CHAPTER XIII

REORGANIZING THE EQUITABLE

"We can better afford to slacken our pace than to abandon our old simple American standards of honesty."
—GROVER CLEVELAND.

DURING the first eight years of Mr. Cleveland's life at Princeton, many attempts were made to lure him into business, where his hold upon the confidence of the public would have been of inestimable value; but he resisted them all, despite the tempting financial offers of many of them. In 1905, however, there came a call to what Elihu Root later characterized as "distinctly a public service," and one which, as such, he did not feel free to refuse, although it meant leadership in a field wholly new to him.

The Equitable Life Assurance Society, an association designed to benefit its policyholders, had by slow stages been transformed into a gigantic engine for their exploitation. Its funds were in the hands of directors who did not direct; its policyholders had become the victims of officials who did direct; while factional differences within the board had brought about a condition in which a receivership was inevitable, unless a thorough reorganization could be speedily effected. As a step toward such reorganization, its President, James W. Alexander, had asked the directors to mutualize the society by extending the voting privilege to all policyholders; and, in March, 1905, the committee appointed to effect this change unanimously recommended that the charter be so amended

350

as to provide that a majority of the directors, 28 out of 52, be elected by the policyholders.

Before the change was actually made, however, Mr. Thomas F. Ryan purchased 502 of the 1000 shares of Equitable capital stock, a block which had belonged to Henry B. Hyde, and with it the right to cast the majority vote upon all questions. Mr. Ryan later gave the following explanation of the motives which led him to make this purchase, involving the payment of $2,500,000: "I saw in the virtual necessity of a receivership of the Equitable . . . disaster impending unless the factional differences in the company among the directors and the management should be radically changed. To avert this and to prevent the frightful losses that would occur from the violent breaking up of the Equitable, not only to the policyholders but to the financial community at large, as well as to myself, I thought that someone ought to take over the business."

For one man to intervene to protect the interests of six hundred thousand policyholders, interests amounting to $400,000,000, was a venture of enormous proportions, and Mr. Ryan knew that if his plan were to succeed he must secure as the head of the trustees, in whose hands he intended to place the administration of his majority stock, a man whom the public would fully trust, since with the majority stock went the full control of the Equitable Corporation. Ex-President Cleveland appeared to him the man best fitted for this task, and he accordingly sent him the following letter:

New York, *June 9, 1905.*

DEAR MR. CLEVELAND:

You may be aware that a bitter controversy exists regarding the management of the Equitable Life Assurance Society and that public confidence has been shaken in the safety of the funds under the control of a single block of stock left by the late Henry B. Hyde. This loss of confidence affects a great public trust of more than $400,000,000, representing the savings of over 600,-000 policyholders, and the present condition amounts to a public misfortune.

In the hope of putting an end to this condition and in connection with a change of the executive management of the Society, I have . . . purchased this block of stock and propose to put it into the hands of a board of trustees having no connection with Wall Street, with power to vote it for the election of directors—as to twenty-eight of the fifty-two directors, in accordance with the instructions of the policyholders of the Society, and as to the remaining twenty-four directors in accordance with the uncontrolled judgment of the trustees. This division of twenty-eight and twenty-four is in accordance with a plan of giving substantial control to policyholders already approved by the Superintendent of Insurance.

I beg you to act as one of this board with other gentlemen, who shall be of a character entirely satisfactory to you.

I would not venture to ask this of you on any personal grounds; but to restore this great trust, affecting so many people of slender means, to soundness and public confidence would certainly be a great public service, and this view emboldens me to make the request.

The duties of the trust would be light, as, in the nature of things, when a satisfactory board is once constituted there are few changes, and all the clerical and formal work would be done by the office force of the Company.

I have written similar letters to Justice Morgan J.

O'Brien, Presiding Justice of the Appellate Division in our Supreme Court, and to Mr. George Westinghouse, of Pittsburgh, two of the largest policyholders in the Society.

Very truly yours,

THOMAS F. RYAN.

Hon. Grover Cleveland
    Princeton, N. J.

After some hesitation, Mr. Cleveland answered:

Princeton, N. J.
June 10, 1905.

THOMAS F. RYAN, ESQ.,
DEAR SIR:

I have this morning received your letter asking me to act as one of the three trustees to hold the stock of the Equitable Life Assurance Society, which has lately been acquired by you and certain associates, and to use the voting power of such stock in the selection of directors of said Society.

After a little reflection I have determined that I ought to accept this service. I assume this duty upon the express condition that, so far as the trustees are to be vested with discretion in the selection of directors, they are to be absolutely free and undisturbed in the exercise of their judgment, and that, so far as they are to act formally in voting for the directors conceded to policyholders, a fair and undoubted expression of policy-holding choice will be forthcoming.

The very general anxiety aroused by the recent unhappy dissensions in the management of the Equitable Society furnishes proof of the near relationship of our people to life insurance. These dissensions have not only injured the fair fame of the company immediately affected, but have impaired popular faith and confidence in the security of life insurance itself, as a provision for those who in thousands of cases would be otherwise helpless against the afflictive visitations of fate.

The character of this business is such that those who manage and direct it are charged with a grave trust for those who, necessarily, must rely upon their fidelity. In those circumstances they have no right to regard the places they hold as ornamental, but rather as positions of work and duty and watchfulness.

Above all things, they have no right to deal with the interests intrusted to them in such a way as to subserve or to become confused or complicated with their personal transactions or ventures.

While the hope that I might aid in improving the plight of the Equitable Society has led me to accept the trusteeship you tender, I cannot rid myself of the belief that what has overtaken this company is liable to happen to other insurance companies and fiduciary organizations as long as lax ideas of responsibility in places of trust are tolerated by our people.

The high pressure of speculation, the madness of inordinate business scheming, and the chances taken in new and uncertain enterprises, are constantly present temptations, too often successful, in leading managers and directors away from scrupulous loyalty and fidelity to the interests of others confided to their care.

We can better afford to slacken our pace than to abandon our old simple American standards of honesty; and we shall be safer if we regain our old habit of looking at the appropriation, to personal uses, of property and interests held in trust, in the same light as other forms of stealing.

Yours very truly,
GROVER CLEVELAND.

On June 15th a deed of trust was executed transferring control of the Equitable Life Assurance Society from its one majority owner to Mr. Cleveland and his two co-trustees. At the same time Paul Morton, ex-Secretary of the Navy, and a son of J. Sterling Morton, of Cleveland's second Cabinet, was made President of the Equitable, but he was in effect a President without a Board of Directors, as the old board had nearly all resigned, and the new one was as yet to be created.

During the days which intervened between his appointment and his first formal meeting with his co-trustees, Mr. Cleveland set himself to the task of mastering the problems and the complicated machinery of the insurance business. He sought advice from neither Mr. Ryan himself nor from Mr. Ryan's able counsel, Mr. Elihu Root, although fully conscious of their skill in matters of large business. He had friends also on the Board of Directors, but he asked no help from them, declaring that they had made a mess of things, and that now he, by his own methods, must find his "own blundering way." Disregarding the summer heat, he worked at his task of discovering the facts, which he later summarized thus:

"A majority of the directors of this Company were each qualified as stockholders and directors, by a colorable holding of five shares of the stock of the Company, placed in their hands by its President and subject at any time to his recall, or such other disposition as he should request. Nearly all of them were men of such wealth and were so distinguished and prominent in business and financial operations that their names were familiar throughout the United States, and some of them throughout the world. All of them were connected with the control and management of other large companies, numbering in some cases twenty or more. Their honorable business reputations repelled any suspicion of deliberate wrongdoing or willful neglect of obligations. They were simply non-directing directors, holding their places at the request of the President of the Company, and doing what a vicious system dictates in such cases—precisely nothing except drift with the current. Thus it came about that before their eyes and within their reach, peculation and breach of trust flourished, scandals grew, the beneficent designs of the Company, pending its thorough reformation, were discredited, and its policyholders were distressed with fear and gloomy forebodings."

As soon as he had mastered the situation, he sent an announcement to the policyholders, informing them that the trustees had assumed their posts as representing the majority stock, and asking that suggestions be made or names proposed for the vacant directorships. Although he refused expert advice, he instinctively sought the guidance of popular opinion.

While the replies were coming in, the question of the salary of the Chairman of the Trustees was taken up by a committee of the directors, which, on June 20th, reported that in view of "the nature and extent of the services rendered by Mr. Cleveland . . . $1000 per month is a fair sum."

By June 27th, some two hundred suggestions had been received in answer to Mr. Cleveland's request, and on that day the second meeting of the trustees was held, nine directors were chosen, and a longer and more elaborate address adopted, to be sent out under date of June 28th. Each of these documents was drawn with as much care as though it had been a presidential message to Congress. Paul D. Cravath, one of the counsel who had executed the deed of trust, recalls the following incident: "At his request I had drafted a statement or paper of some kind, I forget just what it was, for which he was to become responsible. One afternoon I went to Princeton to submit it to him. He seemed to like it. I went to bed at a normal hour, say eleven o'clock. When I came down to early breakfast the next morning Mr. Cleveland greeted me with an entirely new paper which he had prepared after I had gone to bed. He must have stayed up most of the night. It is needless to say that his paper was very much better than the draft which I had proposed."

By the end of June, the Society was reorganized, with a board of trustees ready to take the responsibilities of their trust in the spirit of the "old simple American standards of honesty," to which Mr. Cleveland always pinned his faith. As Chairman he had furnished men for vacant places, destroying the practice of furnishing places for vacant men. As each new director had been appointed he had called upon Mr. Cleveland, nominally to pay his respects, but really to receive his instructions. Each came from the interview with a clear vision of the dangers which beset directors, and with the knowledge that there was no room for dummy directors on the new board.

In his letter accepting the trust, Mr. Cleveland had said: "What has overtaken this Company is liable to happen in other companies." And, on July 20th, acting perhaps upon this hint, the New York Legislature made provision for a committee to investigate the entire business of life insurance within the state.   Senator Armstrong was its Chairman, and its chief counsel was Charles E. Hughes.

Their report laid bare a sordid and humiliating situation in which senators, masters of industry, political machine-men, bankers, railroad presidents, and directors of insurance companies had wrought together to exploit a helpless public.   But it emphasized the value of the changes which Mr. Cleveland had brought about in the Equitable before the Armstrong Committee had even been appointed, and forced other companies to make similar changes in the interest of the public.

In commenting upon the report, Mr. Cleveland said of Mr. Hughes: "No one can better know the causes responsible for such management than the able and fearless man who conducted the investigation which brought it to light.   His universally conceded sincerity and his pre-eminent qualification as a witness give the weight of conclusiveness to the following words addressed by him to his fellow citizens in the state of New York: 'What is the vice in the conduct of those great enterprises which directly affect our interests?   It is the vice of selfishness. It is the vice of setting up self-interest as against service. It is the vice of seeing how much we can get and keep, instead of seeing how much benefit can be bestowed!' "

No sooner had the affairs of the Equitable been set in order than there came a new call:

Dec. 15th, [1905]
120 Broadway, New York

My dear Mr. Cleveland:

I am authorized by The New York Life Insurance Company, The Mutual Life Company, and this Society to offer you $12,000.00 per year salary to act as the referee between the three companies in matters of dispute concerning the respective agents of the three institutions rebating the commissions they receive from premiums paid.

This will not be arduous work and I doubt if there will be many cases. They can be submitted to you at Princeton generally by correspondence and any expenses for clerk hire will also be allowed you.

You were the only man suggested for the position and I sincerely hope you will decide to accept it commencing January 1st.

Mr. Thos. B. Reed once held this same relation to these companies.

Respectfully yours,
PAUL MORTON.

To
Hon. Grover Cleveland
Princeton, N. J.

To this Mr. Cleveland replied:

Princeton, *Dec. 19, 1905.*

MY DEAR MR. MORTON:

I have duly considered your letter of the 15th instant in which, on behalf of The New York Life Insurance Company, The Mutual Life Insurance Company, and The Equitable Life Assurance Society you offer me the position of Referee to determine disputes that may arise between the organizations mentioned concerning the allowance by their respective agents of rebates on their premium commissions.

I believe this to be a vice that can have no place in well-conducted life insurance.

I accept the proposition contained in your letter; but in doing so I assume that those for whom you speak are seriously determined to present the claims referred to, and will unreservedly second every effort directed to that end.

Yours very truly

GROVER CLEVELAND.

Hon. Paul Morton
President of The Equitable
Life Assurance Society.

To the duties of these two posts, the Equitable trusteeship and this refereeship, there was added a year later a third, also in the field of insurance. The revelations of the Armstrong Committee having produced a nation-wide tendency on the part of legislatures to make unnecessary and ill-advised attacks upon the insurance business, representatives of the larger companies came together and formed an organization for mutual protection: "The Presidents' Association of Life Insurance Companies."

As head of this new organization, and therefore in effect the titular head of life insurance in America, they selected Mr. Cleveland, offering him a salary, liberal though not large in comparison with those which Americans had come to associate with high insurance posts. The duty of this office was to examine and elucidate measures of legislation as they were presented, a duty for which his public experience had admirably equipped him.

For a time he hesitated, accepting at first, and later sending a telegram of refusal, which he explained in the following letter to Mr. Morton:

Princeton, *Feby. 6, 1907.*

MY DEAR PAUL:

I have just sent you a dispatch which has brought me a great deal of regret, and a consciousness that I have caused you disappointment and embarrassment. I am altogether to blame for these and confess my fault without any claim of mitigation. If I had taken a little more time to consider the matter in all its aspects and had trusted a little more thoroughly to the soundness of my first promptings, I should have saved you embarrassment and vexation, by declining the place you offered me, at the proper time.

My interest in insurance affairs, I now realize more than ever, is related exclusively to the success and prosperity of the Equitable, and my great desire to be of service to you and Mr. Ryan as well as to the company. It is such a different proposition to make this new connection and to be related to other companies and their officials whom I know nothing about and which have not enlisted any personal attachment, that I cannot, all things considered, bring myself to its acceptance.

I know, too, that on the actual basis of service to be rendered—that is, real work to be done, I would not earn anything like the salary offered me.

I fully appreciate the generous compensation paid me for past services; but I have had no very serious twinges of conscience on account of its acceptance.

Conditions have, however, so changed and the work which I might do in the future will be so much diminished that I insist upon an entire suspension of the compensation heretofore allowed me in connection with my trusteeship and refereeship, or the relinquishment of both positions.

Perhaps, if continued, I ought to be reimbursed

actual expenses and a fair compensation for such matters as should be submitted to me as referee.

I want you to understand that my interest in the Equitable and your success as its President and the satisfaction of my relationship with Mr. Ryan, is as strong as ever (and that means as strong as it can be); and I would be glad if I could continue a serviceable connection.

In my judgment the head of the Presidents' Association would more naturally be an insurance man. I believe you do not agree with me in this.

Finally, if you will let me off from this new engagement with as much complacency as you can muster, I will be glad to render any other possible service to the institution and the persons with whom I am already associated, on the conditions which I believe you understand.

Yours faithfully,
GROVER CLEVELAND.

Hon. Paul Morton,
President, &c.,
120 Broadway, New York.

Mr. Morton and his associates, however, persisted in their demand that Mr. Cleveland accept the proffered post, and in the end he yielded. The field of his activities was nation-wide, but his audience was world-wide; and the influence exerted by his carefully considered statements concerning the business of life insurance was comparable with that which he had so long exerted as a political leader. His method of pinning the crime on the criminal was employed as fearlessly as in the old days of Sheriff, Mayor, Governor or President. One of his addresses bore the title, "Directors Who Do Not Direct," and into it he put his philosophy of representative responsibility. When a bank has been looted, he declared, it is not enough for the Directors to tell the plundered depositors that "someone must be trusted." Their proper reply is, "Yes! but we have trusted you."

Despite his frank acknowledgment of the fact that the insurance idea had at times been used as a cloak to cover many crooked deals, his examination of the entire field confirmed his earlier view that insurance companies had rendered invaluable service to the great majority. And his frank approval of the system reassured many minds and helped greatly to restore the confidence so rudely shaken by the findings of the Armstrong Committee.

Thus, in the last years of his life, was he able to apply his statesmanship to big business, carrying through promptly, efficiently, and without seeking the spotlight, a series of reforms whose ultimate influence extended far beyond the field of nation-wide insurance. The abuses that had disgraced the insurance business had but reflected others in a hundred kindred lines; and the reforms wrought by the practiced hand of Grover Cleveland, not skilled in insurance but an expert in reform, reacted upon many of these businesses as well. Men had come to believe that the existing system of interlocking directorates was essential to the conduct of big business, because the men capable of managing such enterprises were considered few. This bubble vanished at the first prick of Cleveland realism, for within five weeks after beginning his work as Chairman of the Equitable Trustees he had found enough new men not connected with the insurance business to conduct successfully a great enterprise which had been brought to the brink of ruin by the older system. He had proved that there is no mystery about big business, and that there is no need to erect its leaders into a mystic priesthood.

"It has been interesting to me," declared Judge Day, who entered the Equitable during Mr. Cleveland's reorganization, and later became its President, "to see how life insurance was revolutionized. . . . The new owner's courage in buying a majority of the stock, and his act in divesting himself of any vestige of control over it, by turning it over to the one man in the country who would inspire confidence, has always seemed to me one of the striking events in modern business. . . . The immediate return of confidence, the success of the open appeal to the great public which at once carried its effects beyond the policyholders of the Society, marked it as an outstanding event." And he added, "the one predominant influence was the name and character of Grover Cleveland. . . . The value of Cleveland's services to the cause of sound life insurance in the days of its trial cannot be overestimated."

CHAPTER XIV

SUNSET DAYS

"I have tried so hard to do right."
—Grover Cleveland.

MR. CLEVELAND'S sixty-ninth birthday found him in Florida, seeking the health which never would return. Although not old, he was aging fast. The physical strength which had made possible strenuous days and deliberately sleepless nights was gone, and he dared not face the penetrating dampness of a New Jersey March. To him in his retreat came, as usual, a deluge of birthday letters, some from intimate friends, some from mere acquaintances, and many from admirers who knew him only by his works. Commodore Benedict, in playful vein, sounded the bugle call of the 69th:

Indian Harbor, Greenwich, Conn.
March 12, 1906.

My dear Admiral:—

I am credibly informed that you are to join the Sixty-ninth regiment on the 18th inst., the day following St. Patrick's.

As I shall not be present to extend the glad hand, and, as it was my good fortune to join that disorganization something over three years ago, I have thought, perhaps, you might be interested to hear what I think of it after serving the full term of my enlistment, and what you may expect, based on my experience.

You must not be surprised to find at the very outset that you are the youngest member of the whole shooting match, but advancement is very certain, rapid, and continuous. You will not be obliged to carry the pail at the end of the procession for more than a few moments, so rapidly are younger members admitted. You will not be greeted with a display of shamrocks or shillalahs, the regiment is too busy admitting new members and burying older ones to indulge in such luxuries. Your enlistment will be for one year only, at the end of which, if you survive, you will be a veteran.

Although the memberships of this regiment extend throughout the world, you will be surprised to find how few of them you will meet, and, of them, but very few will be found in good marching order, most of them preferring slippers to seven league boots. Never before did you belong to a club, society, or organization which comprised such a lot of rickety humanity. An atmosphere of spring will be found lingering in some hearts, but the most of them will betray a spring halt in their legs or a movement as if getting ready for winter by practicing on snowshoes. And yet the few little boys you will find to play with, some of whom may have been companions of your youth, will all seem to be on their good behavior. They will flatter one another with all sorts of preposterous assurances of youthful looks and actions, and, after swearing off twenty years or so from each other's ages consult a pedometer and a mirror, with the result that, while each admits a claim to youthful feelings, will all agree that they are pretty good imitations of old people. They will be ever ready to give the latitude and longitude of all their wanderings, and, after touching upon a few joys, such as fishing and hunting—shouldering their guns and rods to show how game and fish have been won—will lapse into a state of ecstatic agony as they unload upon each other the stories of their various sufferings.

Not the least of the attractions of this regiment is the fair light guard of grandmothers who belong; for women, of course, are not only admitted, but, for the most part, are drafted in spite of many protestations. There will appear to be more of them than men; and then will dawn upon you, if it never has done so before, the fact that, in spite of a few scuttle-bonnet cripples among them, there are a whole lot who are exceedingly fascinating and attractive, a joy wholly denied us in youth, but fortunately reserved for age. So much for the Sixty-niners.

Your year of service ended, without booming of cannon, earthquakes, lightning, or thunder, you will quietly slide into the very aristocracy of age. All your life long you have wondered if you would live out your natural days. How strange it is that we should spend so many years in fear that we may never attain the seventieth birthday, yet always dreading the day when we will do so! However, this question settled, you will find yourself in the ranks of many great men, particularly in Biblical history, like King David; and later, Columbus, and still later, Mark Twain, who made a joke of the event. He must have had in mind the inscription on Gay's tomb in Westminster Abbey:—

"Life is a jest, all things show it;
I thought so once, and now I know it."

Then you can almost consider yourself honorably mentioned in the burial service. Looking back to the Sixty-niners, they appear like a marked down lot at Macy's. I find little depression of spirits on my side of seventy. I am on velvet, as the gamblers say. Besides, many compensations appear, not the least is to be able to walk into the office of the Commissioner of Jurors, as I have done, with my thumb on my nose and my fingers fluttering in the air. Your value as an antique has increased, and bumps of veneration come to your support on every hand and head.

But I am exceeding the objects of this letter. At this juncture in your career you might follow the advice given by the little Sunday School boy (in a story you told me, by the way). You remember when asked by his teacher —"What about hell and the Devil?" he answered, "Wait and see." Meanwhile, uniting with the congratulations of other friends, and, in the language of Robert Roosevelt, let me "wish that you may live as long as you want to and want to as long as you live."

Very sincerely yours,

E. C. BENEDICT.

Grover Cleveland.

Richard Olney avowed the opinion that, "On your 69th birthday you find yourself the object of higher and more general respect and esteem among your fellow countrymen than any other living American."

Mark Twain's tribute revamped the slogan of 1884: "We love him for the enemies he has made."

21 Fifth Avenue

March 6, 1906.

GROVER CLEVELAND, ESQ.
EX-PRESIDENT.
HONORED SIR:

Your patriotic virtues have won for you the homage of half the nation and the enmity of the other half. This places your character as a citizen upon a summit as high as Washington's. The verdict is unanimous and unassailable. The votes of both sides are necessary in cases like these, and the votes of the one side are quite as valuable as are the votes of the other. When the votes are all in a public man's favor the verdict is against him. It is sand, and history will wash it away. But the verdict for you is rock, and will stand.

With the profoundest respect,

S. L. CLEMENS.

(as of date March 18, 1906)

Woodrow Wilson thus acknowledged his personal debt to the teachings of the Sage of Princeton:

Princeton University
Princeton, N. J.

President's Room   *5 March, 1906.*

MY DEAR MR. CLEVELAND:—

I should think that a birth-day would bring you very many gratifying thoughts, and I hope that you realize how specially strong the admiration and affection of those of us in Princeton who know you best has grown during the years when we have been privileged to be near you. It has been one of the best circumstances of my life that I have been closely associated with you in matters both large and small. It has given me strength and knowledge of affairs.

But if I may judge by my own feeling, what a man specially wants to know on his birth-day is how he stands, not in reputation or in power, but in the affection of those whose affection he cares for. The fine thing about the feeling for yourself which I find in the mind of almost everyone I talk with, is that it is mixed with genuine affection. I often find this true even of persons who do not know you personally. How much more must it be true of those who are near you.

With most affectionate regard and with a hope that you may enjoy many another anniversary in peace and honor and affection,

Faithfully yours,

WOODROW WILSON.

Honorable Grover Cleveland,
    Princeton, N. J.

Illiterate or literary, commonplace or clever, each birthday tribute received its answer in his own handwriting. To Richard Watson Gilder he wrote: "From the height of sixty-nine, I write to assure you that this is a happy day in my life, and to tell you how happy I am that you have made it so—more by your own loving message of congratulations than by those you have inspired. I have been so deeply impressed by it all, that I have had many struggles between smiles and tears as I read the words of affection and praise that have met me at the gate of entrance to another year. Somehow I am wondering why all this should be, since I have left many things undone I ought to have done in the realm of friendship, and since in the work of public life and effort, God has never failed to clearly make known to me the path of duty. And still it is in human nature for one to hug the praise of his fellows and the affection of friends to his bosom as his earned possessions. I am no better than this; but I shall trust you to acquit me of affectation when I say to you that in to-day's mood there comes the regret that the time is so shortened, within which I can make further payment to the people that have honored and trusted me."

To Andrew Carnegie, he sent the following reply:

Stuart, Florida.
March 20, 1906.

MY DEAR MR. CARNEGIE:

Your exceedingly kind letter of congratulation touched me deeply, and I want to thank you for it from the bottom of my heart. With other like manifestations of good will from friends whom I also hold close in affection, I feel that it compensates not only for advancing age, but for all that has been hard and laborious in the past.

I avail myself of the knowledge of your address which your letter furnishes, to thank you for the package from Scotland which arrived in proper condition some time ago. Despite all fanatical medical advice, I insist upon it that at the age of sixty-nine, a man should know himself of at least one thing that meets his physical condition.

Ever since you told me something of your dear daughter's ailment, I have been exceedingly anxious to hear that you had been relieved of solicitude on her account.

Will you please convey to Mrs. Carnegie my dutiful regards and believe me

Faithfully yours
GROVER CLEVELAND.

Andrew Carnegie, Esq.
The Cottage
Dungeness, Fernandino, Fla.

His acknowledgment to the Rev. Wilton Merle-Smith, D.D., beautifully sums up his own high philosophy of life:

Stuart, Fla., *March 21, 1906.*

MY DEAR DOCTOR SMITH:

You don't know how much good your generous letter of congratulation has done me. It has enlivened my sense of gratitude for what I have been able to do in the past, for the joys of the present, and for such friendship and confidence as yours. I have quite often, lately, found myself longing for the rest of idleness, and the peace of inactivity; and I have sometimes even given entrance to the thought that these were my due. But you have written words to me that will help me to constantly appreciate the fact that God who has blessed me above all other men, and directed all my ways, deserves my service, and every good cause deserves my best endeavor, as long as my life and strength shall last.

I know as no one else can know my limitations, and how fixed and inexorable they are . . . but I shall trust God, as I have in the past, for strength and opportunity for further usefulness.

Yours faithfully,

GROVER CLEVELAND.

Rev. Wilton Merle Smith, D.D.
29 W. 54th St., New York.

His letter to Vilas, the only surviving member of his first Cabinet, he wrote, in reminiscent mood:

Stuart, Fla., *March 24, 1906.*

MY DEAR MR. VILAS,

In this rather secluded place where I have come to seek rest and recreation, many kind congratulations upon my sixty-ninth birthday have reached me. They have all been delightful and comforting to me; but none have touched me so deeply as yours. Twenty-one years is really a long time; and yet without dwelling upon their

actual number how short a time it seems since on the
4th day of March, 1885, seven of the best and most
patriotic men in our country joined me in the highest
executive work. It would have been strange indeed if
the national responsibilities and perplexities of the next
four years—nobly shared by all—had not grappled us
together by bands stronger and more enduring than steel.
It is one of the most impressive thoughts that enter my
mind in these days, that of all that circle you and I alone
remain.

And so it is, that your letter recalling this, and bringing to my mind our free, frank and trustful association,
and manifesting the same unrestrained affection as of old,
comes so near my heart. . . .

With thanks for your continued kindly remembrance
of me, and its beautiful expression just at this time, I am,

Faithfully your friend,

GROVER CLEVELAND.

Hon. Wm. F. Vilas,
Madison, Wis.

George Allen Bennett, aged nine, received this reply:

Stuart, Florida.
March 30, 1906.

MY DEAR LITTLE FRIEND:

I am very glad you wrote me a letter of congratulation and good wishes on my birthday. And I thank you
for kindly thinking of me. We ought to be very good
friends, if we were born on the same day of the month,
though there is a difference of sixty years in our ages.
The years seem to pass much more quickly, as a person
grows older and when you arrive at the age of sixty-nine,

as I have done, you will wonder at the short distance between nine and sixty-nine.

I think the 18th of March is the best day in all the year to be born on and I hope you do too. I wish for you a great many Happy Birthdays, and that as each one passes, there will be such increase in your mental and moral growth and such improvement in every way that you will be insured a life of honor and usefulness.

Your friend
GROVER CLEVELAND.

Master George Allen Bennett
   North Ridgefield, Conn.

Mr. Cleveland loved children and this letter is the result of the natural impulse of that affection. One of his law partners in the old days in Buffalo has recorded the fact that in furnishing his bachelor apartments "his fondness for children was shown in a preponderance of children's pictures in the photographs scattered about." And another friend of early days recalls the fact that, while Governor of New York, he used to walk every day from his residence to the Capitol, and always greeted each child whom he met with "Hello, little one!" Not infrequently he received and always enjoyed the retort: "Hello, little one!" During one of Judge Hornblower's visits to Mr. Cleveland, when Ruth was a very new baby, he drew out from his overcoat pocket and displayed to the ex-President a sadly dilapidated doll which his daughter, Susie, aged five, had asked her father to take to little Ruth when she heard that the latter was ill. The conversation then turned to other matters, and when the Judge returned home he carried the doll with him, forgotten. The next day he received from Mr. Cleveland the following letter:

My dear Mr. Hornblower:

I scarcely do anything just now but read the kindest messages of congratulation and receive in every possible way manifestations of the kindness which pervades the people of the Land.

And yet nothing has come near touching me so much as the incident of to-day relating to the gift your little daughter sent to mine.

I do not know why you did not leave the doll with me. Nothing could have been more dear to the mother than the doll which a little girl, *and your daughter,* was willing to give up to our new baby.

I do not want your child to feel that her gift was not valued for what it was worth. It meant so much to her that it means a very great deal to us.

I wish we could have the doll and that its precious little donor could receive our heartfelt thanks, with the assurance that when our child first plays with a doll it shall be with the one she gave her.

Of course if we are to have it, it must be in the exact shape it was in when I saw it to-day.

Yours sincerely

GROVER CLEVELAND.

The closing months of 1906 were uneventful, save for ceaseless pleas for speeches. But he was weary of speaking, and refused every call which did not lay a hand upon his conscience. He did, however, promise, at the urgent request of the Union League Club of Chicago, to deliver the Washington's Birthday address of 1907, under their auspices, although he shrank from the idea of the labor which such a promise entailed. Having completed it, he wrote to George F. Parker: "I have just finished a terrific and not a very victorious struggle in the prepara-

tion of something to say at Chicago on Washington's
Birthday. I am consoled, however, by the reflection that
it concludes probably my perplexities in that direction
for the period of my natural life, and during the ensuing
eternity, unless I fail to 'arrive,' as I hope to do."

Armed with his manuscript he reached Chicago, only
to find that he could not escape with a single address.
Indeed, he had made four before that strenuous twenty-
second of February closed. His principal speech, a tribute to the memory of George Washington, was at once a
eulogy and a warning. He read it from the manuscript
with neither gesture nor sign of emotion, save when he
turned from his praise of the first President to denounce
the corruption, extravagance, and dishonesty of dema-
gogues, or to attack a too slavish adherence to party and
partisan interests.

"If your observance of this day," he said, "were intended to make more secure the immortal fame of Washington, or to add to the strength and beauty of his imper-
ishable monument built upon a nation's affectionate
remembrance, your purpose would be useless. Washington has no need of you. But in every moment from the
time he drew his sword in the cause of American
Independence to this hour, living or dead, the American
people have needed him. It is not important now, nor
will it be in all the coming years, to remind our countrymen that Washington has lived. . . . But it is important
—and more important now than ever before—that they
should clearly apprehend and adequately value the virtues and ideal of which he was the embodiment. . . .
There should be no toleration of even the shade of a
thought that what Washington did and said and wrote
. . . has become in the least outworn, or that in these
days of material advance and development they may be

merely pleasantly recalled with a sort of affectionate
veneration, and with a kind of indulgent and loftily cour-
teous concession of the value of Washington's example
and precepts. These constitute the richest of our crown
jewels."

In the evening he was introduced to the diners at
the Union League Club by President Charles S. Cutting,
who referred to the question: "What shall we do with
our ex-Presidents?" Mr. Cleveland's reply was a genial
comment upon the solution recently proposed by a prominent editor-enemy: "Take him out into a five-acre lot and
shoot him." "That proposition," he said, "has never had
my support. In the first place, a five-acre lot seems
needlessly large, and in the second place an ex-President
has already suffered enough. . . ."

Mr. Cleveland's delight at the attentions received on
his sixty-ninth anniversary prompted his friends to undertake a larger celebration for the seventieth. In fact,
they dared to plan a national observance of the birthday
of the man who, ten years before, had left the White
House a fallen leader, with few, even among his own
party, prepared to do him reverence. Time, the revealer
of all things, had dealt kindly with his fame, until now
he who had never courted favor, even within his own
party, found it in both parties.

John H. Finley, then President of the College of the
City of New York, suggested that the day be kept as the
nation's "out-of-doors day," and a flock of eager reporters
arrived at Princeton to request Mr. Cleveland's reaction
to the suggestion. They were received with cordiality,
and retired primed with an interview upon the benefits
of the simple life.

"I look with apprehension," he said, "upon the mad
rush of American life, which is certain to impair the

mental and physical vigor necessary to every human being. The wholesome sentiments which spring from country life are being overwhelmed by the ambitions and tendencies that flow out from our great cities. Few have the hardihood to withstand the swirl and rush of city life, or to remain indifferent to the promises of sudden wealth and the excitement of speculation in a metropolis, where immense fortunes are made and lost in a single day. . . .

"We are proud of our cities, of course. But we must not allow them wholly to shape our ideals and our ambitions. Nothing that the wealth of a city can buy will atone for the loss of that American sturdiness and independence which the farm and the small town have so frequently produced. . . . In my experience I have found that impressions which a man receives who walks by the brookside or in the forest or by the seashore make him a better man and a better citizen. They lift him above the worries of business and teach him of a power greater than human power."

Just before his birthday, he started south on a hunting trip, thus setting a good example to the millions who were asked to observe "out-of-doors day." Upon his seventieth birthday, therefore, only one letter reached him; but that one made all others unnecessary to his contentment:

Princeton, N. J.
March 15, 1907.

MY DEAREST:

I am so afraid that I will not get your birthday letter to you in time that I suppose it will be a day ahead! And maybe you will reach home anyway and so not get it, but in that case I think I might be able to express

my birthday thoughts to you. I hope you will be well
on Monday, just as well as you can be, then things will
look bright to you and your new year will begin happily.
Then I hope you will keep well, and it will go a long
long way toward making your year happy. I hate to
have you away on your birthday, but I realize that it
will save you some strain—for many people seem to be
thinking of you at this time. We all send much much
love, and all the deepest best wishes of our hearts—and
my heart is full of gratitude for what the years of your
life have meant to me. You know how dearly I love
you. You do not mind my saying it over, any day, and
you won't mind it on this especial day—so I repeat it
and repeat it, and I ask God's blessing on you for all
the days.

Your loving wife
FRANK.

The oak box tells the tale of how many people were
thinking of him on his seventieth birthday, and of how
he cherished the records of their affection. It contains
hundreds of letters and telegrams from men, women, and
children in all walks of life, expressing pride, gratitude,
and affection for this retired leader of men. One of the
tributes which he most valued was an editorial in the
New York *Sun,* so long his relentless persecutor and
defamer. It declared: "As President, Mr. Cleveland
enforced the laws and did not truckle to organized violence or crouch before public clamor. The man who
taught the Chicago labor lords that there was a Government at Washington, the man who wrote the Venezuela
message, is sure of an honorable place in history and of
the final approval of his countrymen." In sending this
editorial to Mr. Cleveland, Edwin Packard wrote: "If

Mr. Dana were living, I think that even he would make amends."

The day was celebrated at Caldwell, New Jersey, by the unveiling of a tablet in the room where he was born. Unsentimental though he appeared to the outsider, his heart was as responsive as that of a child, despite his long life of conflict; and this mark of affection touched the deepest emotions of his nature. To Richard Watson Gilder, one of the prime movers in the plan to make his birthplace also his memorial, he wrote:

Princeton, *March 25, 1907.*

MY DEAR MR. GILDER:

It was a complete misfit—a travesty on things as they should be—that I should be disporting in balmy air and all creature comforts, while you cold, hungry, and miserably forlorn, were finding your way to Caldwell, for the purpose of marking the time and place of my birth. You did what you ought not to have done. There is no process of calculation by which it can be made to appear a profitable investment for you. And yet when men reach the age of seventy, I believe their mental movements grow self-centered to such an extent, that consciously or unconsciously, they sort of believe their gratitude to be in some measure compensatory to those who honor them or suffer discomforts on their behalf.

I am so new to this venerable age of seventy, that I cannot tell at this moment how much I am under the influence of this idea. But my dear friend, one thing I know: Your kindnesses have been so many, and have extended through so many years, that the pages set apart for their record are full; and I long ago abandoned all hope of redeeming the one-sidedness of the account.

You must I think see how impossible it is for me to

do more than to say to you, that I am profoundly moved by the conception of the Caldwell incident and by the beauty of its completed manifestation. It stands for the thoughtfulness and affectionate remembrance of friends nearer my heart than all others.

Yours faithfully

GROVER CLEVELAND.

Richard W. Gilder
   Editor of The Century Magazine
   New York.

Among the many verses written in honor of the day, are the following by Eliza H. Morton:

> "Time's hand has lightly touched thy brow
> With lines of care.
> And as he touched, he whispered 'peace,'
> And stamped it there."

In general, his own reactions were less serious. To Commodore Benedict he wrote, when the day was over: "I am already regarding it as a small performance to do so easy a trick."

So successful had been the plan to encourage a nation-wide crop of birthday letters that he found it impossible to send personal acknowledgments. He therefore inserted in the New York *Times* the following grateful confession of helpless appreciation: "It seems to be impossible for me to acknowledge, except through the press of the country, the generosity and kindly consideration of my countrymen, which have been made manifest by congratulatory messages and newspaper comment on the occasion of my seventieth birthday. These have deeply touched me, and in the book of grateful recollection they are written where every remaining day of my life I can turn a page and read them."

The drift of politics during the next few months left him still uncertain which national organization was most entitled to be called by disciples of the "True Democracy" the common enemy. Eagerly he watched for signs of the long-hoped-for Democratic redemption, and found none. Bryanism was still Democracy, and Cleveland was as unwilling as ever to acknowledge the identity. Of Republican regeneration he had long since ceased even to dream, for the promises of McKinleyism, which his influence had done so much to enthrone, had bitterly disappointed him; while its successor, Rooseveltism, had never appealed to him as having even promise. "Concerning . . . political affairs," he wrote to Benedict, on August 17, 1907, "I feel like the farmer who started at the bottom of a hill with a wagon load of corn and discovered at the hill top that every grain of his load had slid out under the tail board. Though of a profane temperament, he stood mutely surveying his disaster until to a passing neighbor, who asked him why he didn't swear, he replied: 'Because by God I cannot do the subject justice.' "

For the Commodore's further delectation, he thus pictured his conception of the politics of the day, in which both parties looked strangely alike to him:

"I see our President has been making another 'Yes, I guess not' speech on business, corporations, etc., and has told the farmers how completely they should have the land and the fullness thereof; Gov. Hughes seems to be attempting neck-breaking acrobatics; Bryan smiles at both of them while performing his continuous tight-rope dance; and Hearst in his cage of wild beasts waits his turn to surprise and shock the multitude—'Open every hour of the day and night gentlemen; wonderful vaudeville performance—all seen under one tent.' "

He did not hesitate to declare, however, that if Bryan should be again nominated by the Democrats, he would vote for a Republican, should a satisfactory man be selected. When pressed for his opinion as to "a satisfactory man," he declared that he would consider Secretary Cortelyou such an one, and added: "I know of no one whom I could more heartily and conscientiously support." When Colonel John J. McCook asked him to name a Democrat whom he would be willing to support, he replied, "either Harmon or Gray."

As the spring approached, the political atmosphere took on the peculiar tenseness familiar to every man who has dreamed of national political power; and the hopefulness which had carried him through so many apparently desperate political battles began to return, despite his physical condition. On March 14th, he bared his heart to his old friend, E. Prentiss Bailey:

"I cannot rid myself of the idea that our party, which has withstood so many clashes with our political opponents, is not doomed at this time to sink to a condition of useless and lasting decadence. In my last letter to you I expressed myself as seeing some light ahead for Democracy. I cannot help feeling at this time that the light is still brighter. It does seem to me that movements have been set in motion which, though not at the present time of large dimensions, promise final relief from the burden which has so long weighed us down. I have lately come to the conclusion that our best hope rests upon the nomination of Johnson of Minnesota. The prospects to my mind appear as bright with him as our leader as with any other, and whether we meet with success or not, I believe with such a leader we shall take a long step in the way of returning to our old creed and the old policies and the old pians of organization which have heretofore led us to victory.

"I received a letter a few days ago from Judge Donahue of New York, an old war-horse of Democracy, now 84 years old, but still active in the practice of his profession. He said to me that, though he was by a number of years older than I, he not only hoped but expected to live to see a Democratic President in the White House. I often think that with my seventy-one years to be completed in four days now, such a hope and expectation on my part can hardly be reasonably entertained; but I confess that I am somewhat ashamed of such pessimistic feeling when I read the cheery and confident words contained in this old veteran's letter. I do not want you to suppose that a feeling of pessimism toward political affairs is habitual with me. On the contrary, such a condition of mind is quite infrequent and so temporary that it yields quickly to a better mood and a settled conviction that our party before many years will march from the darkness to the full light of glorious achievement. . . ."

His seventy-first birthday—and his last—found him with strength greatly depleted by the frequent gastro-intestinal attacks complicated by organic disease of the heart and kidneys from which he had suffered, with increasing violence, for many years. His loss of vitality alarmed his family and his physicians who, however, guarded the secret that his condition was serious. On April 14th, Mrs. Cleveland wrote, in strict confidence, to George F. Parker: "We have tried not to have it known, but he has had another attack within the last few days. While not so serious in itself, it came so soon after the one preceding that he was not so strong as usual, and it has left him in much weaker condition."

As the days passed it became more evident that he

could not rally the strength to resist this new attack, and he prepared to face the final battle of his strenuous life; but with little hope of earthly victory. His affairs were in order. He awaited his summons.

"During these last weeks," writes his sister, Mrs. Yeomans, "he sent to his old home for one of the worn hymn books that were used at family prayers in his boyhood." His mind instinctively reverted to the early lessons of hope which had been the inspiration of his life. "As weakness more encroached," wrote St. Clair McKelway, "he faced toward the inevitable with trust in the Almighty and with good will to mankind. The intent look which often came into his face was not due to apprehension."

On June 24, 1908, at 8.40 in the morning he died, as he had often expressed the wish to die, in his Princeton home, with his beloved wife beside him. His parting words are the key to his life: "I have tried so hard to do right."

His body was buried in the old Princeton Cemetery two days later, just as the setting sun touched the rim of the horizon. There, to-day, stands his simple gravestone, a shaft of granite on which is carved:

GROVER CLEVELAND
Born Caldwell, N. J.
March 18th, 1837
Died Princeton, N. J.
June 24th, 1908.

A mile away rises his national monument, the Cleveland Memorial Tower, erected by the contributions of men and women of varied races and political affiliations, many of whom had never seen his face, but all of whom wished thus to pay their homage to a great American.

Living, he dared to disregard party in the service of principle. Dying, he named no party as his heir. Dead, no party and no faction can fairly claim a monopoly of the glory with which the advancing years are steadily crowning his memory.

In the little oak box by his bedside was found a copy of Whittier's beautiful poem, "At Last":

"When on my day of life the night is falling,
And, in the winds from unsunned spaces blown,
I hear far voices out of darkness calling
My feet to paths unknown,

Thou, who hast made my home of life so pleasant,
Leave not its tenant when its walls decay;
O Love Divine, O Helper ever present,
Be Thou my strength and stay!"

SOURCES

A. PRIMARY SOURCES.

Partly in manuscript form; partly in the form of printed documents. The manuscripts consist chiefly of memoranda, diaries, letters written by Mr. Cleveland, and those written to him, speeches, etc., etc.

The printed primary sources are chiefly public documents, city, county, state or national, which have been published either as public archives or as private collections.

Mr. Cleveland, as have all our Presidents, left an enormous mass of manuscript material, but he left it in chaotic condition. The papers were packed into rough wooden boxes, without systematic arrangement, the important and the unimportant thrown together; and many of the most valuable manuscripts contain neither title, date, nor other indication of the purpose for which they were prepared. In most cases, except personal letters, the very authorship of the manuscript would be in doubt but for the fact that all are written in "copper plate," as he called his own neat but distressingly illegible handwriting. Practically every letter, message, proclamation, executive order, even the publicity notices and the successive copies of addresses often revised, are wholly in his own hand.

He apparently made no attempt to keep his files complete, and frequently the only copy of an important document was given to some friend who wished a specimen of his handwriting.

The forty or fifty thousand miscellaneous documents,

mostly letters to the President, but including the final copies of many of his presidential messages, which he brought from Washington at the end of his public life, he stored in a wing of Colonel Lamont's country house at Millbrook, New York, and apparently forgot. These, with a collection of thirty thousand manuscripts from the Library of Congress, and a smaller one from the attic of his Princeton home, constitute the bulk of the manuscript sources upon which his biography has been based.

I. THE CLEVELAND MANUSCRIPTS

    (1)   Memoranda from the following:

        (a)   Mr. Cleveland's sisters, Mrs. Yeomans and Mrs. Bacon: sketches of his childhood days, giving glimpses such as only the members of his own family could give.

        (b)   Richard Watson Gilder, one of Mr. Cleveland's most intimate friends: a collection of notes made immediately after important conversations with Mr. Cleveland. They are written upon the backs of envelopes, or stray scraps of paper of odd sizes and irregular shapes. Many of them are almost illegible, but all are worth the trouble of deciphering.

        (c)   John G. Milburn, an eminent lawyer, whose friendship extended back into Mr. Cleveland's Buffalo days: a series of comments upon important incidents in Mr. Cleveland's public and private life.

        (d)   Milburn and Locke: documents used by John G. Milburn and Franklin Day Locke in the trial of a suit brought by the Rev. George H. Ball against the Evening Post

Publishing Company, and involving the famous case of Maria Halpin.

(e) A committee of sixteen Republicans and Independents: a report upon the personal character of Grover Cleveland, made to the Mugwump National Committee during the presidential campaign of 1884.

(f) The Reverend Wilton Merle-Smith: bearing upon Mr. Cleveland's religious views.

(g) William B. Hornblower, with a supplementary memorandum prepared from Judge Hornblower's papers by his son, George Hornblower: especial reference to the circumstances connected with Judge Hornblower's appointment as an Associate Justice of the Supreme Court, and his rejection by the Senate.

(h) Otto Gresham, son of Secretary of State Gresham: relating to Mr. Cleveland's dealings with currency problems, and especially with the question of his influence upon the currency declarations of the Republican National Convention of 1896.

(i) Many of Mr. Cleveland's friends or close associates, including Elihu Root, Charles W. Eliot, Cardinal Gibbons, Edward W. Hatch, Thomas Cary, Chauncey M. Depew, Adlai E. Stevenson, etc., etc.: brief memoranda relating to particular incidents or impressions.

(2) Diaries:

A small pocket diary, in pencil, beginning August 27, 1898, and ending September 27, 1905. It contains 122 closely written pages.

Most of the entries relate to fishing. Diaries for the years 1898, 1899, 1901, 1903, 1904, and 1905. Many of the pages are left blank, many contain only a few lines of notes, but they are of sufficient biographical value to cause regret that the volumes for 1900 and 1902 are missing.

(3)   Letters:

For the most part Grover Cleveland's letters were gathered from garrets and dusty private files all over the land. Their locations were discovered by studying Mr. Cleveland's own personal papers, noting the names of all persons with whom he appeared to have been upon terms making likely a personal correspondence, and writing to the persons in question, or to descendants or relatives. In this way about 1500 manuscript letters were recovered:

(a)   Letters to Cabinet members:
102 to Wilson S. Bissell; 38 to Judson Harmon; 29 to Don M. Dickinson; 120 to Daniel S. Lamont; 117 to Richard T. Olney; 90 all told to the following: William C. Endicott, Walter Q. Gresham, Charles S. Fairchild, Thomas F. Bayard, William F. Vilas.

(b)   Letters to personal friends, acquaintances, etc.:

Louis L. Babcock
E. Prentiss Bailey
Commodore E. C. Benedict
Mrs. W. Cabell Bruce
Dr. Joseph B. Bryant
Andrew Carnegie

Thomas Cary
Mrs. Julius C. Chambers
Mrs. Robert W. Chapin
Joseph H. Choate
James Freeman Clarke
William Clausen

George B. Cortelyou   George W. Hayward
Frederic R. Coudert   D-Cady Herrick
Paul D. Cravath   F. W. Hinrichs
Mrs. A. B. Creasey   William B. Hornblower
William J. Curtis   Joseph Jefferson
L. Clarke Davis   Daniel M. Lockwood
Bernard S. Deutsch   Dr. Wilton Merle-Smith
Mrs. Louis R. Ehrich   Alton B. Parker
Dr. Charles W. Eliot   George F. Parker
Admiral Robley D. Evans Theodore Roosevelt
A. B. Farquhar   Edward M. Shepard
Dr. John H. Finley   Oscar Straus
Mrs. Roderick E. Fletcher Henry T. Thurber
Colonel David M. Flynn   Mrs. Charles Tracy
Cardinal Gibbons   Lambert Tree
Richard Watson Gilder   Dr. Samuel B. Ward
A. C. Goodyear   Dean Andrew Fleming West
John Temple Graves   A. A. Wilson
John S. Green   Woodrow Wilson
M. D. Harter   Dr. Charles Wood

Of these, the letters to Commodore Benedict alone number 279, and all touch upon the
lighter things of life: fishing, hunting, boat-
ing, cribbage, etc.

Mr. Julian B. Beaty, Mr. Cleveland's pri-
vate secretary in 1904, kindly reproduced
from his notebooks copies of 115 letters dic-
tated by Mr. Cleveland during that year; Mr.
George S. Bixby, the biographer of David B.
Hill, sent a considerable collection which
Mr. Cleveland wrote to Mr. Hill during the
years of political association; and Mrs. H. F.
Reid sent nineteen letters and one telegram to
Ernest Gittings.

In these letters we see the man himself,
simple, frank, and fearless, with the spirit
of a crusader humanized by a sense of humor
and a gift for friendship. Without them it
would be difficult to picture him, for his formal papers are one and all wholly impersonal.

II.   PRINTED SOURCES.

(1)   State Collections
        Public Papers of Grover Cleveland as Gov-
ernor, one volume for 1883 and one volume
for 1884. Argus Co., 1883 and 1884. There
is a later edition in which the two years are
bound together in one volume.

(2)   Federal Collections
        The documents sent by President Cleve-
land to Congress, in connection with his various messages, are printed in the records of
Congress, and are far too numerous for detailed discussion. The following are cited as
having special reference to outstanding questions of foreign policy:
        (a)   The Samoan Affair. The chief docu-
ments are in:

        (1st)   House Exec. Doc., 164, 44th
        Congress, 1st Session, which gives the
        political history of Samoa. Foreign
        Relations, 1894, Appx. I, for Bates
        report.
        (2d)   Foreign Relations, 1889, pp.
        204-231, for texts of protocols on
        Samoan Conferences among Euro-
        pean nations.

(3d) House Exec. Doc., 238, 50th Congress, 1st Session.

(4th) Senate Exec. Doc., 31, 50th Congress, 2d Session; Senate Exec. Doc., 68, 50th Congress, 2d Session.

(b) The Hawaiian Affair:

(1st) Foreign Relations, 1891.

(2d) Foreign Relations, 1894, Appx. II.

(3d) Foreign Relations, Volume VI.

(4th) House Exec. Doc., 130, 49th Congress, 2d Session, Volume XXIII.

(5th) House Exec. Doc., 48, 53rd Congress, 2d Session.

(c) The Venezuelan Affair:

(1st) The British Blue Book, 97, 1896.

(2d) Senate Exec. Doc., 31, 54th Congress, 1st Session.

(3d) Senate Exec. Doc., 226, 50th Congress, 1st Session.

(4th) Senate Miscellaneous Docs., 54th Congress, 1st Session, Volume I.

(5th) The British-Venezuelan Treaty, which ended the controversy, is in Foreign Relations, 1896, p. 254.

(3) Miscellaneous Collections

(a) *The Public Papers of Grover Cleveland, Twenty-Second President of the United States,* March 4, 1885, to March 4, 1889.

Washington Government Printing Office, 1889.

(b) *Writings and Speeches of Grover Cleveland,* edited by George F. Parker. Cassell Publishing Co., New York, 1892. 571 pages. A collection of Cleveland documents, 1881 to 1892, arranged according to topics.

(c) *Principles and Purposes of our Form of Government as Set Forth in the Public Papers of Grover Cleveland.* Compiled by Francis Gottsberger. George G. Peck, New York, 1892. 187 pages of extracts from Grover Cleveland's speeches, letters, and public papers from 1885 to 1892, without editorial comment.

(d) *Messages and Papers of the Presidents.* Edited by James D. Richardson. Government Printing Office, Washington, 1896 *et seq.* Volumes VIII and IX contain the official executive documents issued by Mr. Cleveland as President.

(e) *The Public Papers of Grover Cleveland, Twenty-Fourth President of the United States,* March 4, 1893, to March 4, 1897. Government Printing Office, Washington, 1897.

(f) *Letters and Addresses of Grover Cleveland.* Edited by Albert Ellery Bergh. The Unit Book Publishing Co., New York, 1909. One vol. 499 pages. The most complete general collection of Mr. Cleveland's papers.

B SECONDARY SOURCES

Mr. Cleveland's own books, pamphlets, and articles written for publication; scrapbooks of newspaper clippings; innumerable biographies, genealogical studies, magazine articles, and pamphlets, published during his life and since his death; and a vast mass of literature containing incidental reference to him. These are obviously too numerous to be catalogued exhaustively, but the following list will be found adequate to most demands:

I. WRITTEN FOR PUBLICATION BY GROVER CLEVELAND

(1)   Books, pamphlets, etc.

(a)   *What Shall We Do with It?* (meaning the surplus). Taxation and revenue discussed by President Cleveland, J. G. Blaine, H. Watterson, etc. Harper & Bros., New York, 1888.

(b)   *Thou Shalt Not Steal.* A few words on the tariff by Grover Cleveland, W. E. Russell, etc. A. J. Philpott & Co., Boston, 1892. 29 pages.

(c)   *Cleveland on the Money Question.* Washington, D. C., 1895. 4 pages.

(d)   *The Selfmade Man in American Life.* T. Y. Crowell & Co., New York, 1897.

(e)   *The Defense of Fishermen.* Privately printed, Princeton, N. J., 1902. 13 pages.

(f)   *Presidential Problems.* Century Co., New York, 1904. One vol. 281 pages. A painstaking description of the major conflicts of his second term. The chapters are in essence republications of his Stafford Little Lectures at Princeton University, which are available also in the form of booklets printed by the Princeton University Press under the following titles:

(1st) The Venezuelan Boundary Controversy, 1913, first printed as articles in the *Century Magazine,* June and July, 1901, Vol. LXII.

(2d) The Government in the Chicago Strike, 1913.

(3d) The Independence of the Executive, 1913.

(g) *Fishing and Shooting Sketches.* Illustrated by Henry S. Watson. The Outing Publishing Co., New York, 1906.

(h) *In the Matter of State Legislation Limiting the Compensation of Officers of Insurance Companies.* Brief in opposition thereto. New York, 1907. 11 pages.

(i) *Compulsory Investment Legislation.* Some considerations as to legislation requiring life insurance companies to make investments in certain states in which they are doing business. The Association of Life Insurance Presidents, New York, 1907. 8 pages.

(2) Magazine and Newspaper Articles

(a) In the *Saturday Evening Post:*

"Does a College Education Pay?" May 25, 1900.

"The Plight of the Democracy," December 22, 1900.

"The Young Man in Politics," January 26, 1901.

"The Uses of Adversity," March 9, 1901.

"Strength and Needs of Civil Service Reform," March 30, 1901.

"The Waste of Public Money," June 1, 1901.

"The Safety of the President," October 5, 1901.

"A Defense of Fishermen," October 19, 1901.

"The Serene Duck Hunter," April 26, 1902.

"The President and His Patronage," May 24, 1902.

"The Shadow of the City," September 19, 1903.

"The Mission of Fishing and Fishermen," December 5, 1903.

"The Democracy's Opportunity," February 20, 1904.

"The Cleveland Bond Issues," May 7, 1904.

"Some Fishing Pretenses and Affectations," September 24, 1904.

"Why a Young Man Should Vote the Democratic Ticket," October 8, 1904.

"Old-Fashioned Honesty and the Coming Man," August 5, 1905.

"Directors That Do Not Direct," December 1, 1906.

By far the most important of these articles is the one on the Cleveland Bond Issues. Its sub-title shows the character of the article: "A detailed history of the crime charged against an administration that issued bonds of the government in time of peace." It is about 10,000 words in length and gives Mr. Cleveland's interpretation of the circumstances which made the bond issues necessary. The original MS. is among the Cleveland papers.

In the New York *World* of May 15, 1904, appears a detailed reply to Mr. Cleveland's arguments.

(b)   In the *Youth's Companion:*
"The Civic Responsibility of Youth," July 2, 1903.
"The Country Lawyer in National Affairs," February 8, 1906.
"Our People and Their Ex-Presidents," January 2, 1908.

(c)   In the *Ladies' Home Journal:*
"Woman's Mission and Woman's Clubs," May, 1905.
"Would Woman's Suffrage Be Unwise?" October, 1905.
"The Honest American Marriage, A Plea for Home-Building," October, 1906.

(d)   In the *Independent:*
"Summer Shooting," June 2, 1904.
"A Word Concerning Rabbit Hunting," June 1, 1905.

(e)   In *Collier's:*
"Steady, Democrats, Steady," July 23, 1904.

(f)   In the *Pacific Monthly:*

"The Plight of Democracy and the
Remedy," January, 1901.

(g)   In the New York *World,* Sunday
Editorial Section, March 15, 1903:
"Adversity as an Aid to Success."

II. WRITTEN FOR PUBLICATION BY OTHERS

(1)   Scrapbooks:

(a)   The White House Scrapbooks, forty
volumes, containing clippings from daily and
weekly papers and magazines. In general
these clippings are grouped into volumes according to topics, four volumes dealing
wholly with Civil Service Reforms, etc., etc.

(b)   Wedding Scrapbooks, three large volumes containing a varied assortment of clippings and pictures relating to Mr. Cleveland's
wedding. They were made by friends at the
time of the wedding and subsequently presented to the President.

(c)   The Fairchild Scrapbooks, three volumes, containing newspaper clippings and
press copies of letters relating chiefly to the
history of the campaign of 1892.

(d)   The McKelway Scrapbooks, a set of
about a dozen large folio volumes, containing
chiefly articles and editorials written by Mr.
McKelway, as editor of the Brooklyn *Eagle.*
As Mr. McKelway was an intimate friend and
a strong political supporter of Mr. Cleveland,
these volumes are rich in biographical material.

(e)   George F. Parker Scrapbook of the
Presidential Campaign of 1884, made up

chiefly of clippings from the New York *World,* and containing many Cleveland cartoons.

(f) 20th Century Press Clipping Bureau of Chicago Scrapbook, covering the incidents of Mr. Cleveland's visit to Chicago in October, 1903.

(g) New York Public Library Scrapbook of the death of Grover Cleveland. New York, 1908.

(h) Princeton University Library Scrapbook, devoted wholly to clippings concerning Mr. Cleveland's death.

(2) Biographies:

(a) *Life and Public Services of Grover Cleveland.* By Pendleton King. G. P. Putnam's Sons, New York, 1884. 224 pages.

(b) *Life and Public Services of Grover Cleveland.* By Honorable William Dorsheimer. Hubbard Brothers, Philadelphia, 1884. A new and enlarged edition was prepared by W. U. Hensel, in preparation for the Campaign of 1888. Hubbard Brothers, Philadelphia. One vol. 588 pages.

(c) *Life and Public Services of Grover Cleveland and Thomas A. Hendricks.* By Chauncey F. Black. Thayer, Merriam & Co., Philadelphia, 1884.

(d) *Building and Ruling the Republic.* By James P. Boyd. Garretson, Philadelphia, 1884. Part 4.

(e) *Campaign of 1884. Biographies of S. Grover Cleveland, and Thomas A. Hen-*

dricks. By Benjamin Le Fevre. Fireside Publishing Co., Philadelphia, 1884.

(f) *The Authorized Pictorial Lives of Stephen Grover Cleveland and Thomas Andrews Hendricks.* By Frank Triplett. N. D. Thompson & Co., Publishers, New York and St. Louis, 1884. One vol. 568 pages.

(g) *Stephen Grover Cleveland.* By Deshler Welch. J. W. Lovell Co., New York, 1884. 222 pages. Also published under the title *Life of Grover Cleveland,* Worthington, New York, 1884.

(h) *Early Life and Public Services of Hon. Grover Cleveland,* the fearless and independent Governor of the Empire State, and candidate for President. . . . Also the Life of Hon. Thomas A. Hendricks, candidate for Vice-President. By Thomas W. Handford. Caxton Publishing Co., Chicago and New York, 1884. 510 pages.

(i) *The Life of Honorable Grover Cleveland,* including his early days, District Attorneyship, Mayoralty of Buffalo, Governorship of New York, nomination at Chicago. Edited by J. B. McClure. Rhodes and McClure, Chicago, 1884. One vol. 218 pages.

(j) *Life and Public Services of Grover Cleveland,* with incidents of his early life, and an account of his rise to eminence in his profession; also containing his addresses and official documents as Mayor of the City of Buffalo, and Governor of the State of New York. By Frederick E. Goodrich. B. B. Russell, Boston, 1884. One vol. 504 pages.

A valuable campaign biography. Abundantly supplied with copies of documents accurately transcribed, many of which are not easily available elsewhere. As a campaign biography, however, it is history written with the intention of making the Democratic party appear spotless and the Republican party crooked and unreliable, a thesis scarcely consistent with fact in that period of the history of New York or of the United States.

(k) *A Man of Destiny.* Edited by W. P. Nixon. Belford, Clarke & Co., Chicago, 1885. 226 pages.

(l) *Life and Public Services of Grover Cleveland.* By William U. Hensel and George F. Parker. Guernsey Publishing Co., Philadelphia, 1888 and 1892.

(m) *Life and Public Services of Our Great Reform President, Grover Cleveland.* By Col. Herman Dieck. J. Dewing & Co., San Francisco, 1888. Also S. I. Bell & Co., Philadelphia. 554 pages.

(n) *Age of Cleveland.* By Harold Fulton Ralphdon. F. A. Stokes & Bros., New York, 1888. 135 pages. Compiled from contemporary journals. Copy in Library of, Congress.

(o) *Grover Cleveland.* By Wm. O. Stoddard. Frederick A. Stokes Co., New York, 1888. One vol. 263 pages. The best campaign biography of Grover Cleveland, covering a much wider field than that of Frederick E. Goodrich, the only one comparable to it.

(p) *Distinguished American Lawyers.*

By Henry W. Scott. Webster, New York, 1891. "Grover Cleveland," pp. 161-172.

(q) *The History of the Democratic Party from Thomas Jefferson to Grover Cleveland.* . . . Lives of Cleveland and Stevenson. By Chandos Fulton. P. F. Collier, New York, 1892. 608 pages.

(r) *Life and Public Services of Grover Cleveland.* By William U. Hensel. Edgewood Publishing Co., Philadelphia, 1892. 556 pages.

(s) *A Life of Grover Cleveland,* with a sketch of Adlai E. Stevenson. By George Frederick Parker. Cassell Publishing Co., New York, 1892. 333 pages.

(t) *Cleveland and Stevenson, Their Lives and Record.* The Democratic campaign book for 1892, with a handbook of American politics up to date, and a cyclopedia of presidential biography. Compiled by Thos. Campbell-Copeland. C. L. Webster & Co., New York, 1892. One vol. 438 pages.

(u) *Grover Cleveland.* By James Lowry Whittle. Bliss, Sands & Co., London, 1896. F. Warne & Co., New York, 1896. One vol. 240 pages. In series, "Public Men of Today." A badly digested sketch of Mr. Cleveland's life. Its strong British point of view appears especially in Chapter XIV, "America and Great Britain," where the chief topic is the Venezuelan controversy. It is a volume of what is called popular history, showing little research and no special grace of style or conception.

(v) *Four Great American Presidents,
Garfield, McKinley, Cleveland, Roosevelt.*
J. M. Stradling & Co., New York, 1903. 309
pages.

(w) *Recollections of Grover Cleveland.*
By George F. Parker. Century Co., New
York, 1909. One vol. 427 pages. A book of
considerable interest, containing the personal
recollections of a man closely associated with
Mr. Cleveland, especially during the latter
years of his life. It contains many personal
letters not elsewhere attainable. The same
author has written many magazine articles
about Mr. Cleveland, notably a series in the
Saturday Evening Post ending in 1923, and an
earlier series in *McClure's Magazine,* as follows:

(1st) "Cleveland the Man." The
first administration and the second
campaign. v. 32, pp. 337-346.

(2d) "Cleveland's Estimate of
His Contemporaries." v. 33, pp.
24-34.

(3d) "Cleveland's Opinion of
Men." v. 32, pp. 569-581.

(4th) "Cleveland's Venezuela
Message." v. 33, pp. 314-323.

(x) *Mr. Cleveland, A Personal Impression.* By Jesse Lynch Williams. Dodd,
Mead & Co., New York, 1909.

(y) *Grover Cleveland, A Record of
Friendship.* By Richard Watson Gilder.
Century Co., New York, 1910. First printed
as articles in the *Century Magazine,* New

York, 1909, v. 78, pp. 483-503, 687-705, 846-860; v. 79, pp. 24-31. An artistic little volume, of much literary merit; depicting the human side of Grover Cleveland.

(z) *Grover Cleveland, A Study in Political Courage.* By Roland Hugins. The Anchor-Lee Publishing Co., Washington, D. C., 1922.

(3) Genealogical Works:

(a) *A Genealogy of Benjamin Cleveland, the Great-Grandson of Moses Cleveland of Woburn.* By Horace Gillette Cleveland. Rand McNally & Co., Chicago, 1879.

(b) *A Genealogical Register of the Descendants of Moses Cleveland of Woburn, Massachusetts.* Munsell, Albany, 1881.

(c) *An Account of the Lineage of Gen. Moses Cleveland of Canterbury, Conn., the Founder of the City of Cleveland, Ohio.* Also a sketch of his life. By H. Rice. W. W. Williams, Cleveland, Ohio, 1885.

(d) *The New England Ancestry of Grover Cleveland.* By W. K. Watkins and E. Putnam. The Salem Press, 1892. Privately printed. 35 copies made. Contains twenty-five pages, the first fifteen being taken up with charts by Walter K. Watkins and Eben Putnam. The rest is given up to notes presenting items of particular interest in connection with various members of the Cleveland family and collateral branches.

(e) *The Genealogy of the Cleveland and Cleaveland Families.* Compiled by Ed-

mund James Cleveland and Horace Gillette
Cleveland. Three vols. 3000 pages. The
Case, Lockwood and Brainard Company,
Hartford, Conn., 1899. An enormously de-
tailed work, covering a vast range of genea-
logical records. By far the most valuable
Cleveland genealogical work.

(4)   Magazine Articles:
(a)   "The President's Policy." By J. B.
Eustis, Wm. R. Grace, and Theodore Roosevelt. *North American Review,* October,
1885, pp. 374-396. An attempt to combine in
a single three-headed article a defense and a
denunciation. The article by Mr. Roosevelt
is the most interesting of the three, by virtue
of its picturesque, violent language, and its
frankly partisan criticisms.

(b)   "Southern View of the Election of
Cleveland." By A. G. Bradley. *Macmillan's
Magazine,* 1885. Vol. 51, p. 372.

(c)   "Possible Presidents: President
Cleveland." By D. B. Eaton, *North American Review,* 1887. Vol. 145, p. 629, *et seq.*

(d)   "Democracy Photographed. The
Record of a Bogus Reformer. President
Cleveland, a Wanton Pledge-breaker." New
York *Tribune* Extra, No. 100. New York,
1888.

(e)   "The Political Effect of the Message." By B. Smith. *North American Review,* 1888. Vol. V., p. 146, *et seq.*

(f)   "La Lutte pour la Presidence aux
Etats-Unis." By A. Moireau. *Rev. d. Deux
Mondes,* 1889. Vol. 91, p. 642, *et seq.*

(g) "Regierung des Praesidenten Cleveland." *Unser Zeit,* 1889. Vol. 2, p. 208, *et seq.*

(h) "Defeat of President Cleveland." *Contemporary Review,* 1889. Vol. 55, p. 283, *et seq.*

(i) "Cleveland a Popular Leader." By Wilbur Larremore. *The Arena,* January, 1891. Vol. 3, pp. 147-156.

(j) "What Mr. Cleveland Stands For." By Charles Francis Adams. *Forum,* July, 1892. Vol. 13, pp. 662-670. A brilliant, characteristically frank defense of Mr. Cleveland's record on the tariff, civil service, the currency, and the pension question. It is also a promise that the Independents will support Mr. Cleveland in 1892.

(k) "Mr. Cleveland as President." By Woodrow Wilson. *Atlantic Monthly,* March, 1897. Vol. 79, pp. 289-300.

(l) "Second Administration of Grover Cleveland." By Carl Schurz. *McClure's Magazine,* May, 1897. Vol. 9, pp. 633-644. An article of great value by one of the recognized leaders of Civil Service Reform, and a Mugwump of great influence and ability.

(m) "Character Sketch of Grover Cleveland." By William Allen White. *McClure's Magazine,* February, 1902. Vol. 18, pp. 322-330.

(n) "Grover Cleveland." By Lyman Abbott. *New York Genealogical and Biological Record.* New York, 1908. Vol. 39, pp. 237-241.

(o) Tribute to the Memory of Grover Cleveland, June 26, 1908. New York Chamber of Commerce, 1908.

(p) "Grover Cleveland." By Henry Loomis Nelson. *North American Review,* New York, 1908. Vol. 188, pp. 161-187.

(q) "Grover Cleveland, a Princeton Memory." By Andrew Fleming West. *Century Magazine,* New York, 1908. Vol. 77, pp. 323-337.

(r) "Cleveland as a Teacher in the Institution for the Blind." By Fanny J. Crosby. *McClure's Magazine,* March, 1909, pp. 581-583. A series of recollections prepared for the Democratic Campaign Committee, and containing little of interest or value.

(s) "Cleveland as a Lawyer." By Wilson S. Bissell. *McClure's Magazine,* Vol. 32, pp. 583-585. New York, 1909.

(t) "Grover Cleveland Memorial Meetings in Brooklyn and Manhattan, 1909." Addresses by Dr. St. Clair McKelway, President William H. Taft, Senator Elihu Root, etc., Brooklyn *Daily Eagle,* 1909. Eagle Library No. 148.

(u) "Official Characteristics of President Cleveland." By Charles R. Lingley. *Political Science Quarterly,* Lancaster, 1918. Vol. 33, pp. 255-265.

(5) Pamphlets:

(a) Address by Henry Ward Beecher at the Brooklyn Rink, October 22, 1884. Circular No. 13 of National Committee of Republicans and Independents, New York, 1884. 8 pages.

(b) *Cleveland and the Irish,* true history of the great Irish Revolt of 1884. By John Devoy. Issued by the Irish-American Anti-Cleveland and Protective League, New York, 1888. 8 pages.

(c) *Tell the Truth,* an anonymous pamphlet dealing, in a manner most unfair to Mr. Cleveland, with the scandals of the presidential campaign of 1884.

(d) *The Democratic Party and Civil Service Reform.* By the Young Men's Democratic Club of Brooklyn. Issued on January 26, 1885, and containing a collection of extracts bearing upon the Civil Service Reform movement and Mr. Cleveland's relation thereto. 16 pages.

(e) *The Inauguration of Grover Cleveland, the President-elect,* March 4, 1885. A book for fifty million people. By Henry J. Kintz. W. F. Fell & Co., Philadelphia, 1885.

(f) *Defense of Grover Cleveland, in Regard to His Treatment of the United States Attorneys in Pennsylvania and Missouri.* By Edward M. Shepard. New York, 1887. Privately printed. 23 pages.

(g) *The Imaginary Conversations of "His Excellency" and Dan.* By C. W. Taylor with illustrations by F. H. Blair. Cupples and Hurd, Boston, 1888. A burlesque very popular in the days of Mr. Cleveland's second presidential campaign.

(h) Souvenir of the Reception and Dinner given by the Young Men's Democratic Club of the City of New York, to the Honorable Grover Cleveland, New York, May 27, 1889. Contains the addresses of Mr. Cleveland, W. C. P. Breckinridge, David B. Hill, Governor Hoadley of Ohio, Frederic R. Coudert and Ashbel P. Fitch.

(i) Tammany Hall Souvenir of Inauguration of Cleveland and Stevenson. J. W. McDonald & Co., New York, 1893. 148 pages.

(j) *King George. Chronicles of His Reign According to Simonides, the Scribe of the Tribe of Lechay.* First book. Published by the author, Allentown, Pa., 1894. 128 pages. Written in the style of the Scriptures.

(k) Souvenir of the Annual Dinner of the Reform Club, held at the Waldorf Hotel, New York City, April 24, 1897. Martin B. Brown Company, New York, 1897. Contains Mr. Cleveland's address entitled "Present Problems," and addresses by John G. Carlisle, William L. Wilson, Edward M. Shepard, and others, all bearing more or less directly upon the history of Mr. Cleveland's fight for a sound currency.

(l) *Cleveland's Last Message:* Life insurance and its relationship to our people. Spectator Publishing Co., New York, 1908.

(m) *Good Citizenship.* Henry Altemus, Philadelphia, 1908.

(n) *Tribute to Memory of Grover Cleveland,* June 26, 1908, by Chamber of Commerce of the State of New York. New York Chamber of Commerce, 1908.

(o) *Cleveland's Last Message, A Literary Forgery.* By Broughton Brandenburg. New York, 1908. 15 pages.

(p) *Proceedings of the Second Annual Meeting of the Association of Life Insurance Presidents,* including an account of the Cleveland Memorial Meeting. Printed by the Association of Life Insurance Presidents, New York, 1909.

(q) *Grover Cleveland Memorial,* the eighteenth of March, in the year one thousand, nine hundred and nine. DeVinne Press, New York, 1910.

(r) *Grover Cleveland:* Address delivered at the unveiling of the memorial tablet at the Buffalo Historical Society, May 20, 1912. By John G. Milburn. Buffalo Historical Society Publications, 1913, v. 17, pp. 121-126.

(s) *Proceedings at the Passing of Title to the "Old Manse," Grover Cleveland's Birthplace, Caldwell, N. J.* March 18, 1913. Grover Cleveland Memorial Association, 1913.

(t) *Was New York's Vote Stolen?* By Francis Lynde Stetson and William Gorham Rice. Reprint from *North American Review,* January, 1914. A critical examination of the contest over the election of 1884.

(u) *The Surgical Operation on President Cleveland in 1893.* By Wm. W. Keen. G. W. Jacobs & Co., Philadelphia, 1917. 52 pages.

(v) *Address on Grover Cleveland,*

March 18, 1919, Cleveland Memorial Service
in New York City. By Leonard Wood. Published by the Cleveland Memorial Association, 1919.

(w) *Memorial Exercises of the Boston
Bar Association before the Supreme Judicial
Court in Memory of Richard Olney,* June 28,
1919. Geo. H. Ellis & Co., Boston, 1919. A
pamphlet containing many items of interest
with reference to the Chicago Strike, the
Venezuelan Controversy, etc.

III. BOOKS CONTAINING IMPORTANT INCIDENTAL BIO-
GRAPHICAL MATERIAL CONCERNING GROVER CLEVE-
LAND

(1) *The President and His Cabinet,* indicating the
progress of the Government of the United States under the administration of Grover Cleveland. By
Charles B. Norton. Cupples & Hurd, Boston, 1888.
249 pages.

(2) *Biography of James G. Blaine.* By Gail
Hamilton. Norwich, 1895.

(3) *History of Presidential Elections.* By Edward Stanwood. Houghton Mifflin Co., Boston, 4th
ed., 1896.

(4) *The First Battle.* By William Jennings
Bryan. A story of the campaign of 1896, together
with a collection of his speeches and a biographical
sketch by his wife. W. B. Conkey Co., 1897. 629
pages.

(5) *A History of the American People.* By
Woodrow Wilson. Harper & Bros., New York, 1902.
Five vols. See v. 5, pp. 170-253.

(6) *Our Presidents and How We Make Them.*

By A. K. McClure. Harper & Bros., New York, 1902. 481 pages.

(7) *American Tariff Controversies in the Nineteenth Century.* By Edward Stanwood. Houghton Mifflin Co., Boston, 1903. Two vols.

(8) *Autobiography of Seventy Years.* By George F. Hoar. Chas. Scribner's Sons, New York, 1903. Two vols. "President Cleveland's Judges," v. 2, pp. 172-181.

(9) *The Republican Party.* 1854-1904. By Francis Curtis. G. P. Putnam's Sons, New York, 1904. Two vols. "Convention of 1884—Nomination of Blaine—Moral Issue—Election of Cleveland," v. 2, pp. 116-162. "Administration of Cleveland," v. 2, pp. 163-179. "Conventions of 1892," v. 2, pp. 239-270. "Second Administration of Cleveland," v. 2, pp. 271-303.

(10) *Autobiography of Andrew D. White.* The Century Co., New York, 1905. Two vols. "Arthur, Cleveland, and Blaine," pp. 192-212.

(11) *The Democratic Party of the State of New York.* By James K. McGuire. 1905. Three vols. Grover Cleveland, v. 2, pp. 126-162.

(12) *James Gillespie Blaine.* By Edward Stanwood. Houghton Mifflin Co., Boston, 1905. 378 pages.

(13) *Recollections of Thirteen Presidents.* By John S. Wise. Doubleday, Page & Co., New York, 1906. Grover Cleveland, pp. 171-194.

(14) *A Political History of the State of New York.* By DeAlva Stanwood Alexander. Henry Holt & Co., New York, 1906-9. Three vols. "Cleveland's Enormous Majority," v. 3, pp. 483-499. A fourth volume has just appeared (1923), which covers

Mr. Cleveland's later political career in so far as it touched the field of New York politics.

(15) *Twenty Years of the Republic, 1885-1905.* By Harry T. Peck. Dodd, Mead & Co., New York, 1907. "The Return of the Democracy," pp. 1-48. "Two Years of President Cleveland," pp. 49-96. "President Cleveland Once More," pp. 306-349. In general, the best history of the Cleveland period, journalistic in style, but accurate in detail.

(16) *National Problems—1885-1897.* By Davis Rich Dewey. Harper & Bros., New York, 1907. The work of a well-known financial historian, and especially valuable upon the financial questions of Mr. Cleveland's administrations.

(17) *Speeches and Addresses, 1884-1909.* By Henry Cabot Lodge. Houghton Mifflin Co., Boston, 1909. 462 pages. Contains important incidental comment upon Mr. Cleveland's public actions, written by a leader of the opposition party.

(18) *The Autobiography of Thomas Collier Platt.* Compiled and edited by Louis J. Lang. B. W. Dodge & Co., New York, 1910. A frank discussion of American politics by a master politician. Of particular interest is the discussion in Chapter XVI, "The Gold Plank Controversy and How I Won It."

(19) *Random Recollections of an Old Political Reporter.* By William C. Hudson. Cupples & Leon, New York, 1911. Several chapters relate to Cleveland's administrations as Governor and President. Contains interesting material regarding Mr. Cleveland's personal characteristics, and is written in a light, journalistic style.

(20) *The United States in Our Own Time.* By E. Benjamin Andrews. Chas. Scribner's Sons, New

York, 1912. A rather forbidding volume, written from the point of view of a champion of Free Silver, and covering the period from Cleveland to Roosevelt.

(21) *Speeches, Correspondence and Political Papers of Carl Schurz.* Selected and edited by Frederic Bancroft. G. P. Putnam's Sons, New York, 1913. Data relating to the Mugwump campaign of 1884, Civil Service Reform, etc. Six vols.

(22) *Life of Thomas B. Reed.* By Samuel W. McCall, Houghton Mifflin Co., Boston, 1914. Contains an account of Cleveland's administration as viewed by the leader of the opposition.

(23) *American Diplomacy.* By Carl Russell Fish. Henry Holt & Co., New York, 1915. Third edition revised, 1919.

(24) *Sixty Years of American Life.* By Everett P. Wheeler. E. P. Dutton & Co., New York, 1917.

(25) *History of the United States from Hayes to McKinley,* 1877-1896. By James Ford Rhodes. The Macmillan Co., New York, 1919. One vol. 484 pages. The eighth volume of Dr. Rhodes' monumental history of the United States from the Compromise of 1850, includes the entire period of Mr. Cleveland's public life, and is invaluable as the interpretation of an historian of the first rank.

(26) *The Return of the Democratic Party to Power in 1884.* By Harrison Cook Thomas. Columbia University Press, New York, 1919. One vol. 225 pages.

(27) *Life of Walter Quintin Gresham,* 1832-1895. By Matilda Gresham. Rand, McNally & Co., Chicago, 1919. Contains many letters and other material bearing upon the public actions of Grover Cleveland. Two vols.

(28) *Marcus Alonzo Hanna; His Life and Work.*
By Herbert Croly. The Macmillan Co., New York,
1919. Important with reference to the gold plank of
the Republican platform of 1896. 495 pages.

(29) *Theodore Roosevelt and His Time, Shown
in His Own Letters.* By Joseph Bucklin Bishop.
Charles Scribner's Sons, New York, 1920. Two vols.

(30) *Since the Civil War.* By Charles Ramsdell
Lingley. The Century Co., New York, 1920.
A volume of unusual interest, designed as a college
text. Especially valuable in its treatment of financial
questions, and questions connected with the trust
problem.

(31) *Recent History of the United States.* By
Frederic L. Paxson. Houghton Mifflin Co., New
York, 1921. One vol. 602 pages. A scholarly sketch
of the history of the United States from Hayes to
Harding, written from the point of view of a liberal.

(32) *From McKinley to Harding; Personal Recollections of Our Presidents.* By H. H. Kohlsaat.
Charles Scribner's Sons, New York and London,
1923. Important with reference to the gold plank of
the Republican platform of 1896.

INDEX

417

THE END